Khalik Allah

Souls Against the Concrete

UNIVERSITY OF TEXAS PRESS AUSTIN

Printed in China
First edition, 2017

Managing Project Editor: Vikki Tobak

∞ The paper used in this book meets the minimum requirements of ANSI/NISO Z39.48-1992 (R1997) (Permanence of Paper).

Names: Allah, Khalik, author.
Title: Souls against the concrete / Khalik Allah.
Description: First edition. | Austin : University of Texas Press, 2017.
Identifiers: LCCN 2017000690
ISBN 978-1-4773-1314-5 (cloth : alk. paper)
Subjects: LCSH: Harlem (New York, N.Y.) – Pictorial works. | Homeless persons – New York (State) – New York – Pictorial works. | Drug addicts – New York (State) – New York – Pictorial works. | Street life – New York (State) – New York – Pictorial works. | Street photography – New York (State) – New York.
Classification: LCC F128.68.H3 A55 2017 | DDC 974.7/1 – dc23
LC record available at https://lccn.loc.gov/2017000690

doi:10.7560/313145

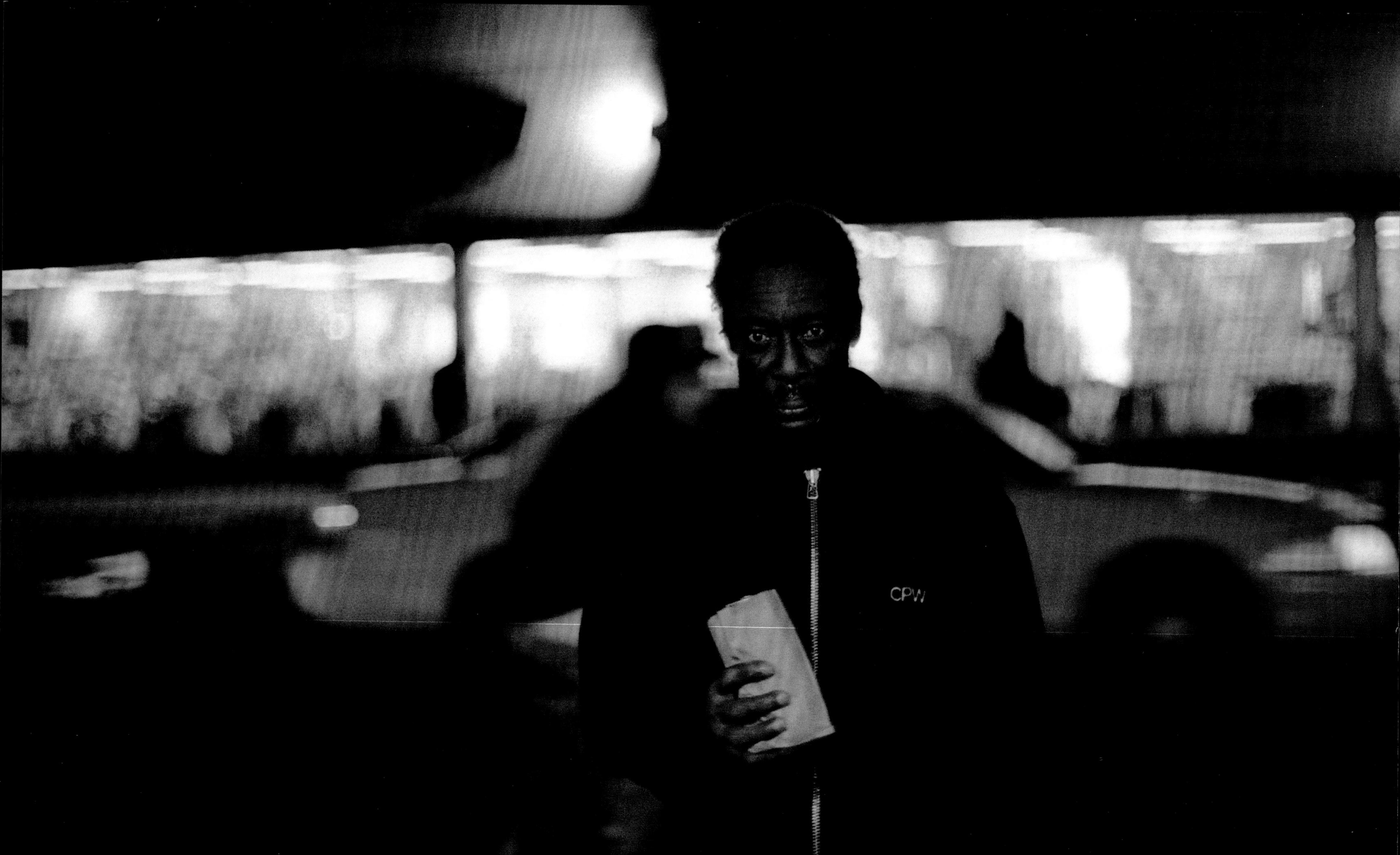
CPW

breakdancing. Back then I thought photography was boring. I never really planned on becoming a photographer, but in retrospect I see that the circumstances that led me toward it weren't random. When I was thirteen I begged my mother for a video camera. I was impressed with the idea of recording motion pictures. After a few months, on my fourteenth birthday, I finally received a Canon ES190 camcorder. I started shooting everything around me: my family, the streets – I was basically capturing the rays of our lives. I'm talking

In '98, after getting left back in the eighth grade, I dedicated myself to the "street science" that I found in New York, Harlem specifically. My journey in Harlem, or Mecca, as the Five-Percent Nation refers to it, began at that same time. I became a student enrolled in a curriculum I found on the corner. I was sparked early by the Five-Percent Nation of Gods and Earths. The Five-Percent Nation is a cultural awareness group dedicated to the growth and development of youth. The teachings of the Five-Percent – the Supreme

to find in the traditional school system. When I first started studying I felt desperate for knowledge. My life was spiraling downward, but I had enough insight to see that I needed to make a perpendicular shift. I come from a lineage of teachers and felt compelled to uphold that legacy, somehow, in my own way.

I began reading these obscure books that I was unable to find in school or in the library. I found them on 125th Street. I began feeding myself a wealth of metaphysics, black history, and literature. Some of

my lecturers were people like Dr. Jewel Pookrum, Dr. Sebi, and Delbert Blair. They affected me deeply and helped expand my worldview. I had no serious artistic ambitions at the time. I was just trying to save myself from the savage spell of ignorance. I would travel the Long Island Rail Road from Patchogue to Penn Station to Harlem. Staring out the window was like a feature film for my growing visual imagination. I was going to Harlem for one thing alone: knowledge. Allah School, the Five-Percent Nation's headquarters, at 2122 7th Avenue was always my primary destination. I would eat at Strictly Roots on 123rd Street. I used to play chess with the owner, DeeCee. He repatriated to Ghana.
I was fourteen years old and in Harlem frequently, but 125th and Lexington was a corner I used to avoid. East 125th was markedly different from the street west of Park Avenue. My earliest impressions of the corner were of drugs, selling and using, accented by a heavy police presence, bogus arrests, and clouds of smoke. For me, it was a chaotic world to avoid. I couldn't have predicted that it would eventually become the nucleus of a slang photography style that I'd author later in life.

The Five-Percent Nation gave me a strong foundation. My teacher was an older brother named CeeAaquil Allah. A lot of Five-Percenters got knowledge around the same time I did – I was glad I wasn't learning from their teachers. CeeAaquil was genuinely interested in my learning. He wasn't just testing me. He wove the principles of work and discipline into the science that he taught me. I went back to school and excelled. He said that would be the best way to prove

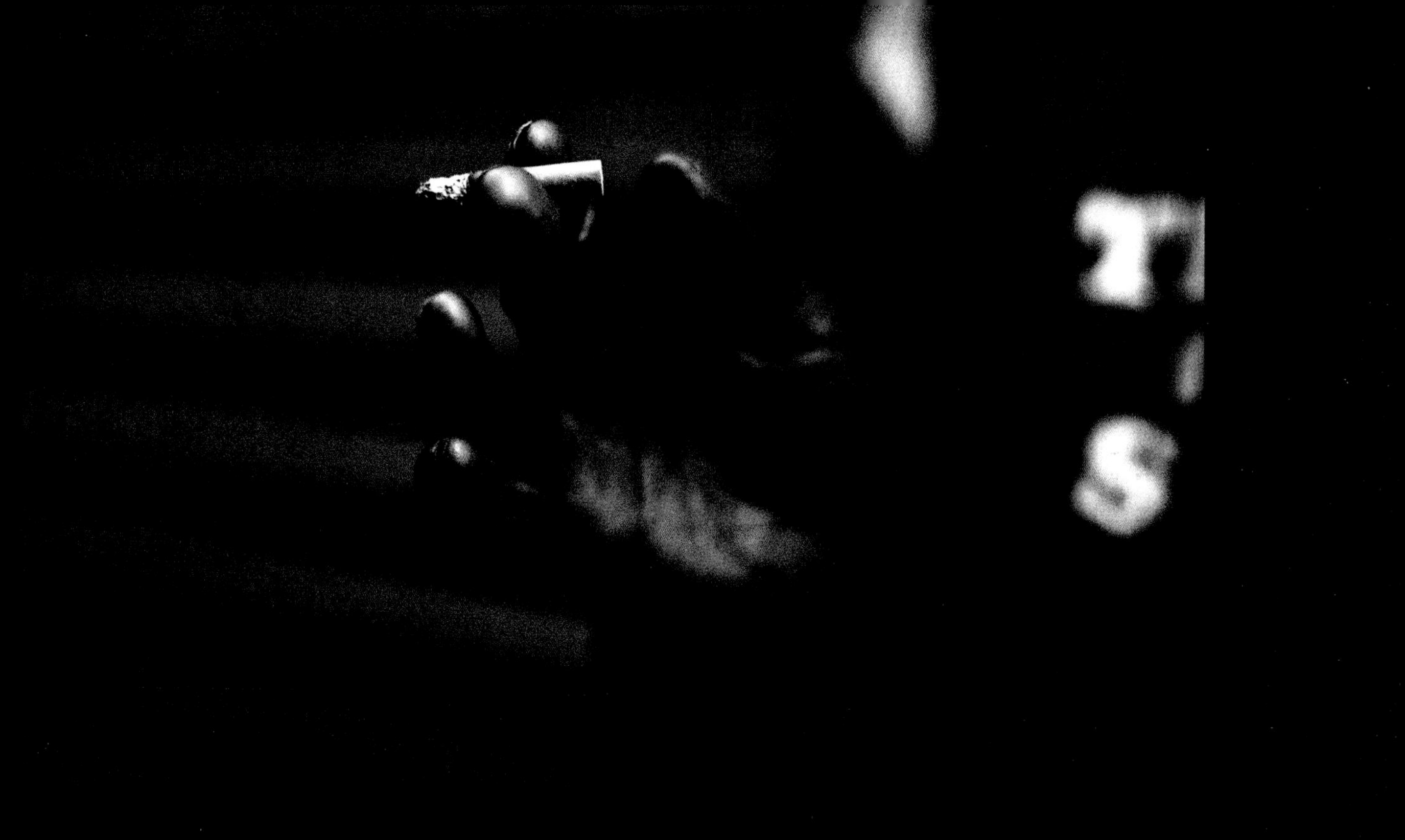

to my parents that the new path I had chosen was profitable. After learning the Supreme Mathematics, the Supreme Alphabet, and the 120 Lessons, I made my first short film, called *The Absorption of Light*. I purchased the camera I shot it with using a $1,000 scholarship I received at the end of high school. The money was meant for college, but I cashed the check immediately and went straight to PC Richard, the electronics and appliance store.

The Absorption of Light was a silent film depicting

the transformation of a misguided youth from "mental death" to a state of awakening. I scored the film using rap songs from the Wu-Tang Clan catalogue. The songs I chose helped flesh out the narrative. When it was done I was adamant that the group see the film. I knew many of the Wu brothers from the Universal Parliaments and Show and Proves, the monthly and annual gatherings of the Five-Percent Nation in Mecca at the Harriet Tubman school on 127th. I'd see the brothers there, but we never really crossed paths. I got in touch with a Wu syndicate named Killah Priest. We spoke over the phone briefly, and he gave me his address. I mailed the film to him, and that was the beginning of my video work with the Sunz of Man, the first rap group to form under the Clan. I remember driving to Park Hill in Staten Island to meet with 4th Disciple, Killah Priest's producer. From there I went on to direct a few music videos for Hell Razah, Masta Killa, and some of the other Wu-Tang family.

Those projects culminated in my first feature-length documentary about Freedum Allah, also known as Popa Wu – the patriarch/mentor of the Wu-Tang Clan. As a self-taught filmmaker I used this project as an opportunity to develop my own style. I didn't have anyone producing me, and I was free to experiment. Throughout the process I became good friends with Allah Just, also known as GZA/The Genius. He took me on tour in 2008. During that time I met many young brothers associated with the Clan who wanted to claim they were a part of the group. I didn't want to do that. I was getting deeper into the rap world but I didn't want to become known as a hip-hop director. I had my own aspirations for film and knew that I wanted to create a unique body of work.

From 2006 to 2010 I worked on the same film project, *Popa Wu, A 5% Story*. I felt like I couldn't get a handle on it; the shooting and editing seemed to go on indefinitely. I was trying to figure out a lot of things about my documentary style. When it was finally complete, I was tired of the arduous filmmaking process. I told myself I was gonna take a break from filmmaking for a while. That's when photography came into my life in an unexpected way.

II

Photography became another way for me to make films. When you shoot film every exposure is connected to the next. I had thirty-six shots to tell a story on one roll. In this way I assumed the role of a visual griot.

GZA called me one day late in August 2010. He said he was about to come check me in Long Island. I thought it would be a good idea to snap some photographs of him. Throughout the time I had known Allah Just, I had never taken any photographs of him; I had only shot some video, while on tour in '08. I asked my older brother if I could borrow his Nikon Rebel for the day. He said, "Na man, I don't let people borrow my shit!" I tried to convince him, but he wouldn't lend me the camera. I didn't give up. I thought to myself, where could I get a camera? Then it came to me. I thought back to when my dad used to take family photographs. I said to myself, surely he must still have that camera. I asked him about it, and he went into his closet, reached to the top, and pulled down his Canon AE1. It was dusty, and he told me I could keep it. That instant changed my life. I was impressed with the solid metallic body, glass lens, and manual features. I knew I had something from the past; it reminded me of my childhood. When I connected with GZA that evening I took a few shots, but when I got home I opened up the

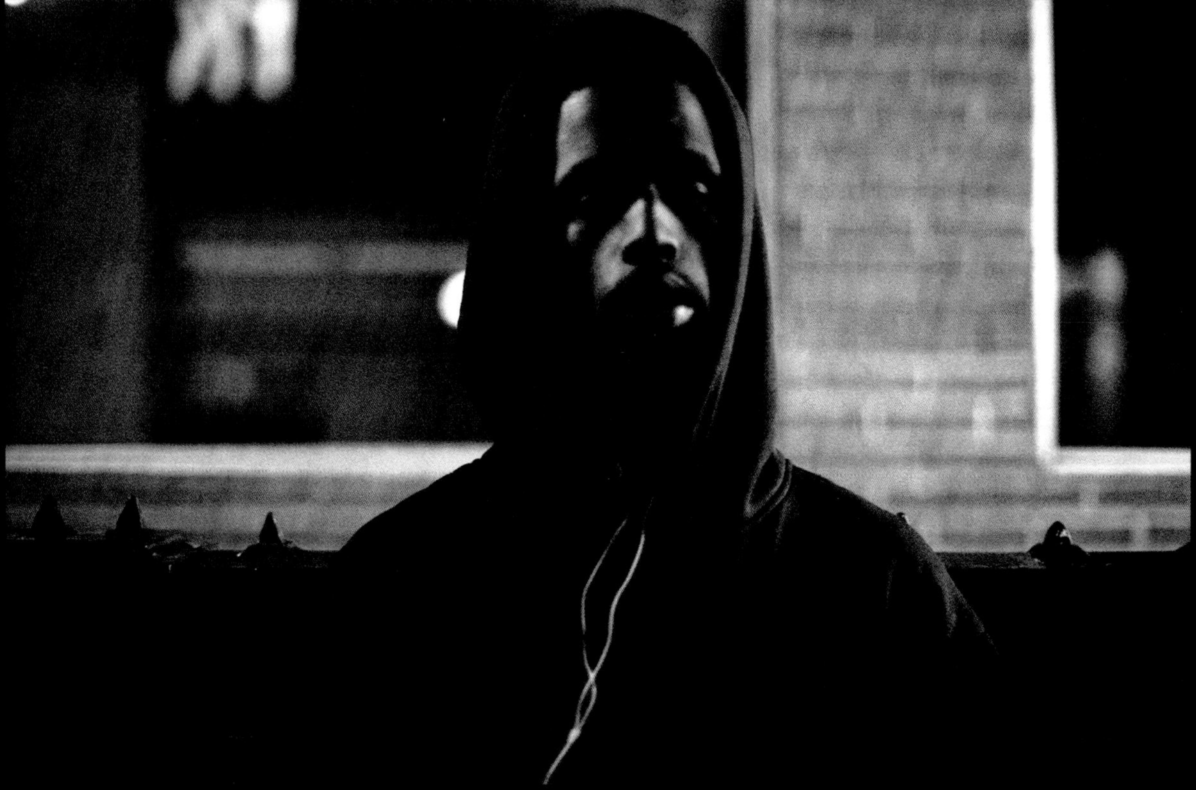

back of the camera and exposed the film to light accidentally. I didn't know how to take the film out of the camera properly. Patience is a virtue that photography taught me much later on.

I remember feeling hyped-up later that night. I walked up to my brother and told him, "Thank you. I thought you were being selfish earlier, and you probably were, but because of that I got this 35mm camera from Pops and I'm gonna pursue photography now." He encouraged me to do that. I stayed up late studying the camera for hours on YouTube. I remember thinking that I had just found a new passion. I was immediately connected to the Canon because it seemed like I was slowing my filmmaking down. I declared myself a photographer that night. It felt like I had reconnected with a part of myself that was lost.

I think all of us agree to a "life contract" before being born. From the narrow perspective of the ego, it's hard to remember many of the things that we agreed to do in our lives during our time on earth. It's like we're born in a state of amnesia and have to work hard to remember what our souls are really striving toward. Sometimes there are people and symbols that help guide us in remembering the real paths that

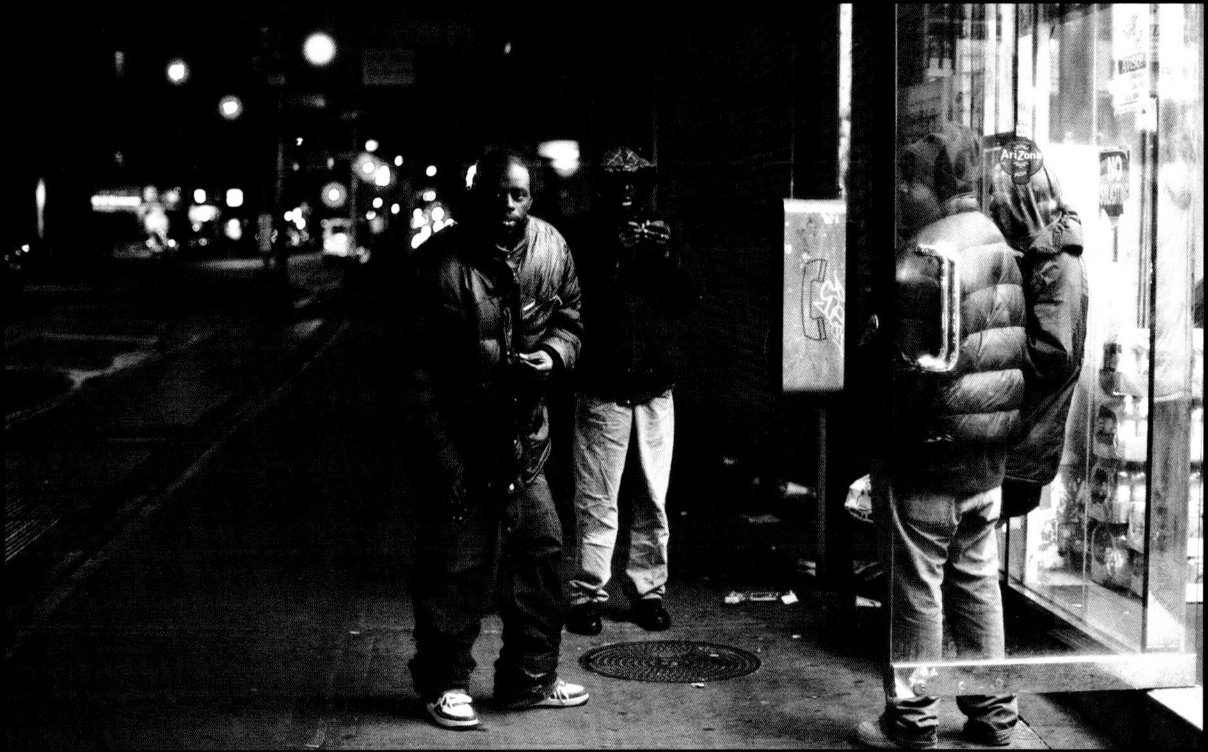

we're supposed to be on. The camera was certainly a symbol for me. I'm glad I recognized it.

I like to say that photography is my inside joke with God, because it's my attempt to make the temporal become eternal, and that's impossible. The world was over a long time ago. These photographs never happened. I shoot at night to remind people that we're in outer time, outer space. Time is over, and the world has ended. Only the Light continues. I shoot people who find themselves in the worst possible situation, but I recognize their invulnerability and reflect it back to them. These are psychic x-rays. I consider my photographs energy charts. During my interactions with people I measure frequencies of soul consciousness.

I began creating a collage of lives photographed in the nighttime. To some, night and darkness represent fear. To me night represents a sense of freedom. But the dark that surrounds my subjects can also represent how the beast swallows them young.

III

This book is about redemption, strength, and resilience amid addiction, poverty, and street life. A comment on the times and the people who birthed civilization, the great Kingdoms of Africa, and how they fell and where they have been scattered. From the Valley of Kings to drug addiction, imprisonment, invisibility, and persecution, just for having frizzled hair. A neighborhood corner brutalized by police. A fragile society opposed by society. Souls Against the Concrete – poor but happy – misunderstood by society at large but still radiating the spirit of kings and queens. This collection of portraits represents a part of black history that shouldn't be avoided – a small part of a great legacy that should be remembered. The struggles of the world desperately call for a different perspective on the problems we face. This book is the result of many nights spent with my Nikon F2 35mm camera on the corner at night. A photography style inspired by jazz: the improvisational click of the shutter fitting into the polyphonic symphony of the corner at night – equal parts psychiatry and photography.

After getting my first camera, I started collecting them. I fell deeply in love with my Nikon F2/55mm

Nikkor 1.2 lens. It's been a solid relationship based on loyalty; other cameras were just side chicks. The world of photography began to fascinate me. I was studying the greats, like Henri Cartier-Bresson, Robert Frank, and Paul Strand. I saturated myself in the art of Nobuyoshi Araki and Daido Moriyama. The work of photographers like Bruce Davidson and Eddie Adams spoke to me. I wanted to emulate them. I wanted to shoot candid and in monochrome the way they did, but after a while I said, "Fuck this! I need my own style now."

I shot photographs between the Lower East Side and Harlem for roughly two years before I narrowed my focus down to one corner at nighttime. A particular experience led me to single out that corner for my work. I was there, at 125th and Lex, one afternoon when a bald female crackhead wearing a baby pacifier connected to rosary beads saw me counting change and asked me for a dollar. I said, "I'll give you a dollar, but I want to take your photograph." She posed with her middle finger up and I took the shot. I said, "That's great, keep giving me the finger but put the pacifier in your mouth." A few brothers standing around me heard that and didn't like it. One man in an MTA uniform, wearing a name tag with "Mike" on it, said, "Yo brother, we don't want to be seen like that. Why are you shooting that? We don't want to expose that!" I said, "Peace, my name is Khalik Allah. I'm a documentarian, I'm depicting the positive, the negative, and the neutral. I'm documenting 360 degrees." He said "You're a Five-Percenter, you should know better." A few people

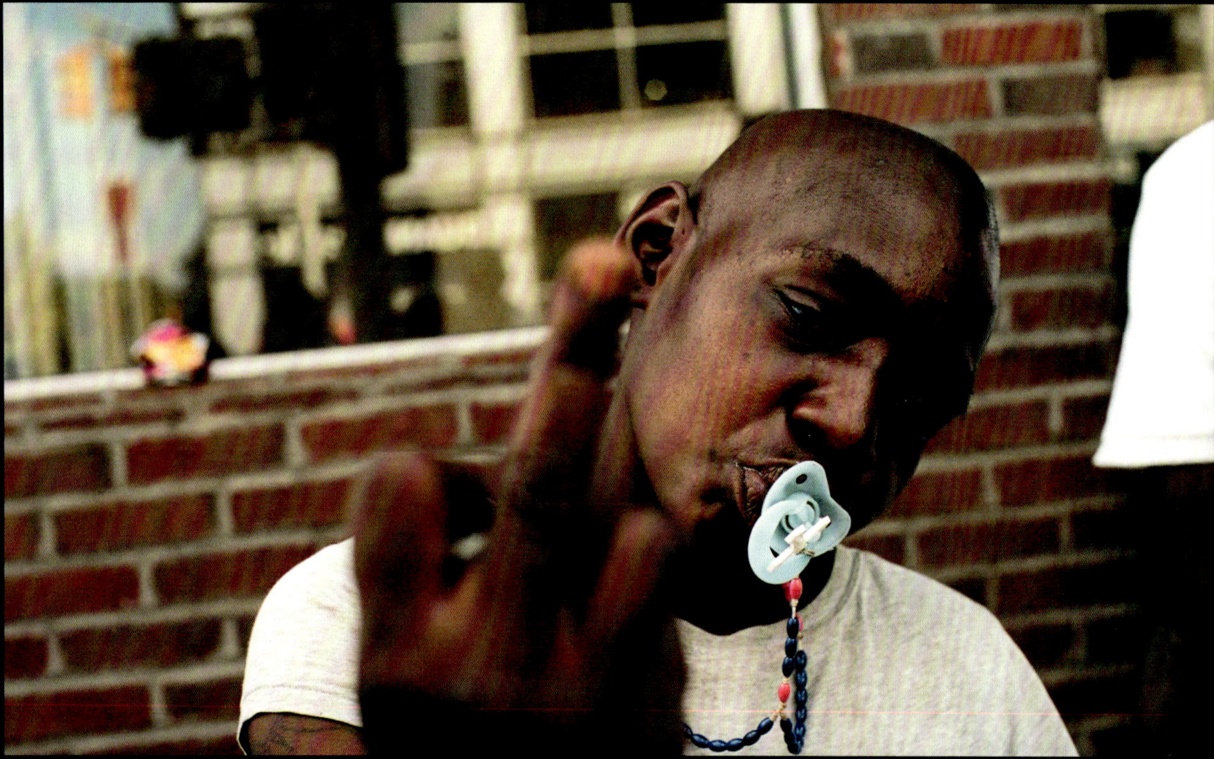

started to chime in, some defending me, some not. There was a NOI (Nation of Islam) bookseller watching the episode. He remained silent but attentive. I said to the MTA officer, Mike, "Peace," and kept moving. Engaging any more than that would have been futile. I shot around Harlem for a few hours, then returned to the corner as it was starting to get dark. It was much emptier. Everyone from earlier seemed to have left except the bookseller, who was still there. He called me over and said, "Peace, young man, I think what you're doing is positive. I like what you said about 360 degrees. Keep working with your camera."

But the night that really set it off for me was November 21, 2011. I drove to the city at 10 p.m. on a very serious mission. I parked on Houston Street in the Lower East Side. It was me, my Nikon, my brown leather jacket, and twelve rolls of film in my cargo pants. My plan was to ride the train all night until dawn I knew I wanted to check 125th and Lex and to see what it was like there in the middle of the night. I shot in the subway for a while, exploring different parts of it. Finally I got to Harlem around 2 a.m. I got out of the subway at Frederick Douglass and 125th, then began heading east toward Lexington Avenue.

It was a quiet walk, as most of the stores had already shut down for the night. 2 Bros. Pizza, which I came to love later – not for its pizza but for the light pouring out of its window – was closed. The entire corner was blacked out. It was the first time anyone from the block had seen me with my camera that late at night. I learned that only a certain element walks the streets during those hours. I was still new to the area, slowly becoming known for what I did, but all of my previous work was shot in the daytime and I didn't recognize anyone who was out that late. I knew it would be either love or fear; either I would be respected, or someone would try to jump me and steal my camera. I shot some prostitutes; some of the hustlers watched. I could tell a few were suspicious, but I told myself: this is New York, and there's nothing strange about this.

I recognized that I'd have to confront my subjects. I asked a brother in a hoodie if he would pose for a quick photograph. He asked me for a few dollars and I blessed him. I was shooting Ilford HP4 35mm. The 125 ISO monochrome film had to struggle to create an exposure with so little light present. I knew the film was struggling. In that moment I saw the concept of struggle become mirrored in my work. Layers of struggle became visible to me. It was something palpable that I felt to my core.

My lens is like the moon reflecting light, but devoid of water and life. The moon pulls on the earth's water, causing high and low tides. In this sense it's struggling for water, just as my lens and film were struggling for light. It all clicked for me. It represented my own struggle for knowledge early in life, when I acted like a lunatic – before I learned that the light was in me.

The night of November 21, 2011, was a profound turning point. It got wilder as the hours progressed. I committed to the idea of only shooting at night.

Around 3 a.m. I walked into a congregation of

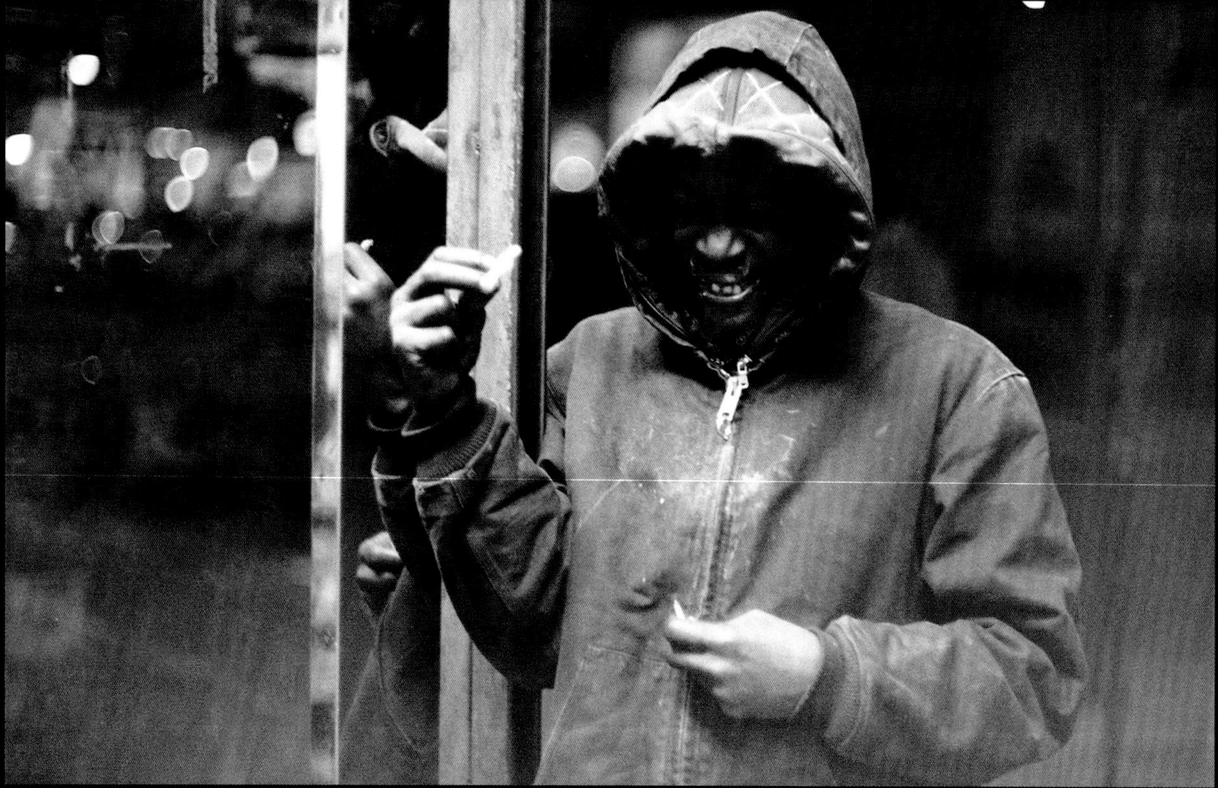

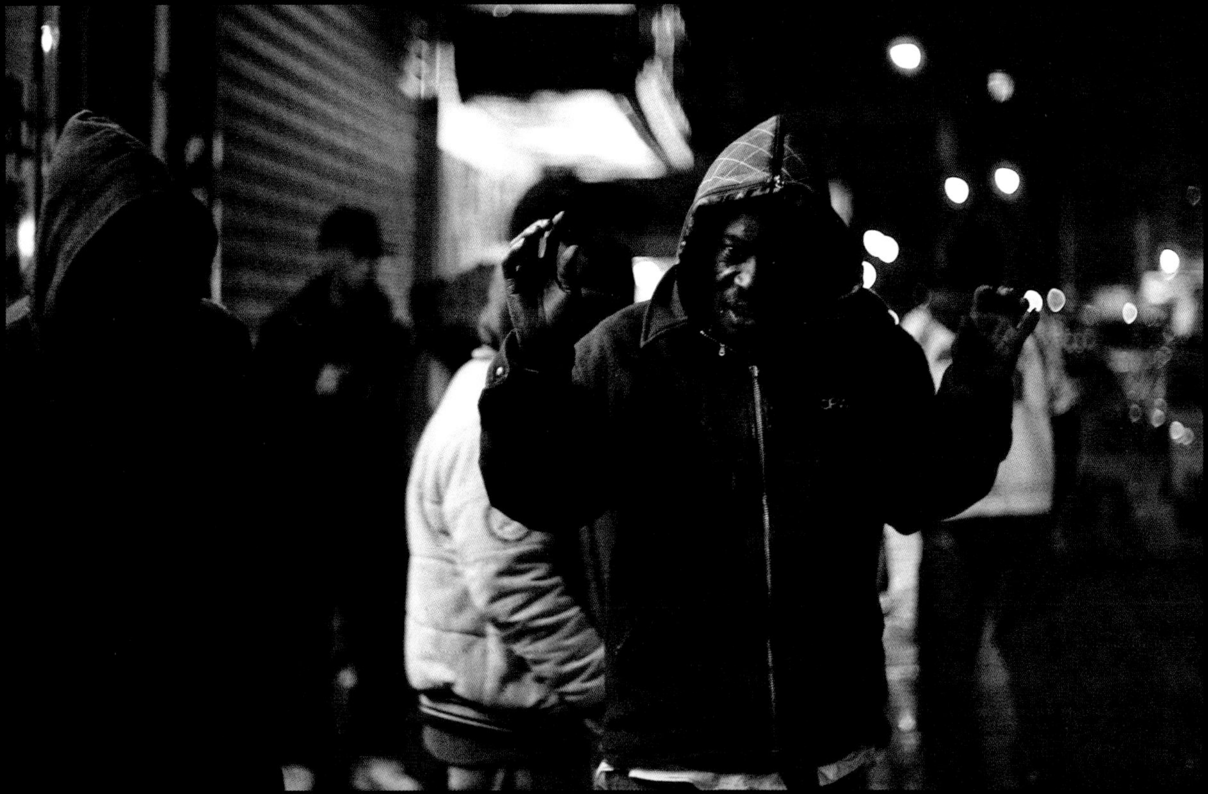

"crack-heads." I learned later that they were smoking a legal synthetic substance called "K2." K2 is a highly dangerous substitute for weed, but it's sold legally from the corner stores on 125th and Lex. I've always looked at it as a tool to further gentrify the area. It's legal to purchase but illegal to smoke in public; because of this, many homeless people are cited and arrested on bullshit charges. It encourages the police to prey on this area where they may easily meet their quotas.

At first I went undetected among the smokers. Lexington Avenue felt like a dark corridor, narrow and wet. I had a new Nikon flash in my pocket but had been debating whether or not to use it. I decided to pull it out. I affixed it to the camera, let it warm up, then took a shot of the smokers in their circle. The flash exploded, and everyone scrambled in different directions. There was one man who stayed with his hands raised in terror. I snapped a quick shot, then he swiftly fled. That's how I met Frenchie. He would eventually become the main character in my photographic work on the corner at night.

I cranked the film advance and heard a snap. I had overcranked the camera and knew the valuable film I had just shot would be ruined if I couldn't get it to a darkroom fast. I could have called it a night, but I still had seven rolls of unexposed film in my cargo pants pocket. It was late at night and I didn't want to call any of my friends. I hopped into the subway and stood on the edge of the platform. I was contemplating jumping on the tracks and walking into the tunnel to use its darkness to take the film out of the camera. Then I turned my head and saw a janitor coming out of the custodial closet underneath the staircase. I approached her with ultimate humility and respect. I told her that I really needed a dark place to take the film out of my camera. She sensed my desperation and allowed me to use the room. I entered first and asked her to please shut the door all the way behind us. There was a little light coming under the door. I took my leather coat off and zipped it closed. I put my camera inside, then I put my arms through the sleeves and began using it as a "dark bag." I began making small talk with her as I was doing this. I'm not religious, but I was saying things like "God bless you! Thank you. Thank God for you!" I was just happy she was so charitable. I sealed the film tightly before running up the subway steps.

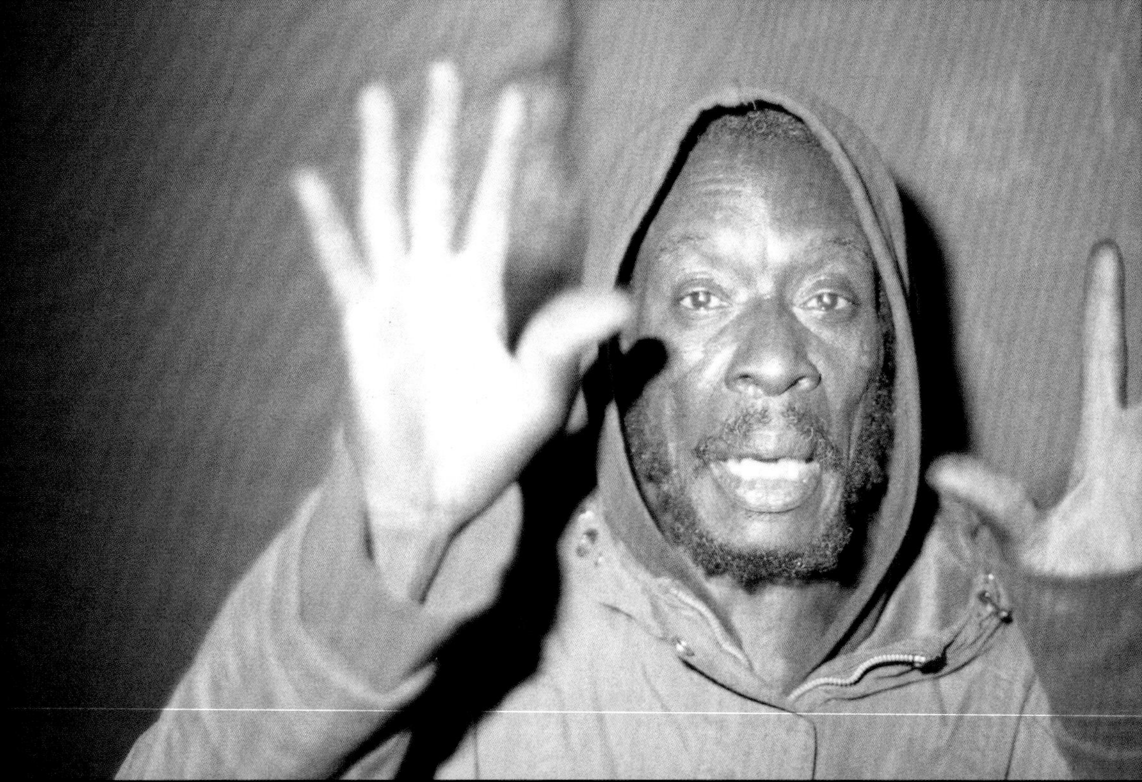

I shot on Lexington Avenue all night, until sunrise, when my camera eventually broke. The advance locked up, and I had torn a roll of film inside the camera. The whole thing had to be overhauled. But I didn't feel I was done for the night. I had hit a rhythm at a level that I had never reached before. I was truly in my element. At 6 a.m. I walked into the Pathmark supermarket on the southeast corner of 125th Street and Lexington Avenue. I bought two disposable cameras. There were a bunch of birds shitting all over the place, and a lot of people were starting their day. Frenchie reemerged from nowhere. He was wearing a blue jacket that matched the morning sky. I took a shot. There was plenty of snot running from his nose, and I loved him that much more for it. He struck me as a powerful soul who was having a hard time cooperating with the nature of this world. I jetted onto the train with a renewed purpose. I saw my own struggle and that of others clearly. My major concern was developing the roll I had saved in the custodial closet. I got home

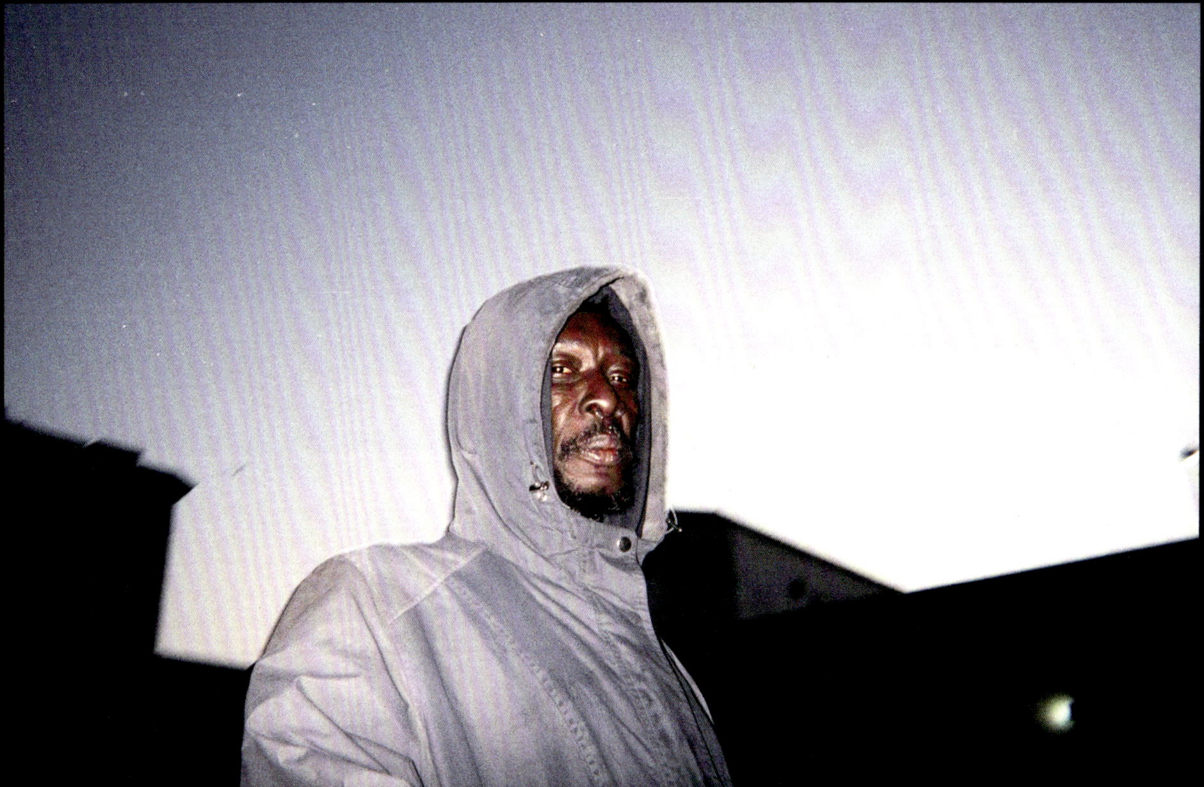

and immediately mixed a fresh batch of chemicals. I developed two rolls of film at the kitchen sink, then went to sleep.

IV

My days began and ended with a rhythm opposite to that of other folks' days. I was swallowed by the camera and the night. I claimed the corner like a drug dealer would have claimed it. I didn't see other photographers there, only surveillance cameras. Periodically I would see Frenchie. Usually I would find him lying on the vents across from Pathmark. Or I'd find him on the corner in a state of excited inebriation. We didn't exchange words much. Our conversation was limited to "stand right there" or "buy me a beer."

After a few months I created a short film that keyframed the images I'd been shooting in monochrome on the corner. I called it *Urban Rashomon* and I put it on YouTube. It was just me telling a story, not too dissimilar to the one I'm telling here. I felt that I had created my first truly personal work. After putting it out there, I went looking for Frenchie in the streets. It was April 2013. I asked a few people if they had seen him, and they said, "Yeah, he's wearing a clean black suit that he got from the Salvation Army. You can't miss him." I took this as a symbol that, on some telepathic level, Frenchie understood the film had just premiered on YouTube.

I stood in front of the store on Lexington where a lot of brothers congregate. I wasn't really taking many pictures that night. I was just chilling, hanging there and hoping that Frenchie would pop up. I stood there vibing on the corner for a few hours before I decided to head off. Then I saw the same MTA officer, Mike, walk past me. We made eye contact, then I saw him whispering to some brothers who were standing on the sidewalk. A kid named Mario walked over to me and said, "You should get out of here, this dude is telling these kids that you work with the police." When I got to the corner I saw Mike there. I said, "Yo, I remember you, we had an argument a while ago, but I'd like you to see some of the work I've been doing." He looked at me coldly and said, "If I was you I would get out of here, those kids over there were talking about fighting you." I said, "Word, because you told them to?" I remember speeding down the FDR, pissed. I was still new to the corner and I thought this dude was fucking up my

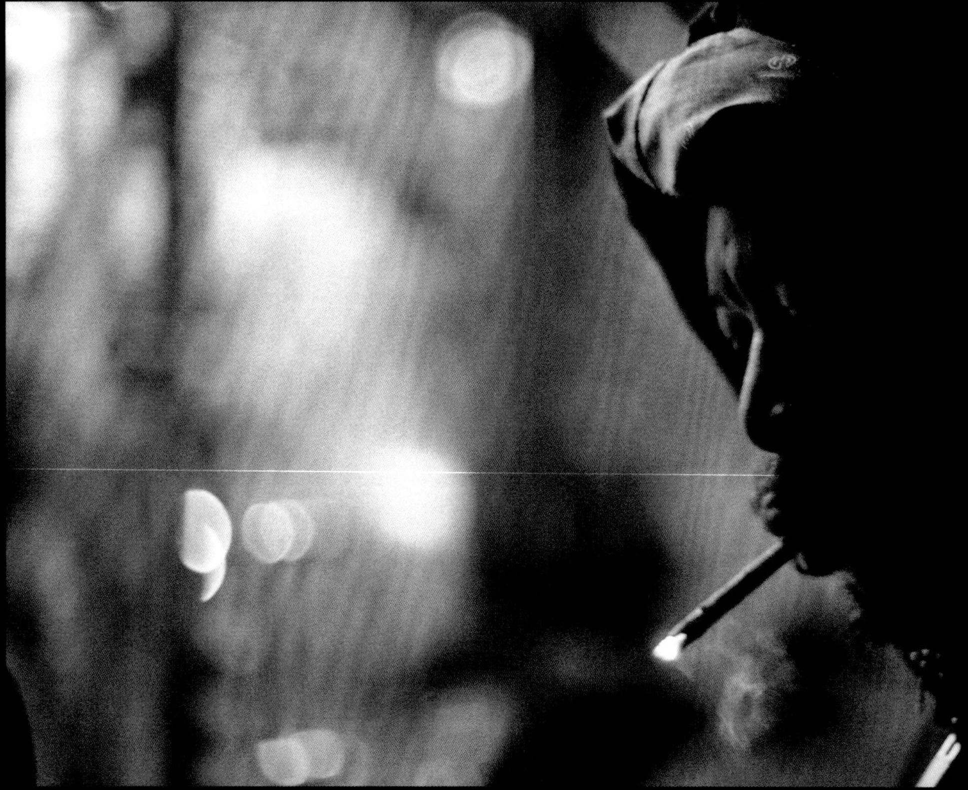

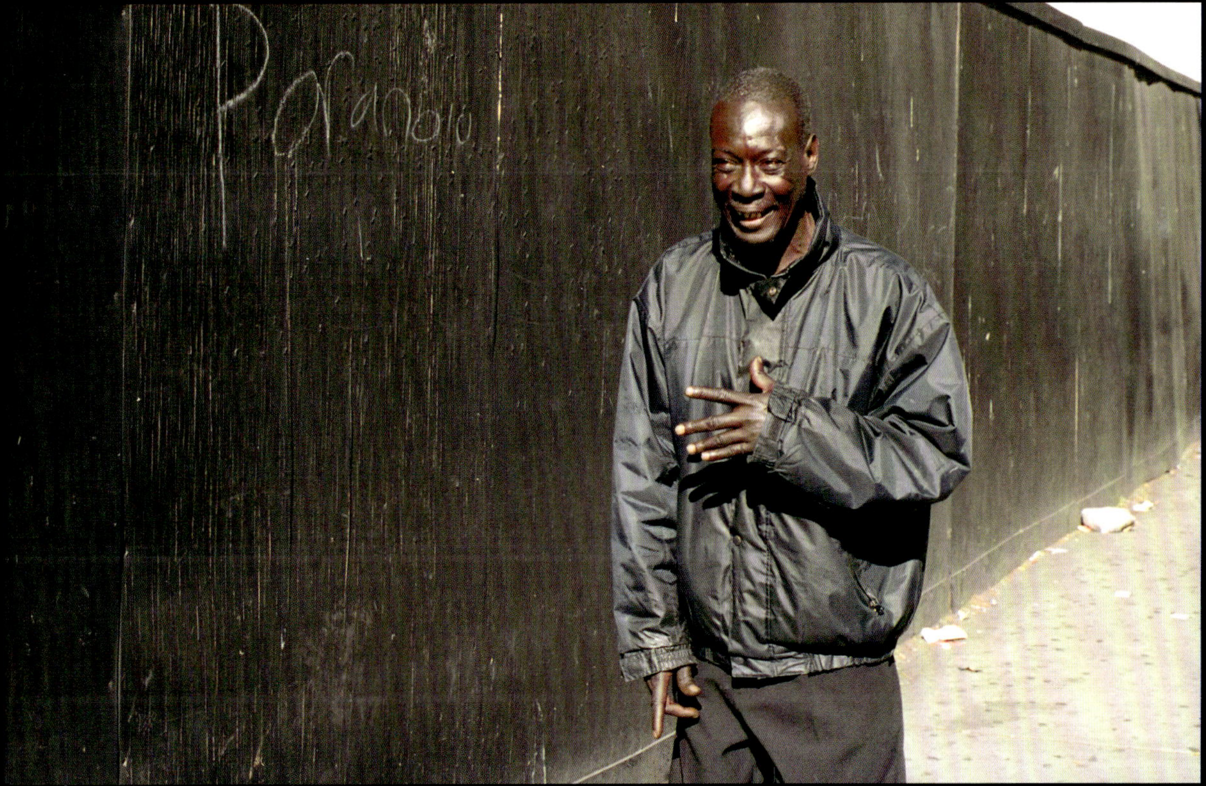

reputation. I couldn't have that. I was resolved to stay out of the area for a few months and let the situation work itself out.

After just one week I hit the block again. It was early in the morning and I was shooting color film. I wanted to avoid the nighttime for a while. My idea was to shoot the morning in color, thus inverting the form, if not the content, of my monochrome night work.

I parked on 125th and made my rounds. A group of officers was making an arrest, throwing a man into an unmarked van. I took some shots of the police and the handcuffs around the man's wrists. I walked to Lexington, where many people were still sprawled out on the vents: some were sleeping, others had been up all night. When I crossed the street, I saw a skinny figure wearing a white knitted beanie and sitting comfortably against the brick wall on the sunny concrete. It was Frenchie. I knelt down to speak to him. "Yo Frenchie, it's me, it's Khalik, get up. Let's go for a walk." People stared at us as we passed them on the street. We must've looked odd together. He was wearing a snot-riddled coat and was still limping from a train accident that broke his pelvis. I told him to stand against a wall where someone had inscribed the word "paranoid." I told him that I'd give him a few dollars. He responded, "No papa, I want something to eat. I want to eat some breakfast."

We walked to a spot called Harlem Delight on 125th. I ordered him three large pancakes with butter and extra syrup. The waiter asked him if he had had any Bacardi today, then he asked him what was his favorite drink. Frenchie sang out, "Champagne." The food came in a foil takeout plate but we sat down anyway. Frenchie began to eat, and I asked him about his life and family and how he ended up in the streets. He told me that he came from Haiti in 1982, when he was twenty-two years old, and after one year of living in New York, "everything got messed up." I was witnessing him speak about his life in a way that I hadn't heard before. There was a chunk of butter on top of the pancakes. I was waiting for Frenchie to spread it around, but he picked it up and ate the whole piece of butter all at once. I had never seen anybody do that.

I started laughing. He smiled, and we kept talking. I continued recording our discussion, and those recordings became part of the film *Antonyms of Beauty*.

That morning, one of Frenchie's friends, Angie, told me something that fascinated me. She said Frenchie had two older brothers that would come through from time to time in a Mercedes Benz and pick him up from the block. They would cut his hair, change his clothes, and give him a warm meal, but then, after a few days, he would run away, back to 125th. She told me Frenchie preferred street life because that's where he felt he was free; his circumstances were by choice. I knew the truth must've been deeper, but that understanding made our bond stronger. I was there by choice, too, as a photographer. Frenchie and I both were swept up in the visceral energy of a slowly gentrifying street corner. I knew I was capturing a future artifact.

I released *Antonyms of Beauty* and, subsequently, decided to keep using the color film but to take it back into the night. I knew I was ready for that. I wanted to see what the incandescent streetlights would do with the color film. I wanted to push my lens to the limit with Kodak Portra 160 ISO film under the lampposts and storefronts, near the bleeding light from ambulances and police sirens; all of these became my sources of light. I couldn't give a fuck about MTA officer Mike or getting jumped. The light pouring from the corner store became my best friend. I trusted it. I tested every light source in the vicinity, over to 124th and down to Park Avenue. I knew I had a lot of power when I made that decision to bring the color film to the corner at night.

From the beginning, I was impressed with the portraits I made, because of the intimacy I achieved. I absorbed and was absorbed by the environment – and then I truly became an adopted son of Harlem. A long way from that fourteen-year-old student enrolled at Allah School, I now took the math to the people that my soul told me to confront on the corner. I don't feel like I could have done what I did without an early foundation of Knowledge of Self. In dark situations I found myself saying to so many of my subjects, "Walk with me into the light." It was a literal command to frame my subjects better, but afterwards I thought about the spiritual implications of the statement. I thought, that's something Christ would say. After that I started calling my work on the street "Camera Ministry." I felt like I was baptizing people with Light: the Light of truth awarded to the mind that withholds judgment, because judgment always obscures truth.

V

A corner is a ninety-degree angle, it's perpendicular and straight up. That's how I knew I had to work when I was shooting. Right and exact. Otherwise the penalty may have been severe. That discipline allowed me to record these color photographs, shot between 2012 and 2016.

Looking at my work, a lot of people have asked me how I approached my subjects and asked for permission to photograph them. I wore a dark green Nikon vest and I fasted all day. I liked to hit the block hungry and shoot from the stomach. It also kept my heart and mind clear, helping me to be sharp and focused. I think that black neighborhoods are feared by many people, but those people aren't aware of how much love exists in the black community, in spite of the destruction that has taken place there. I'm not limited by fear. Fear is always a choice, no matter how involuntarily it seems to arise. Love is its only alternative. Most people prefer love to fear, so when I'm asking people for a photo, I'm

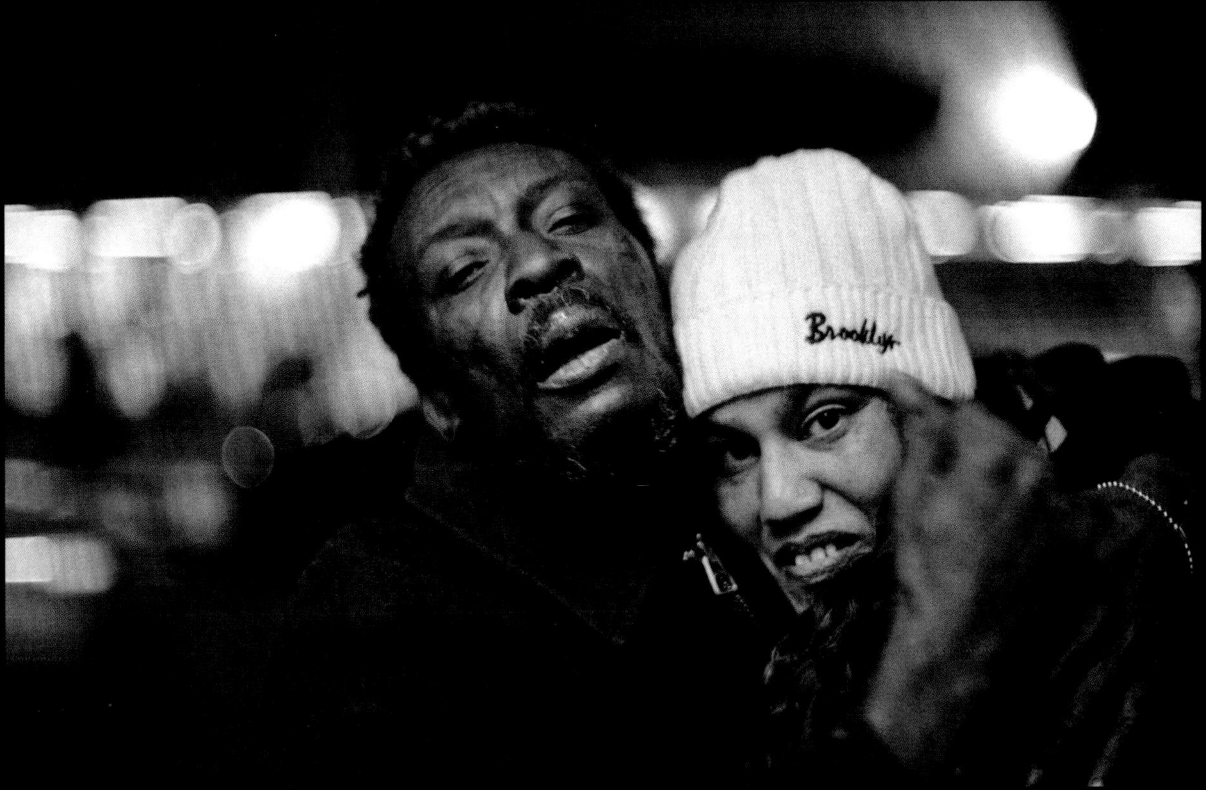

making an appeal to the Light in them, that unforgotten reality. Photographs are memories. I appeal to the spirit in them that remembers the eternal, and this facilitates intimate interactions.

VI

The winter of 2014 was when Frenchie went missing. He had taken to sleeping on the narrow part of the train platform. This was wild because, during the time when I was shooting *Urban Rashomon*, Frenchie had been struck by a train while defecating on the tracks. The irony is that his near-dead emaciated state was what saved his life. If he had been any bigger the train would've killed him. Instead it just broke his pelvis and ripped off one of his ass cheeks. The story was reported on *DNAinfo New York* under the title "Man Fatally Struck by Train, Another Seriously Hurt at Harlem Station." And even after all that, Frenchie still took refuge from the winter on the platform of the 4, 5, 6 subway station at 125th Street and Lexington Avenue.

The last time I saw Frenchie, we met up in front of the pizza shop. He was rushing to buy a bag of K2 and get back down to the warm platform in the subway.

He asked me for five dollars. He came out of the store with a bag of K2 and a pack of blunt wraps. We walked down the steps together. He kept saying, “I’m going home, papa, I’m going home now.” He started telling me all sorts of shit: that he went to the hospital and the doctors diagnosed him as schizophrenic. He told me that he lost all of his medication and also his understanding. I asked him if he thought he was insane; he said yes. It was the first time I had seen him broken down like that. I asked him if he thought it was possible to pick himself up with the help of God. He responded, “Maybe.” We hopped on the 6 train heading into the Bronx. He started singing a song as we sat down in the handicapped seats; all of the passengers were looking at us. He went into his coat and pulled out a blunt of K2 that he had rolled while we were speaking on the benches before the train came. He lit it up right there in the moving train. I didn’t stop him. He reminded me of the late Old Dirty Bastard from Wu-Tang. The girl to my left started barking, saying that she had asthma and he shouldn’t be smoking on the train. I was laughing too hard to do anything about it. Frenchie’s K2 smoke was clouding up the whole car and he was still singing between inhalations. He was happy and I was glad to see him with his spirits raised high. I started to realize that this was it, Frenchie was going to ride the train all night without a destination. I got off at 174th Street in the Bronx. I stood there looking back at him through the scratched train window. The train pulled off, and that was the last time I ever saw him.

VII

I got to a point where I knew everyone on the corner by name, and everyone knew me. There was nothing special about my camera, and I could take photographs of people without asking. Many of the exchanges I had with people didn’t really involve words. I stopped them, framed a shot, and took the photograph, and then they kept walking. Other times my intentions were questioned and the exchange would go on for a while. People poured out many stories. I’d always inquire about Frenchie. Some told me he was dead, others said he was in Bellevue Hospital. I could only hope that his brothers found him and were able to keep him. Frenchie was a soul against the concrete, shouldering the world’s blame. I believe he set himself free from his own imprisonment.

After all that, I felt like I had taken a long enough break from filmmaking. I was becoming frustrated with the limitations of still photography. I felt that I was unable to capture my deeper impressions of the neighborhood. I was seeing and hearing so many things that the medium of photography couldn’t depict. At that moment I knew I had to expand my style. The result was a polyphonic street symphony, a visual poem titled *Field Niggas*. The sincerity of the film was the result of engraining myself deeply into the lives of the people on the corner for three years while I shot the portraits in this book. The title was inspired by Malcolm X’s 1963 speech, “Message to the Grassroots,” in which Malcolm delineated the differences between the “house negro” and the more rebellious “field negro” during the days of slavery in America. My work is predicated on my own attitude of rebellion. I never expected to be accepted, especially not with a title like *Field Niggas*. I expected to be blacklisted, but the opposite happened. *Field Niggas* brought me critical acclaim. It won awards in France, Canada, and all over the United States. It took me to numerous universities to talk about the work and to assume a teaching function. Having been held back in the eighth grade

I was particularly happy to bring my work to schools like Harvard and Princeton. The film was recognized in the *New York Times*, the *Los Angeles Times*, and innumerable other publications. It took me to Copenhagen, Switzerland, London, France, and Canada, and to schools all across the United States.

These days when I go back to 125th to shoot, I tell people where I have been and where they have traveled with me. No one ever sweats it. I'm grateful to be continuing on the path. I ask the Light to lead me, and it has never steered me wrong. 125th and Lex continues to be the cornerstone and central building block to the foundation of my life in photography.

This book. Keep it. Save it. Study it. This is emotion on emulsion. Developed in the dark. From negative to positive. It's my "Camera Ministry." I was appointed to be a minister on the corner; photography was just an excuse to stop people. I baptized them in light and said goodnight and went home, then traveled the planet with the work and came back. I'll be shooting on the corner until I'm no longer, and after I'm gone, my psychic imprint will be visible through the stains of my aura on the sidewalk. Forever, my soul, like varnish against the concrete.

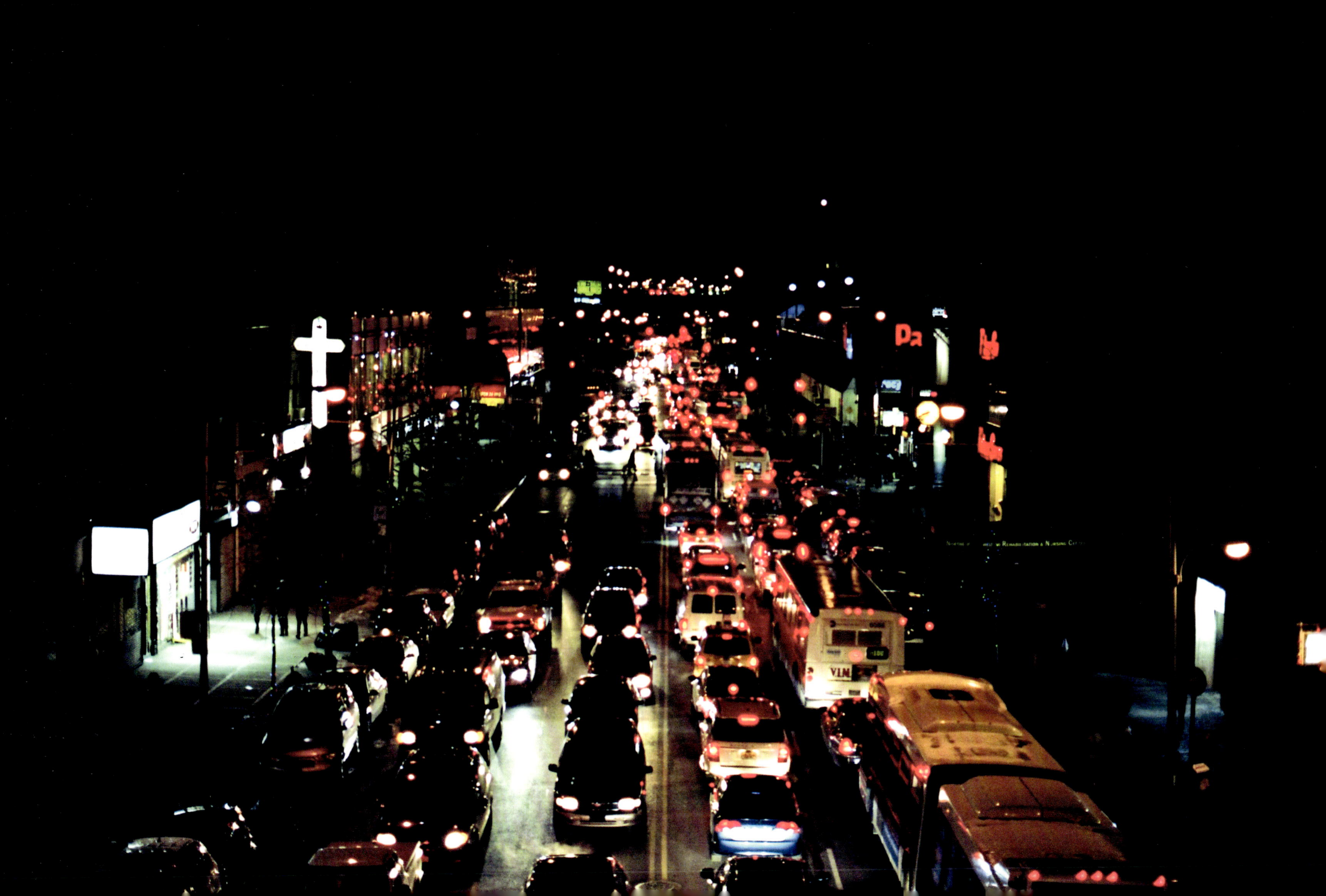

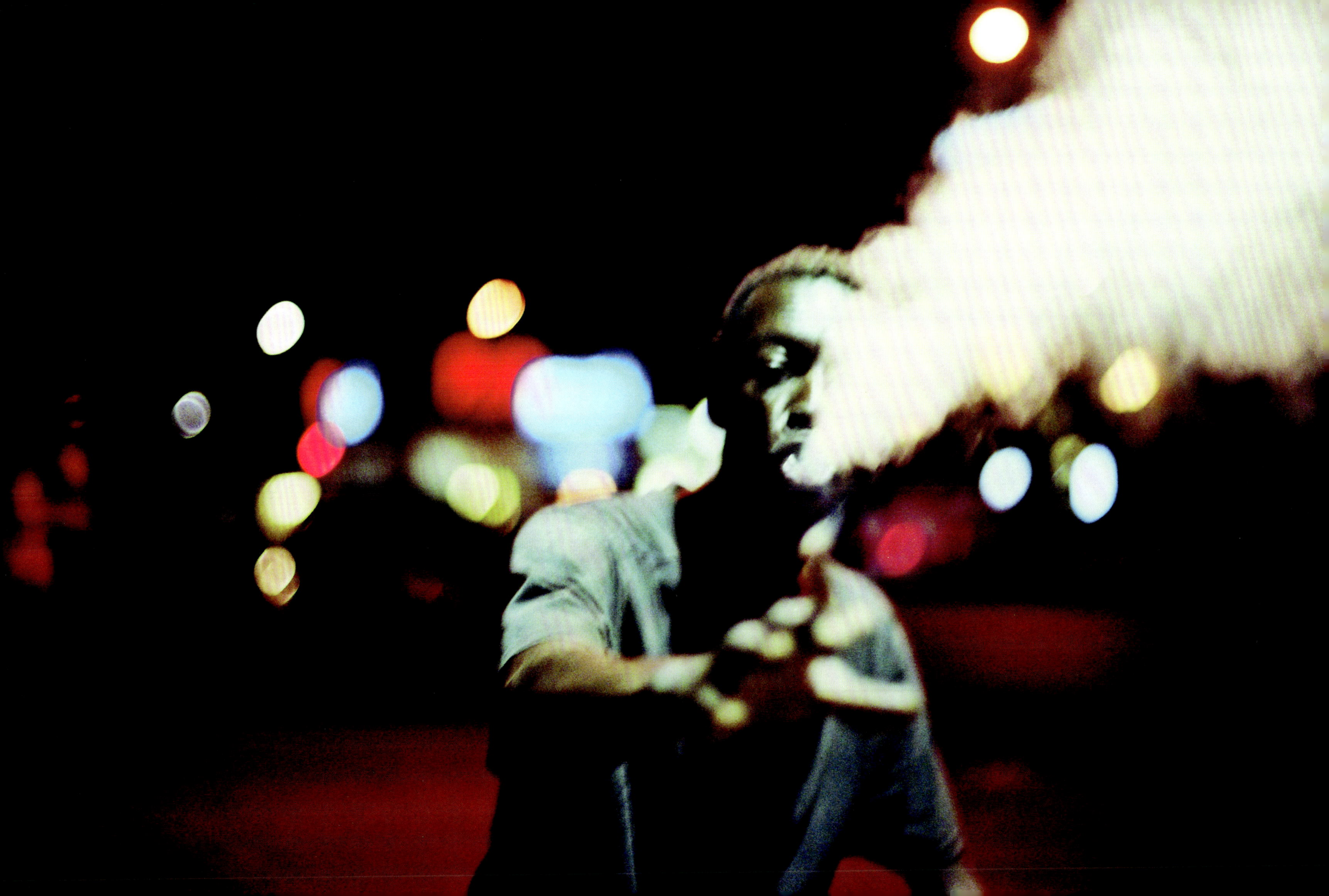

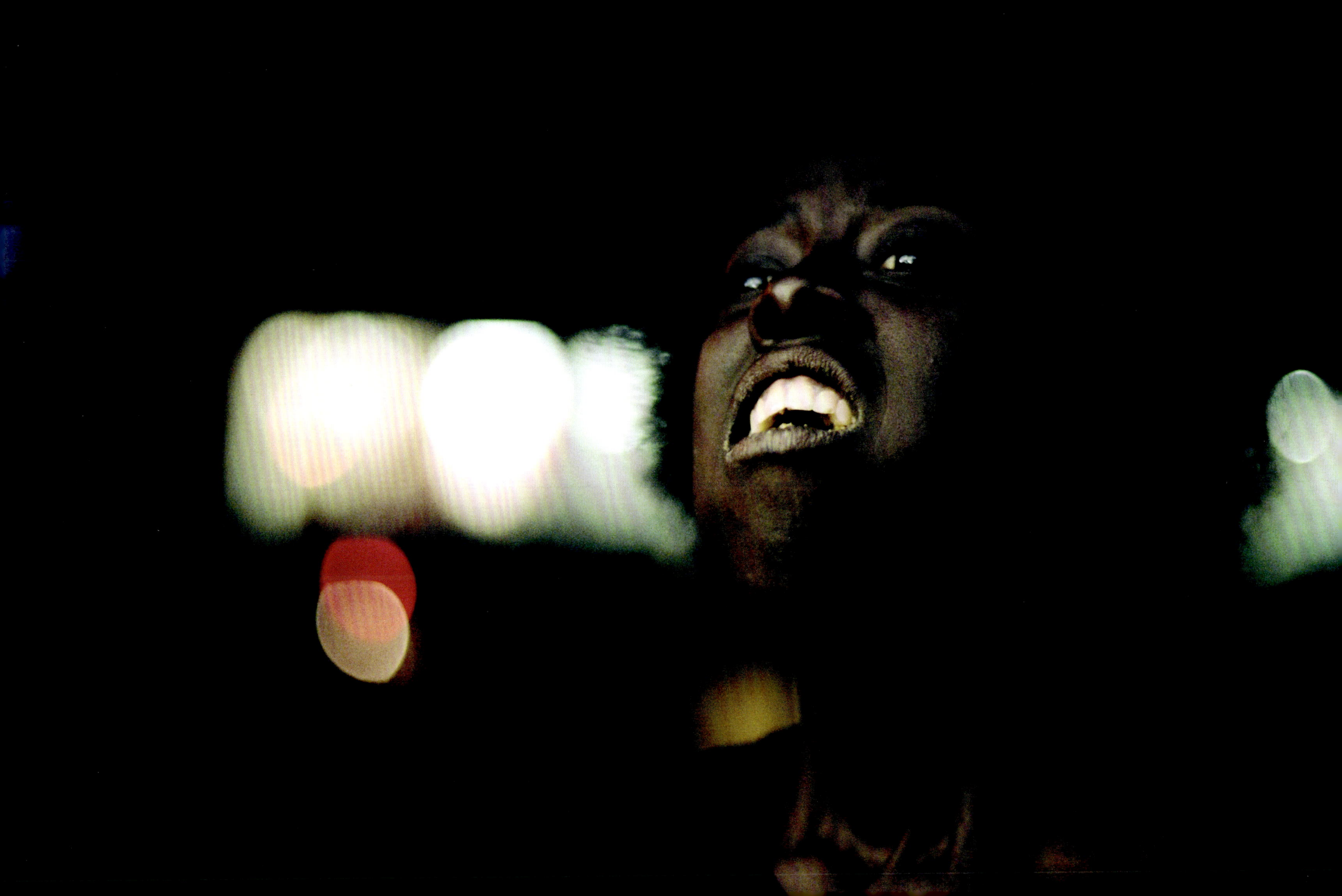

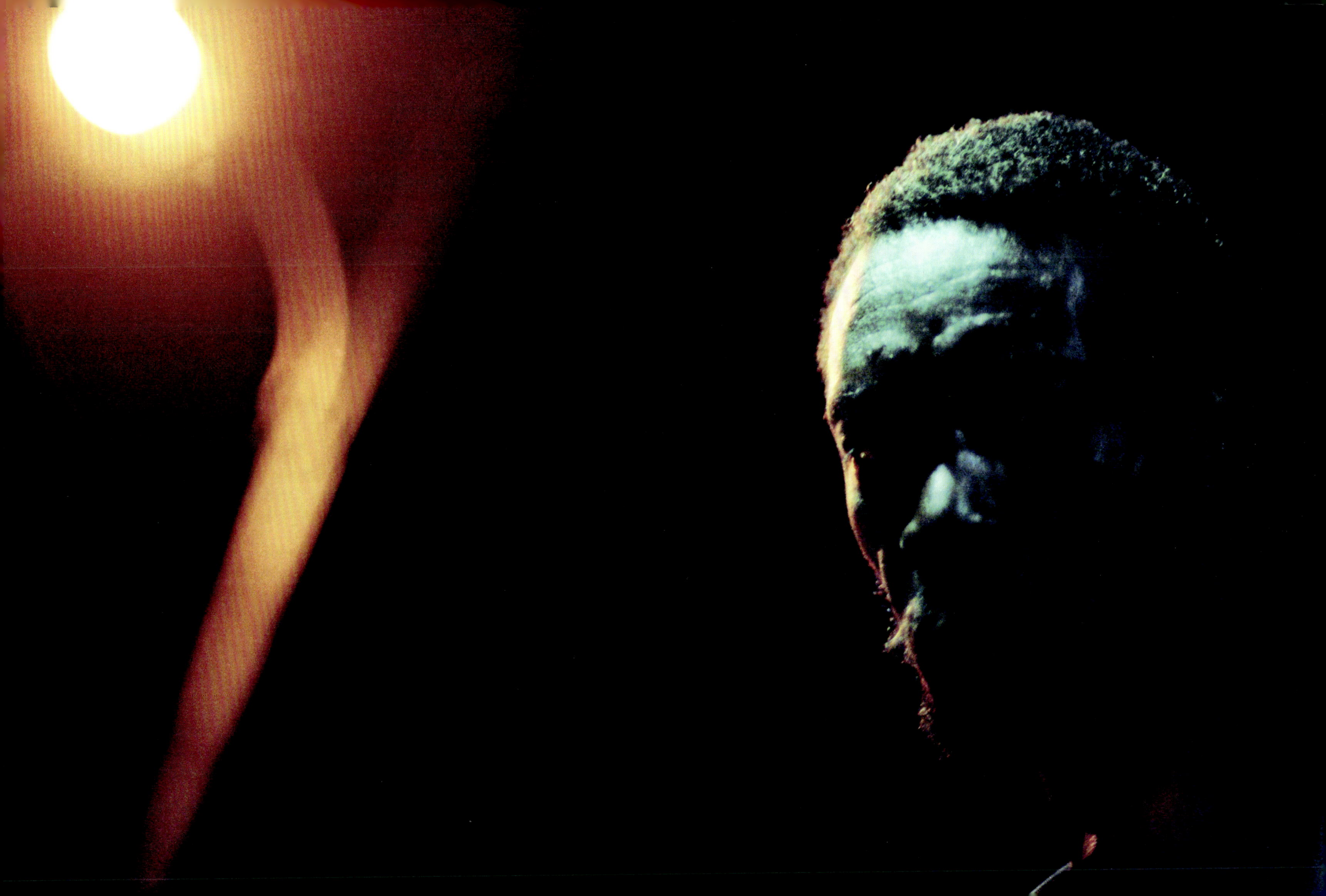

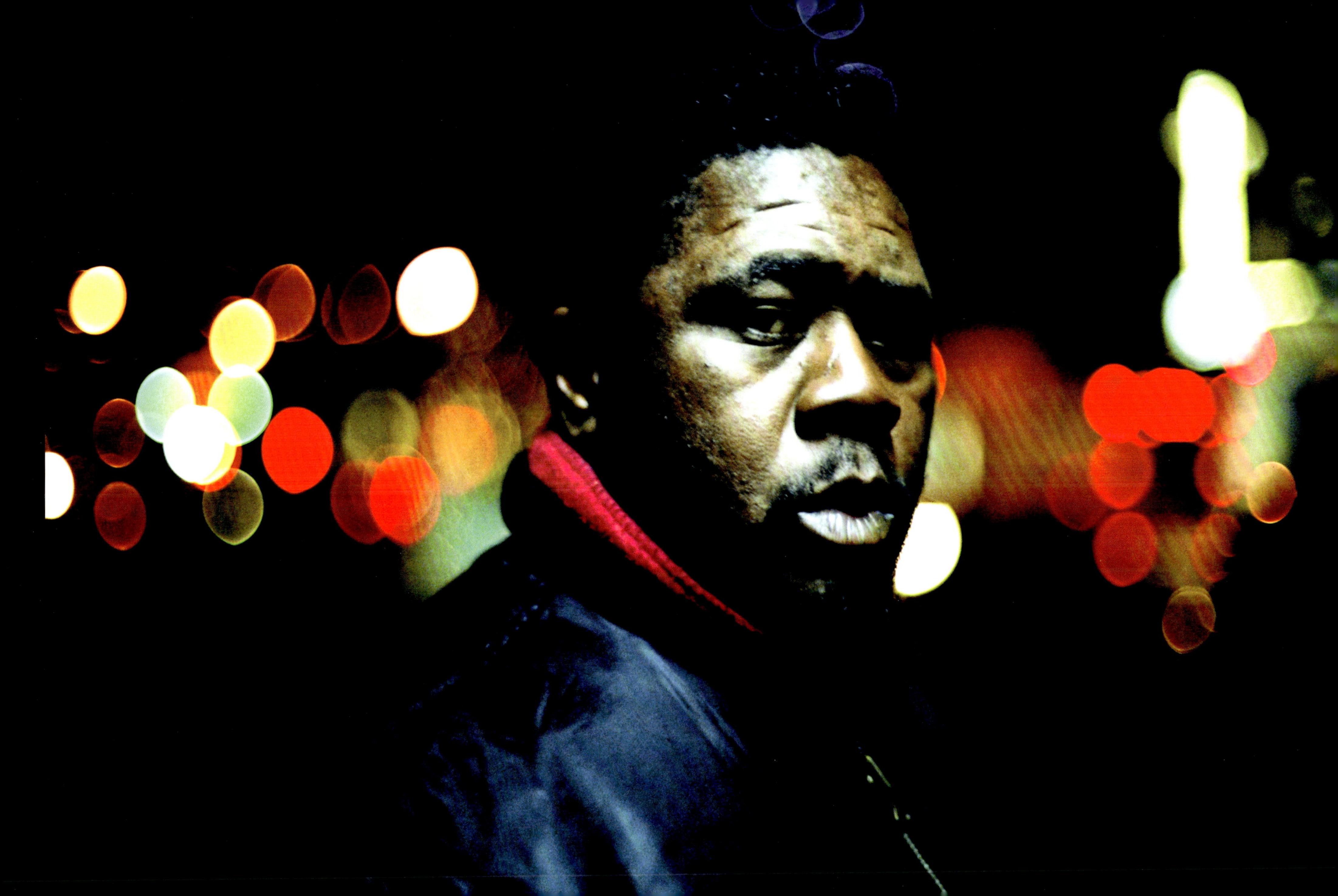

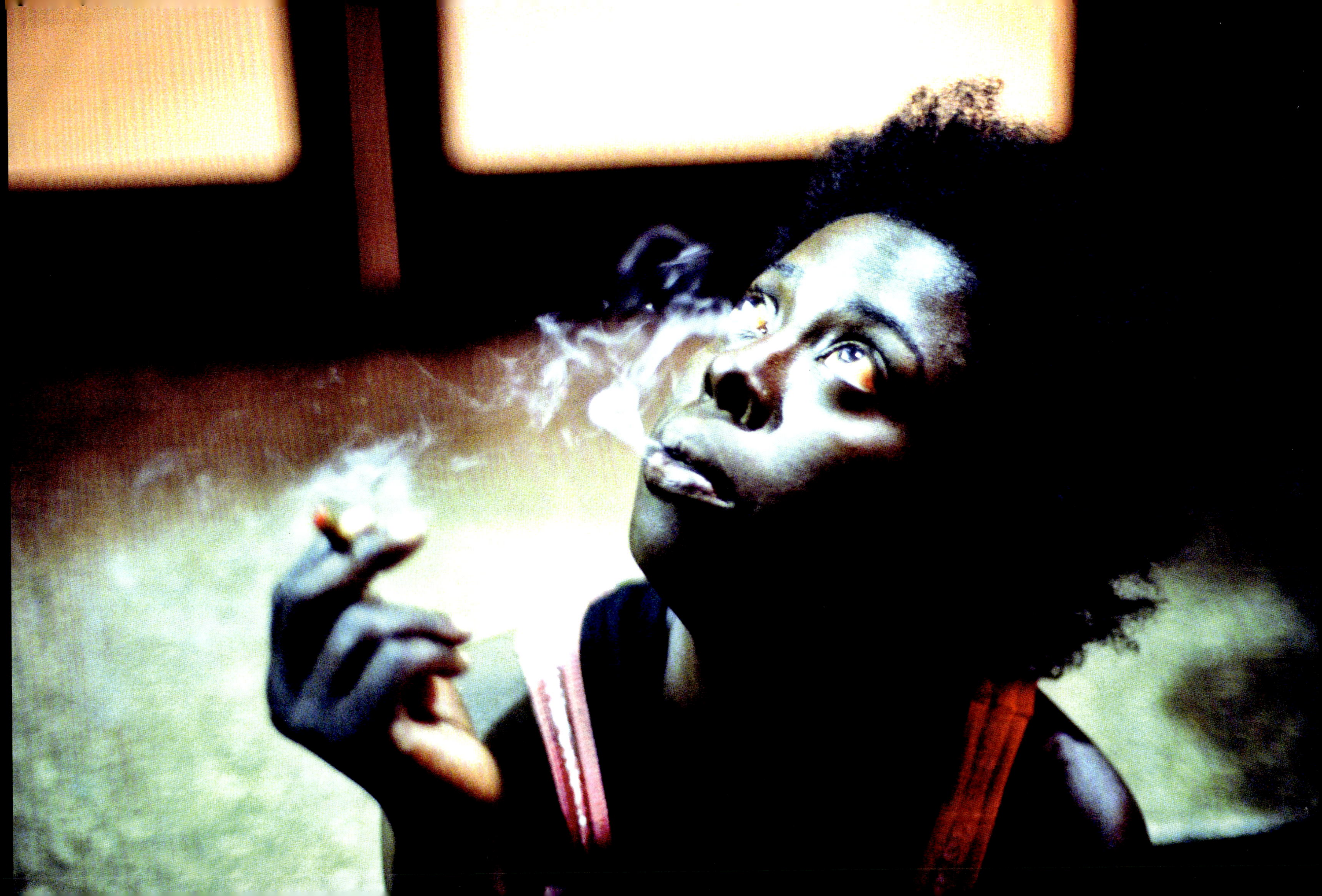

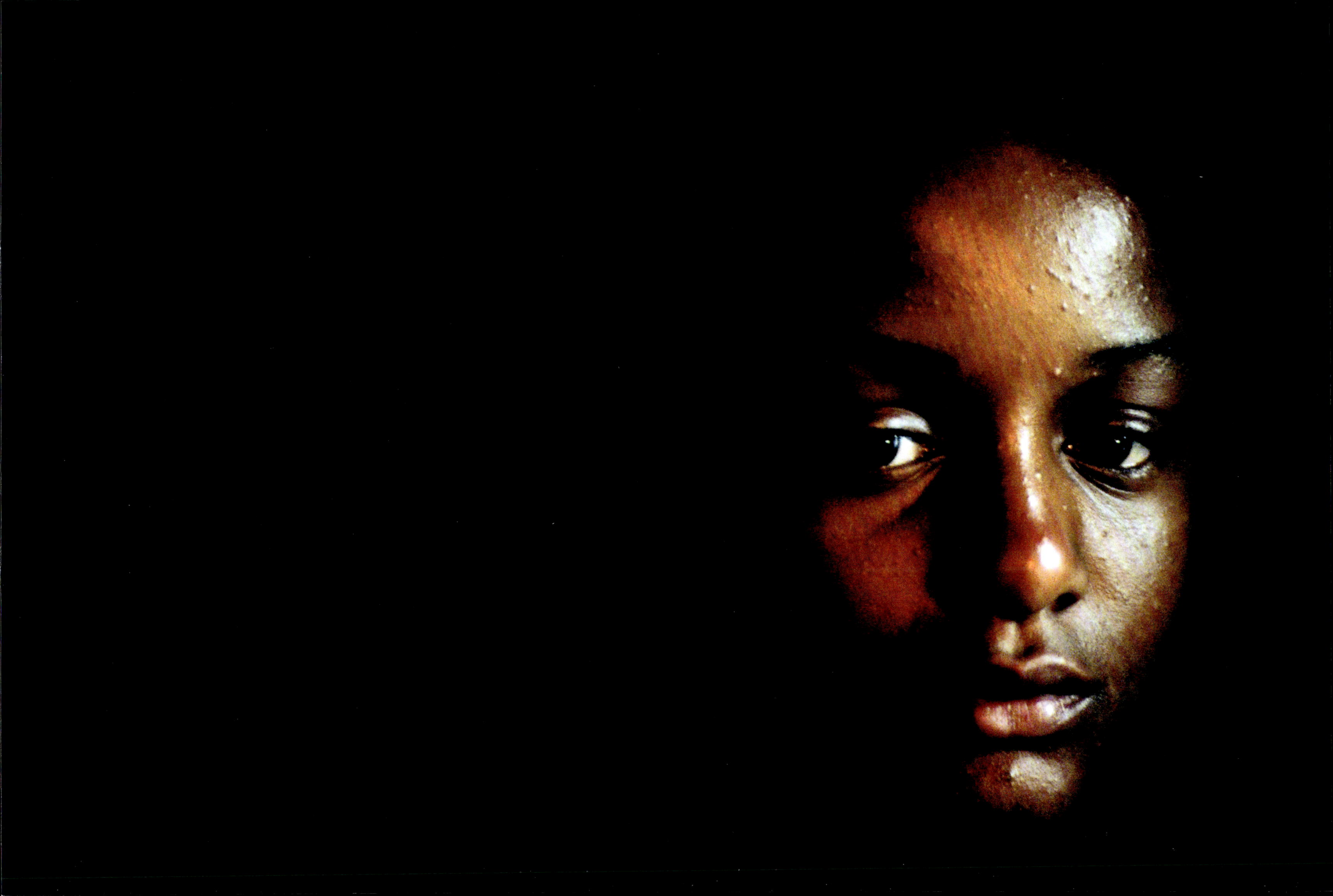

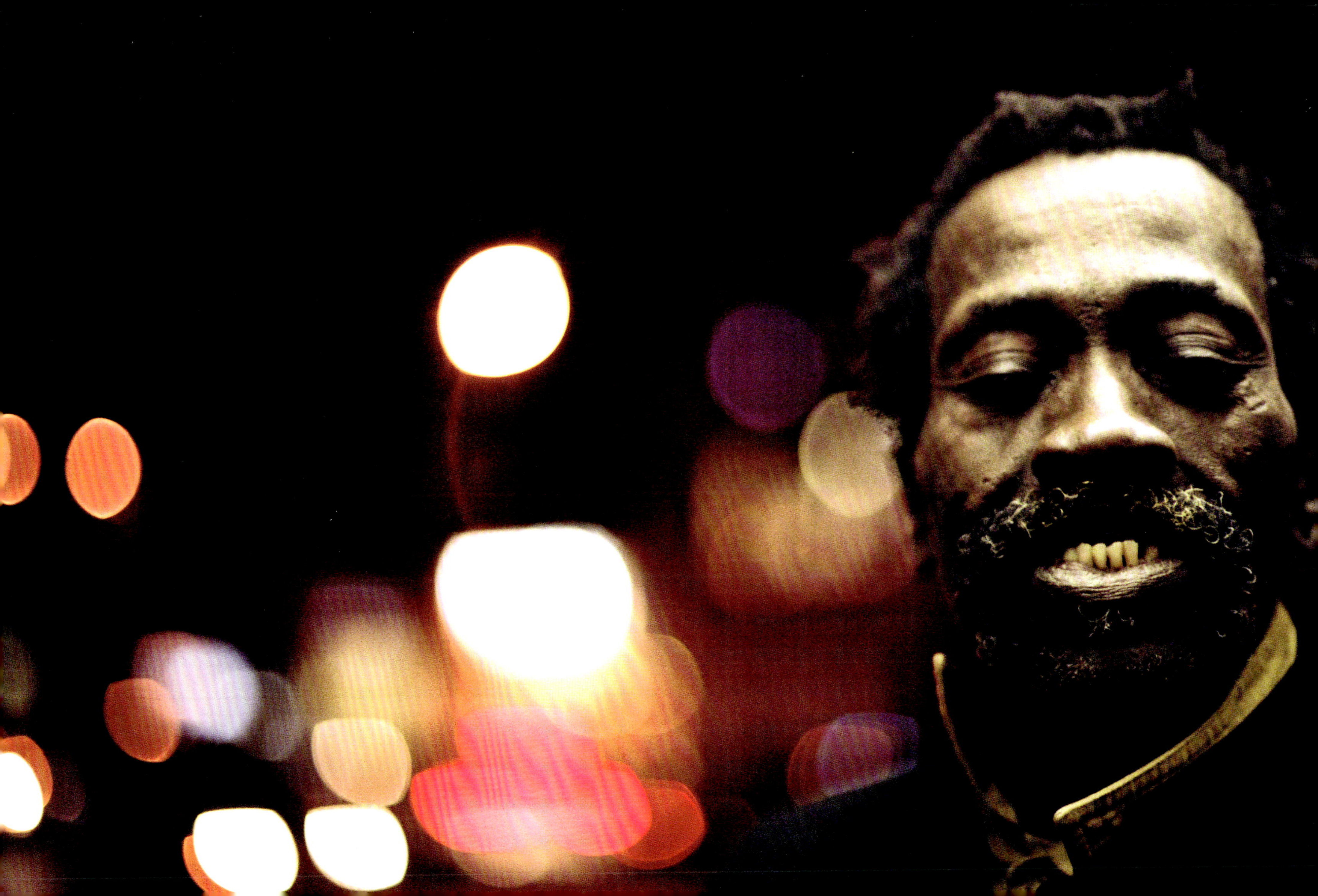

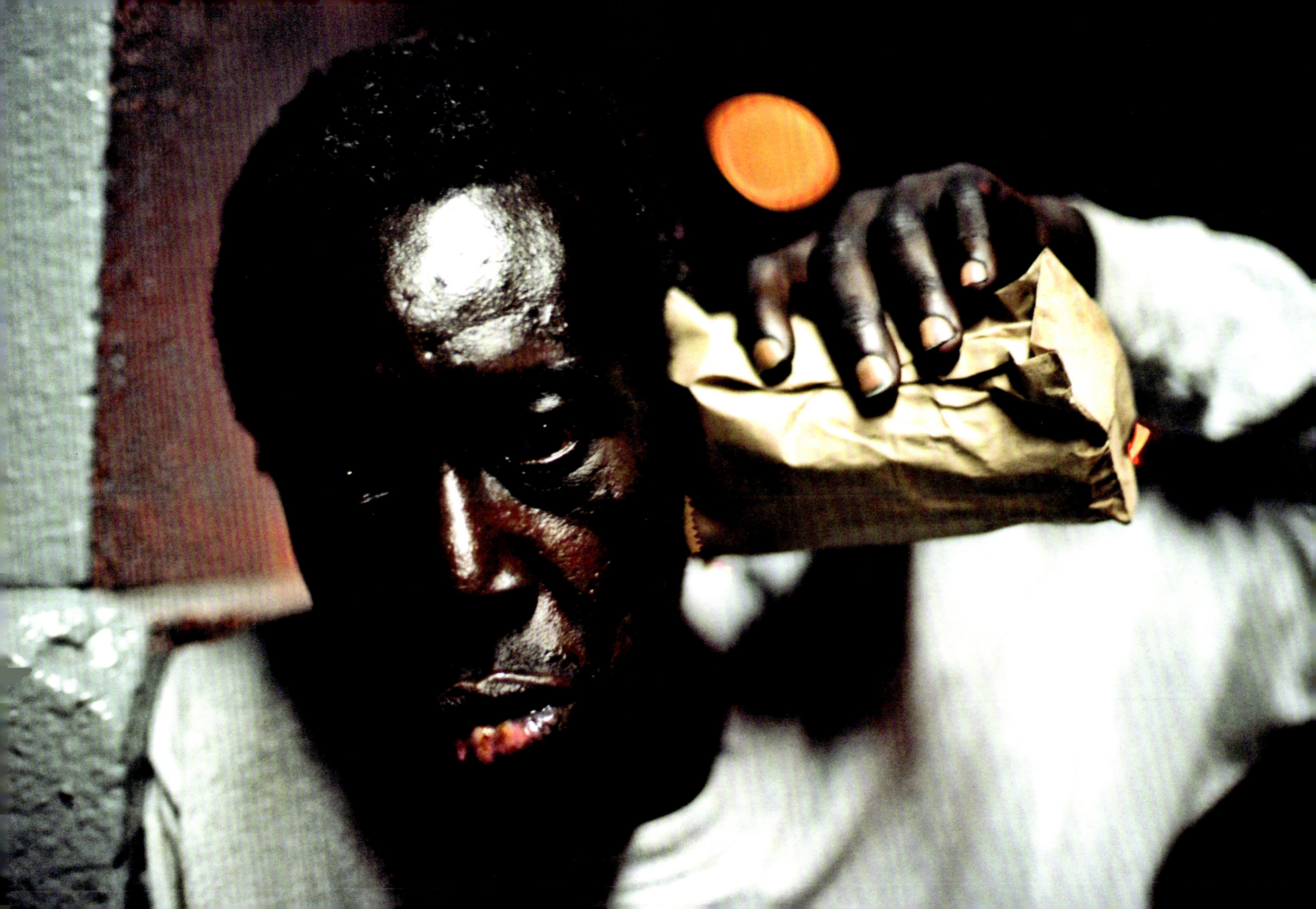

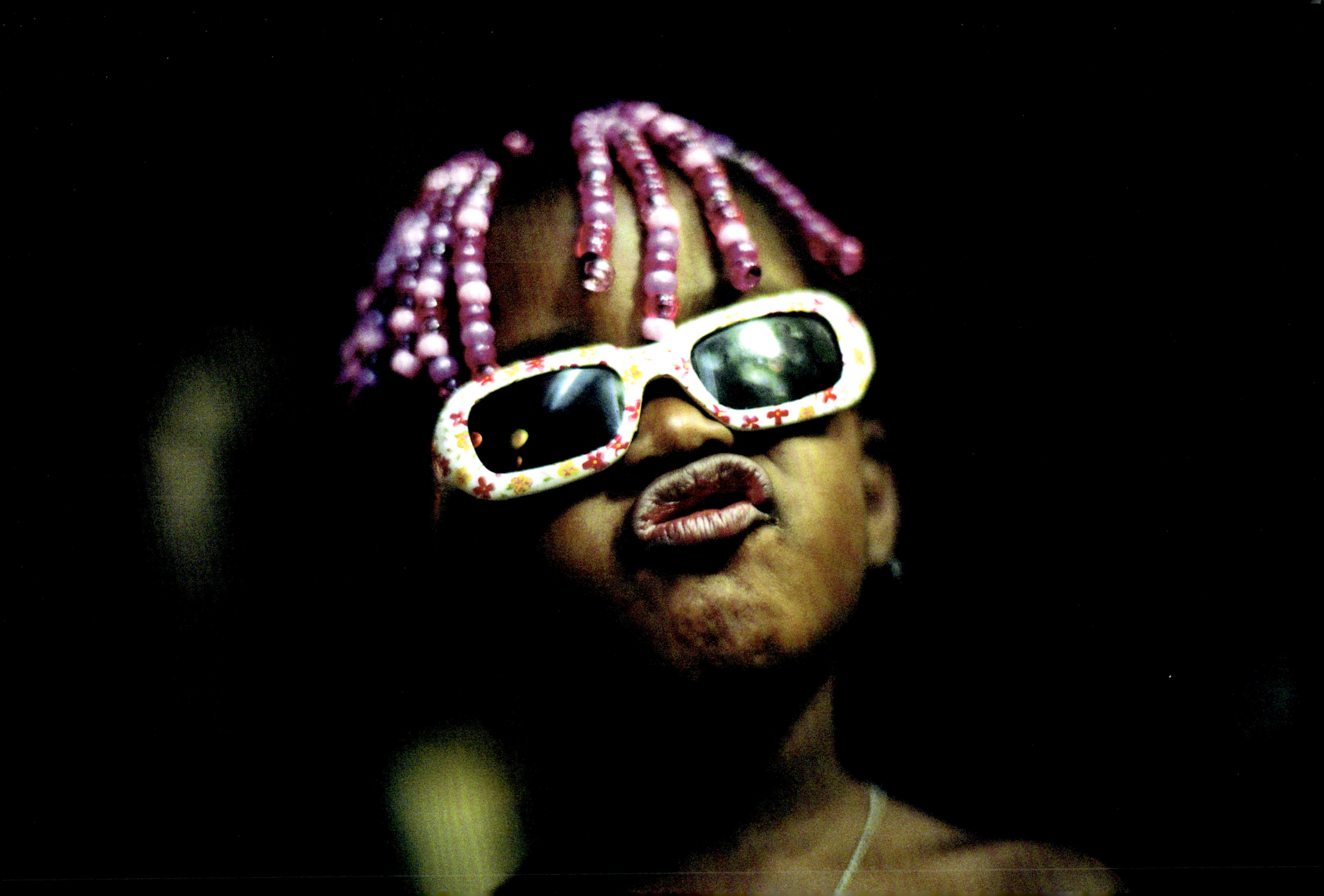

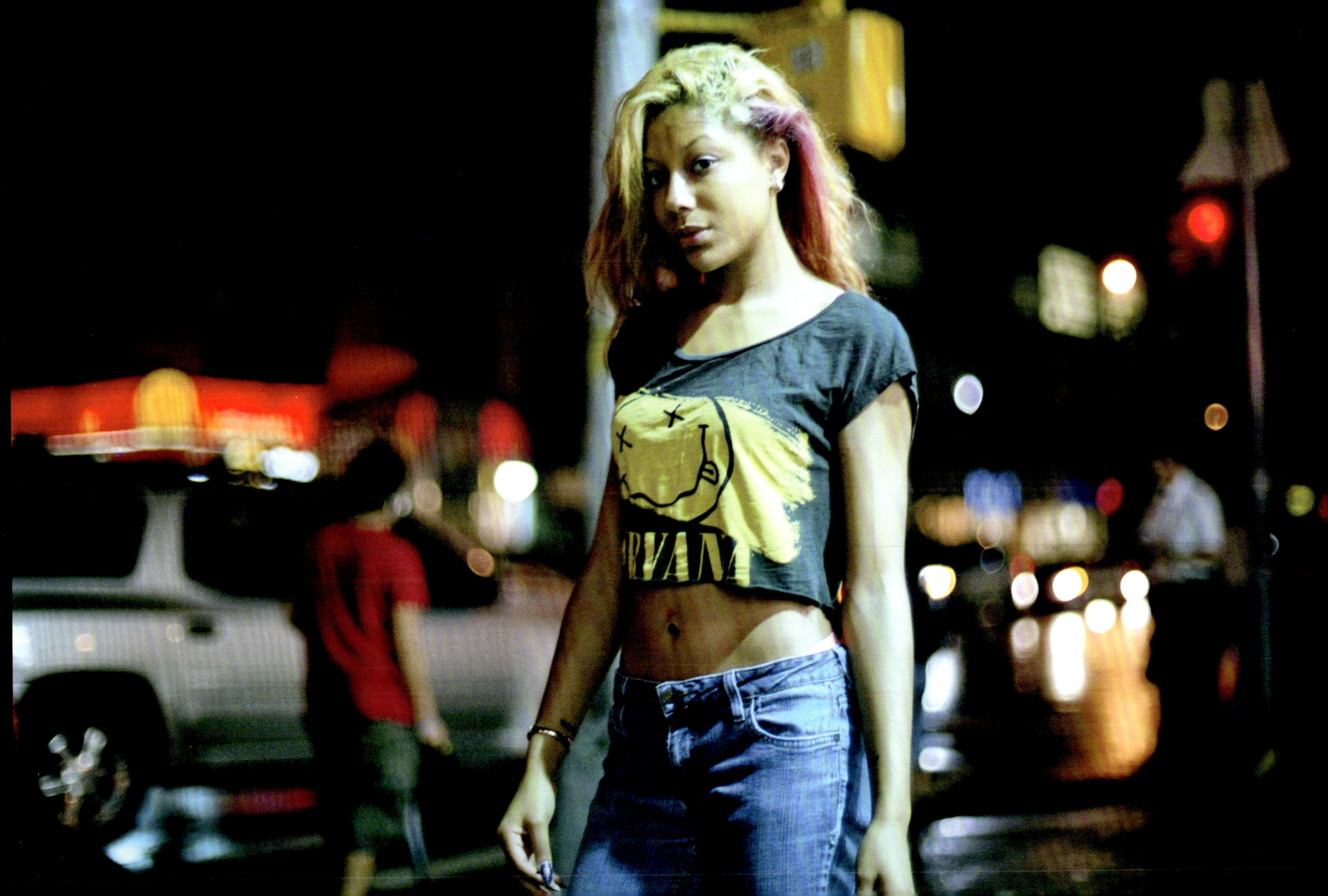

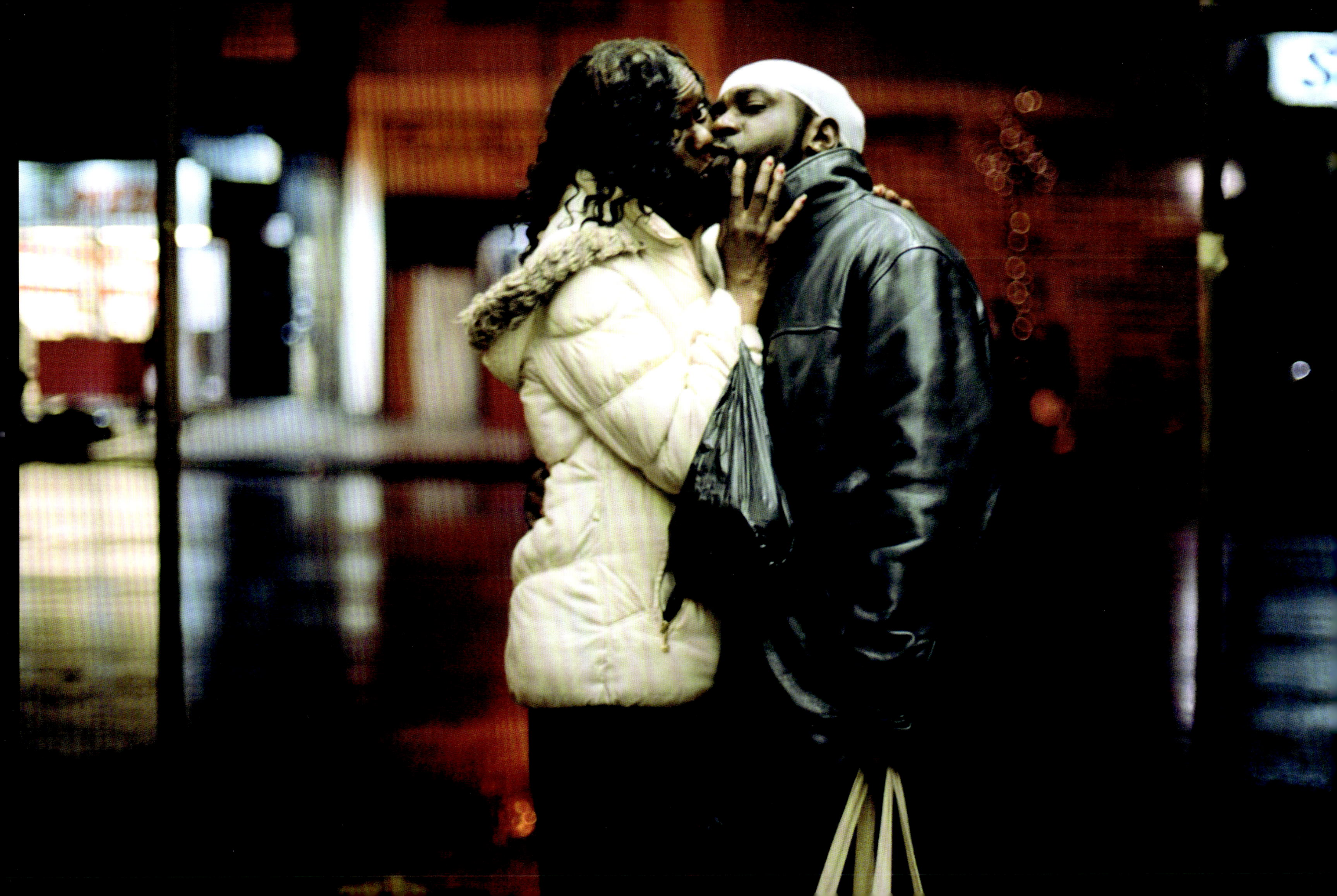

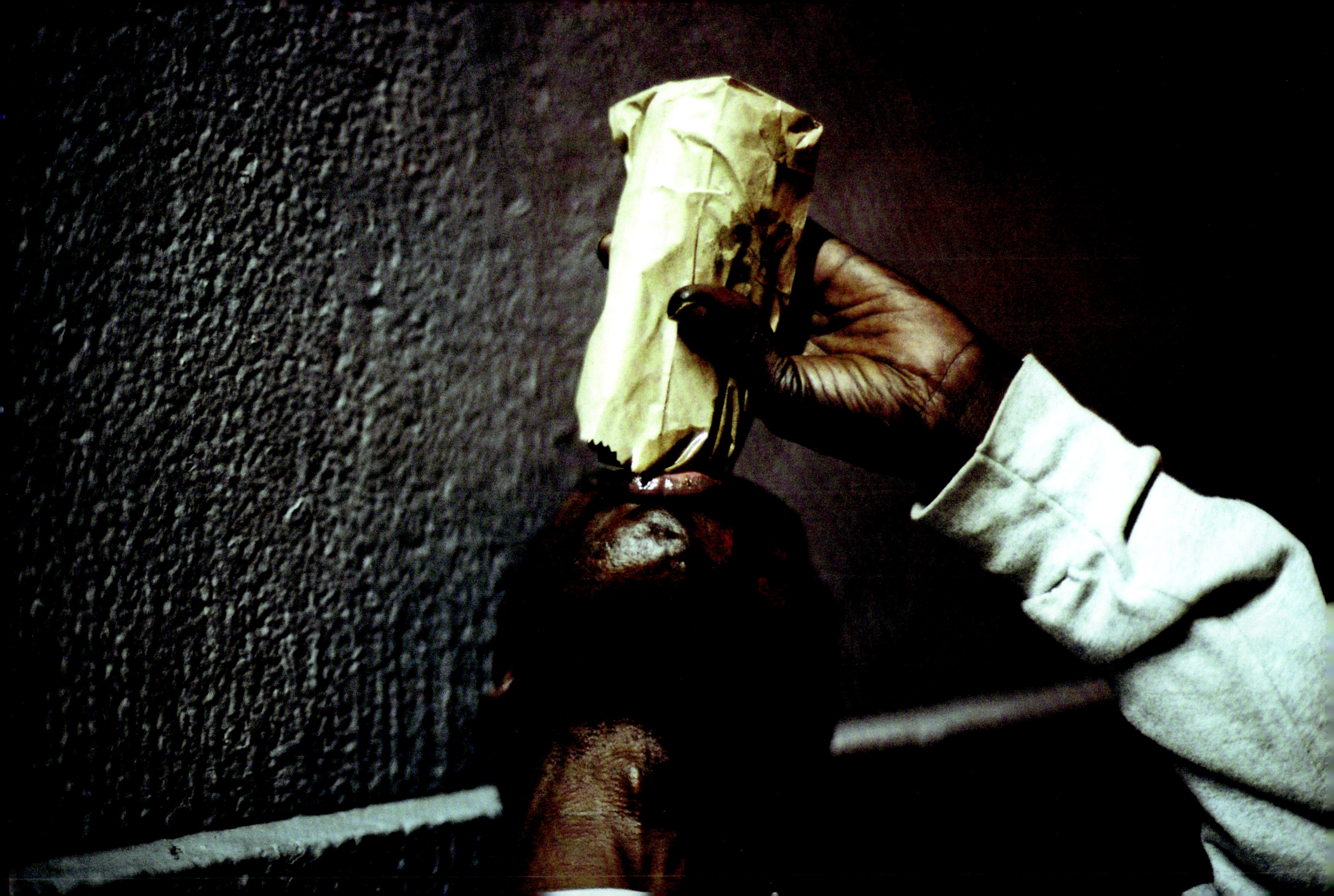

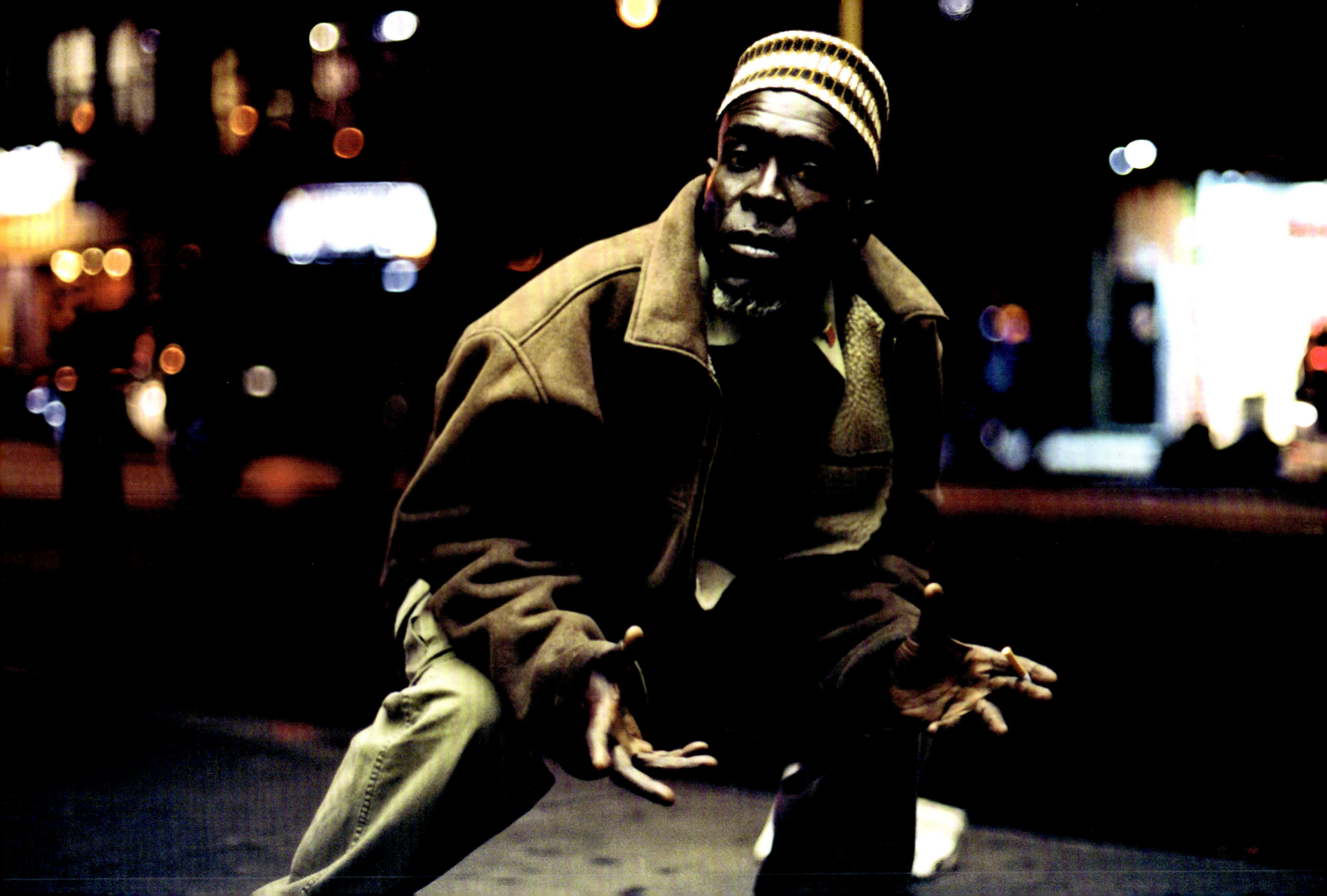

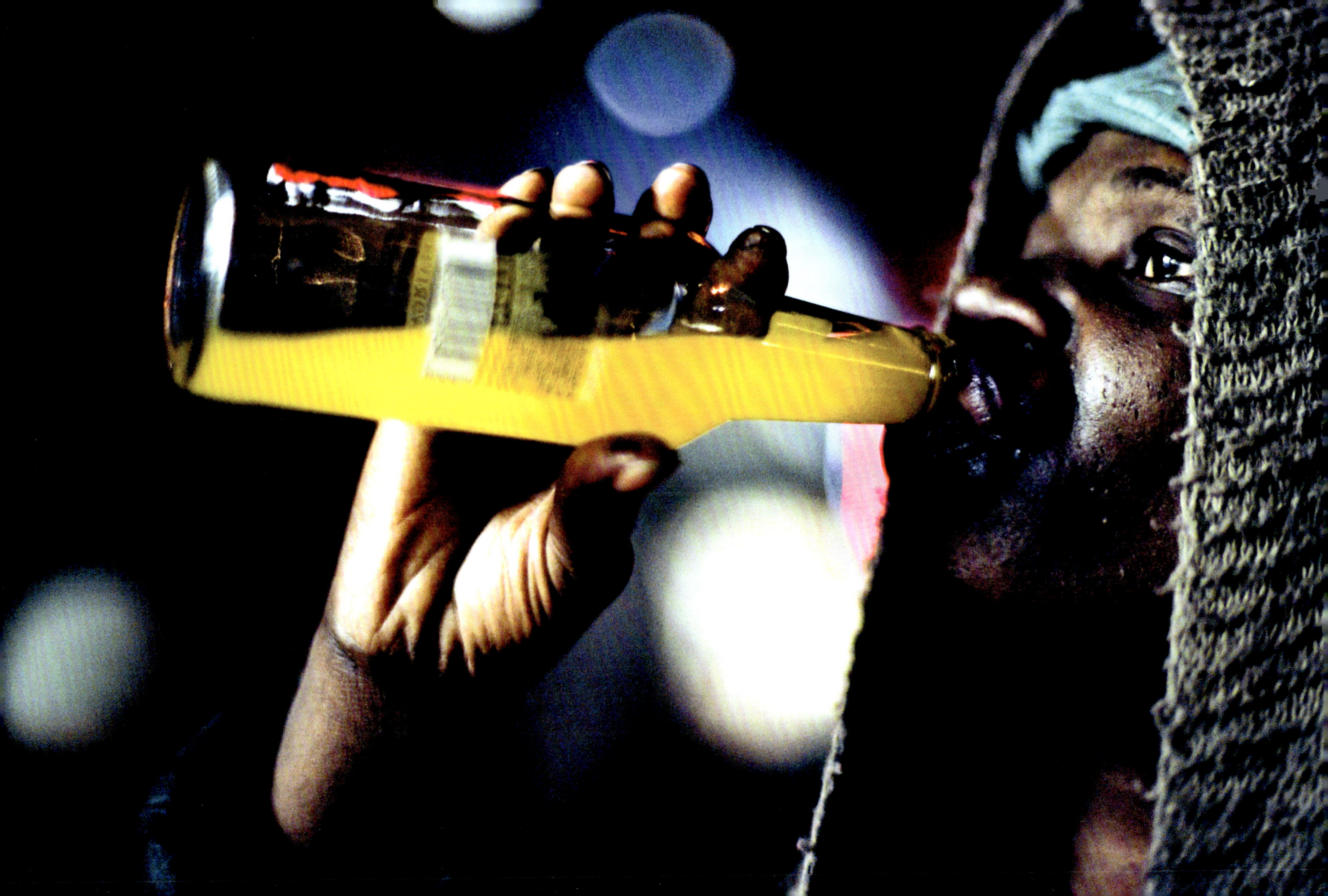

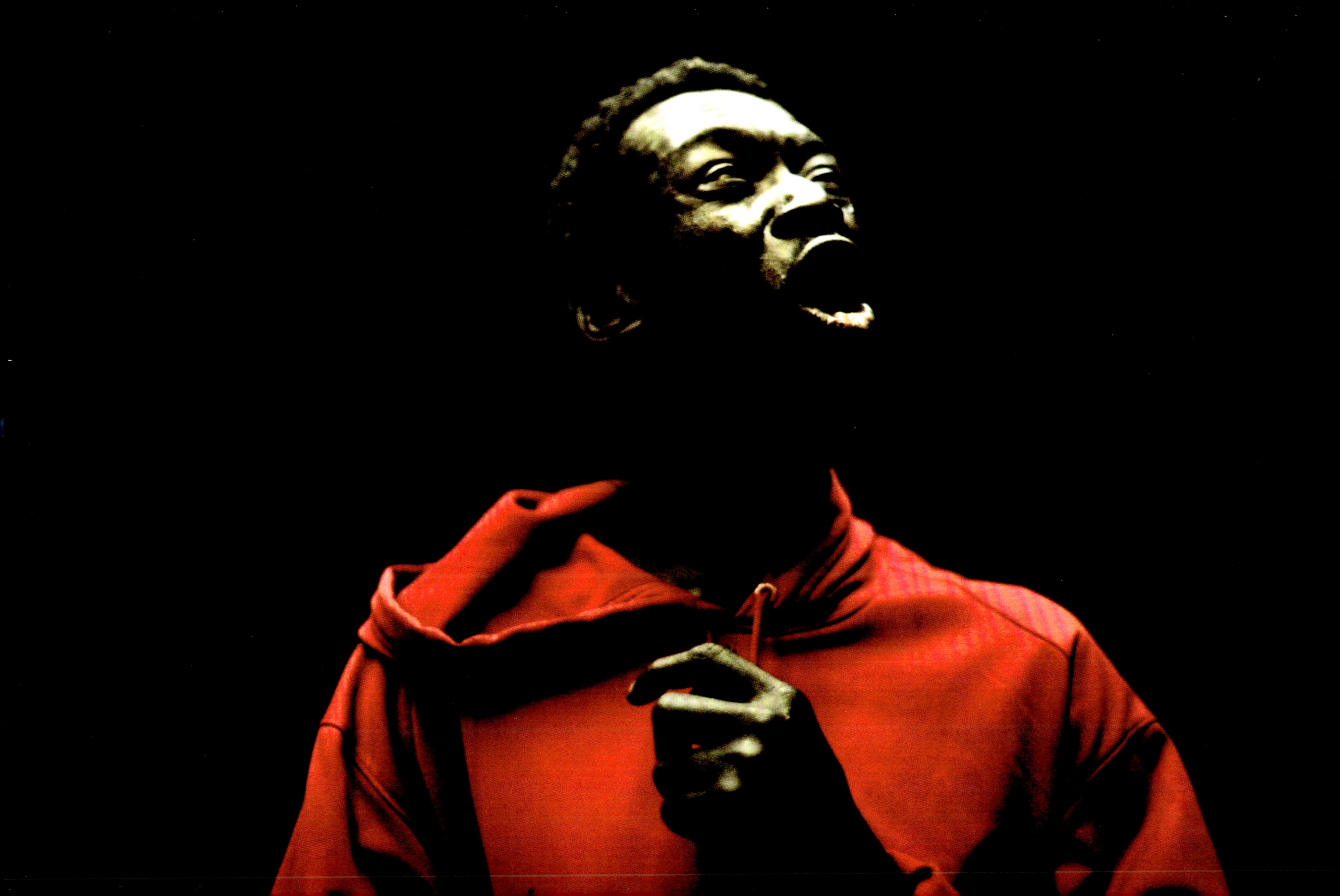

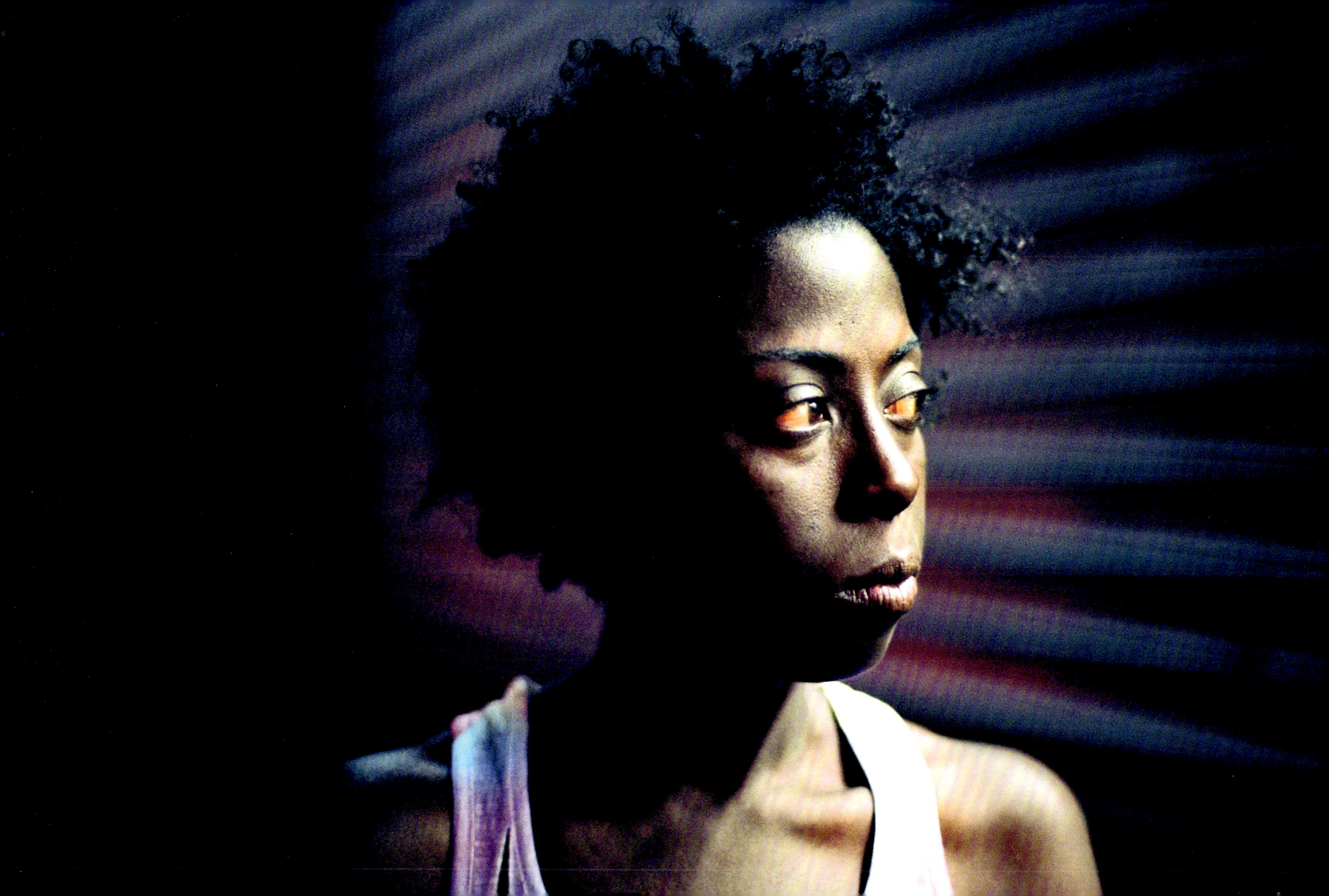

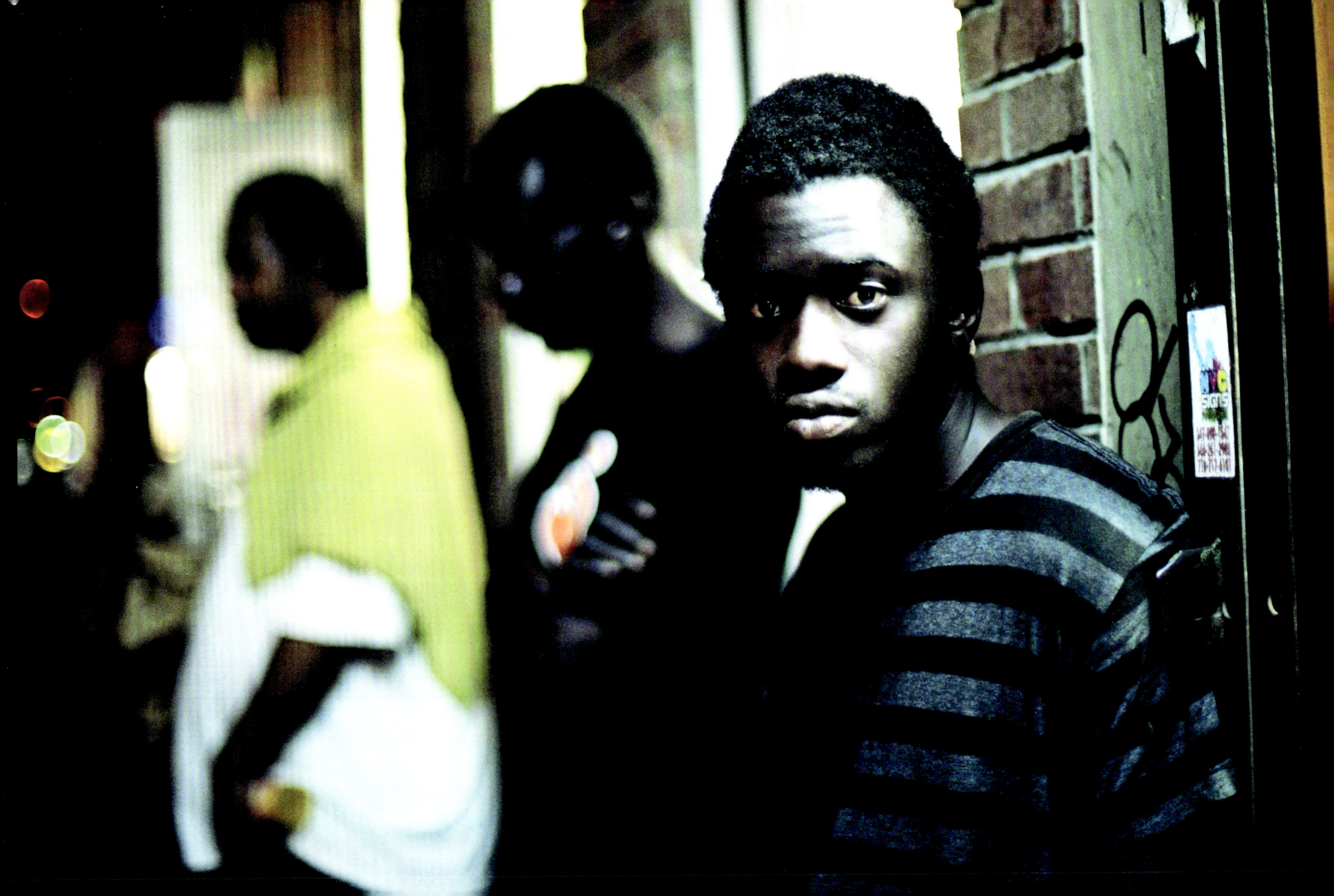
SIGNS

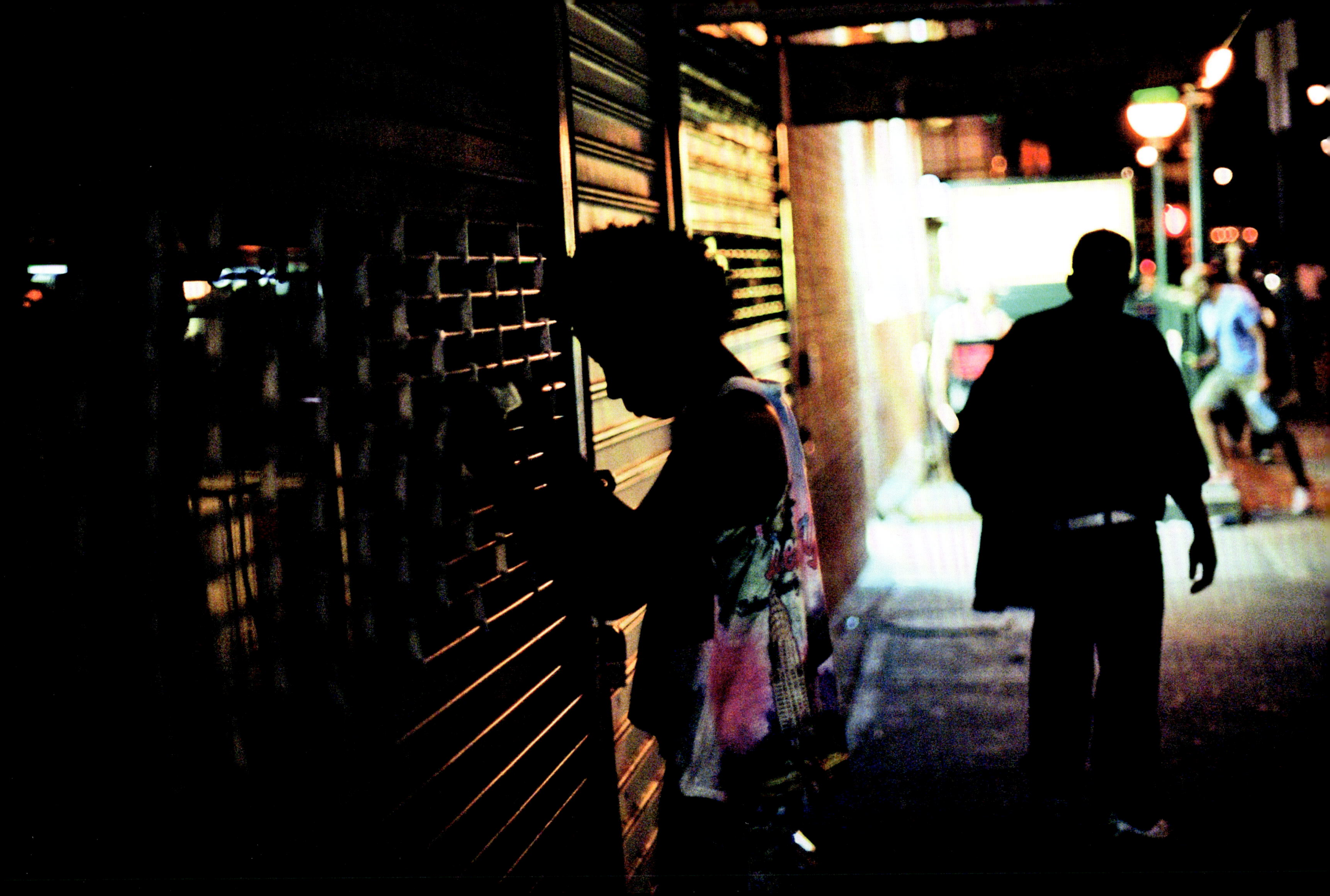

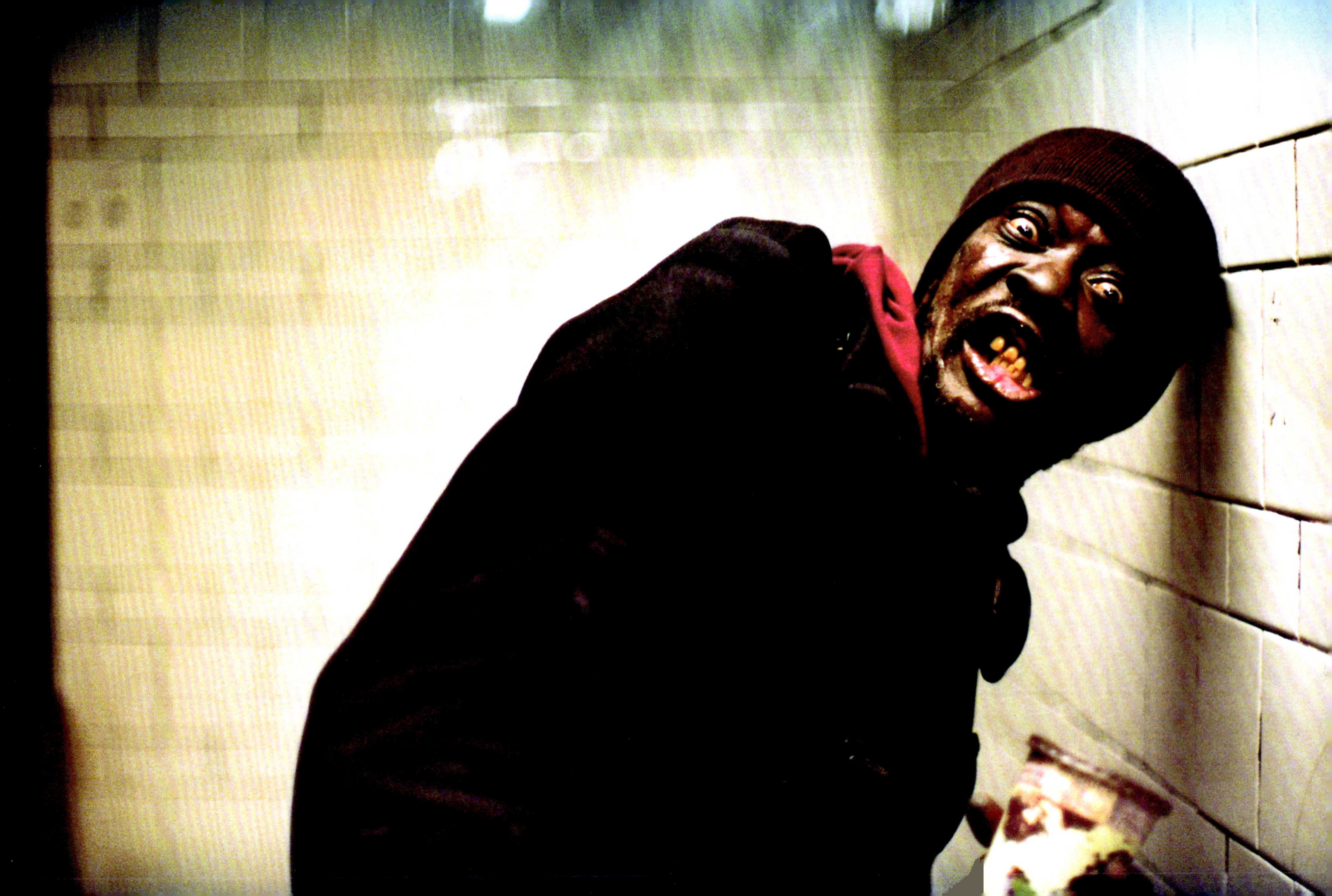

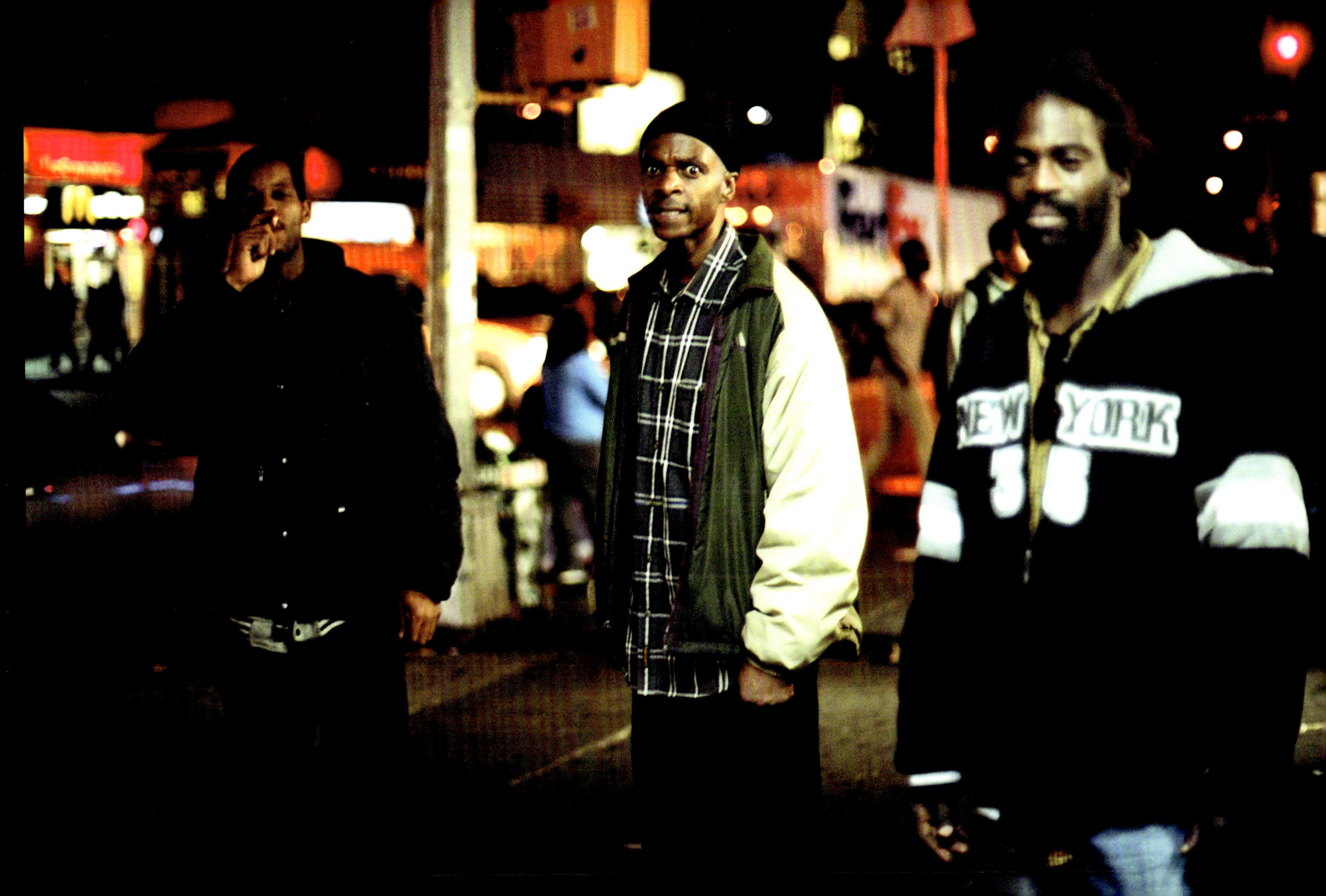
NEW YORK

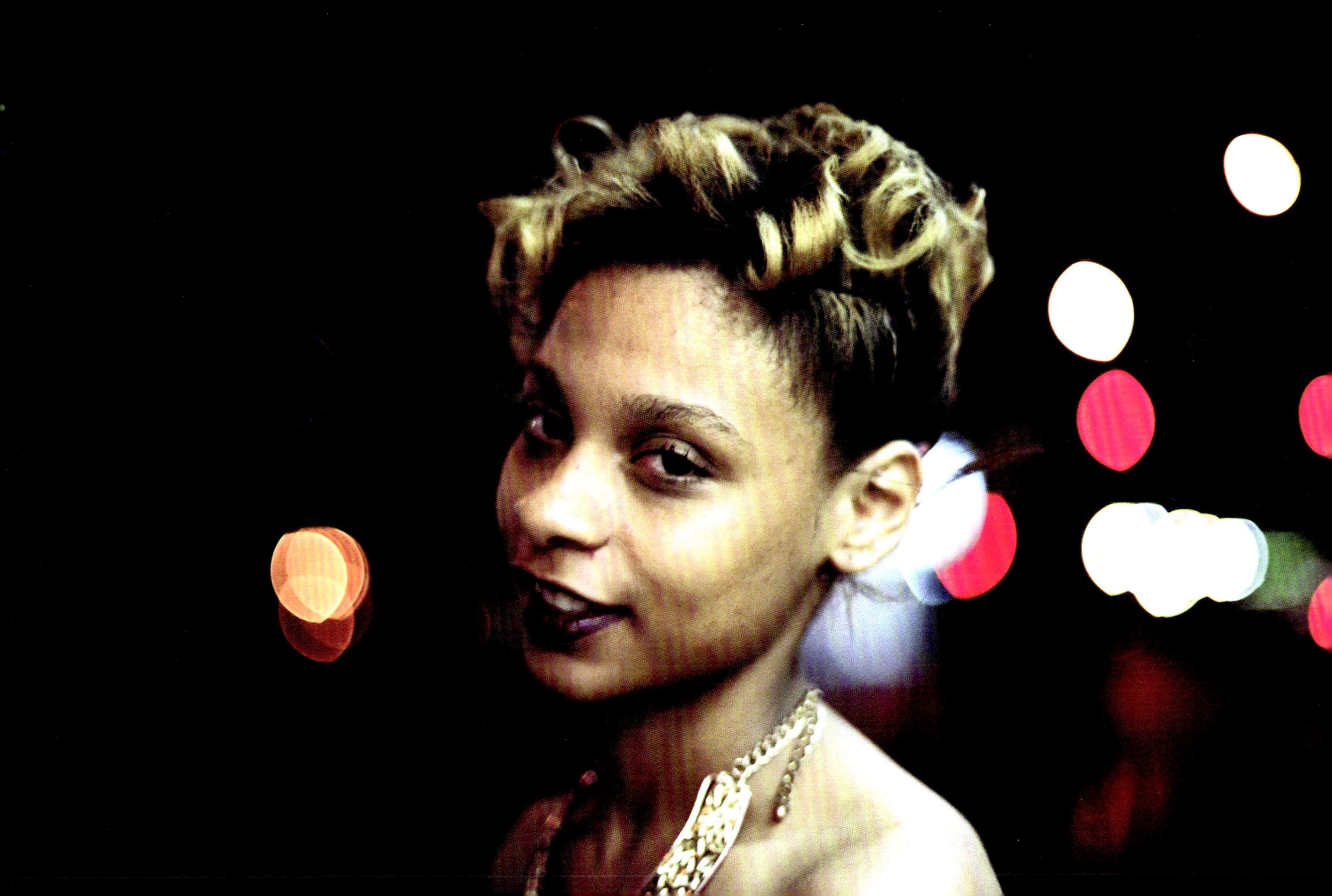

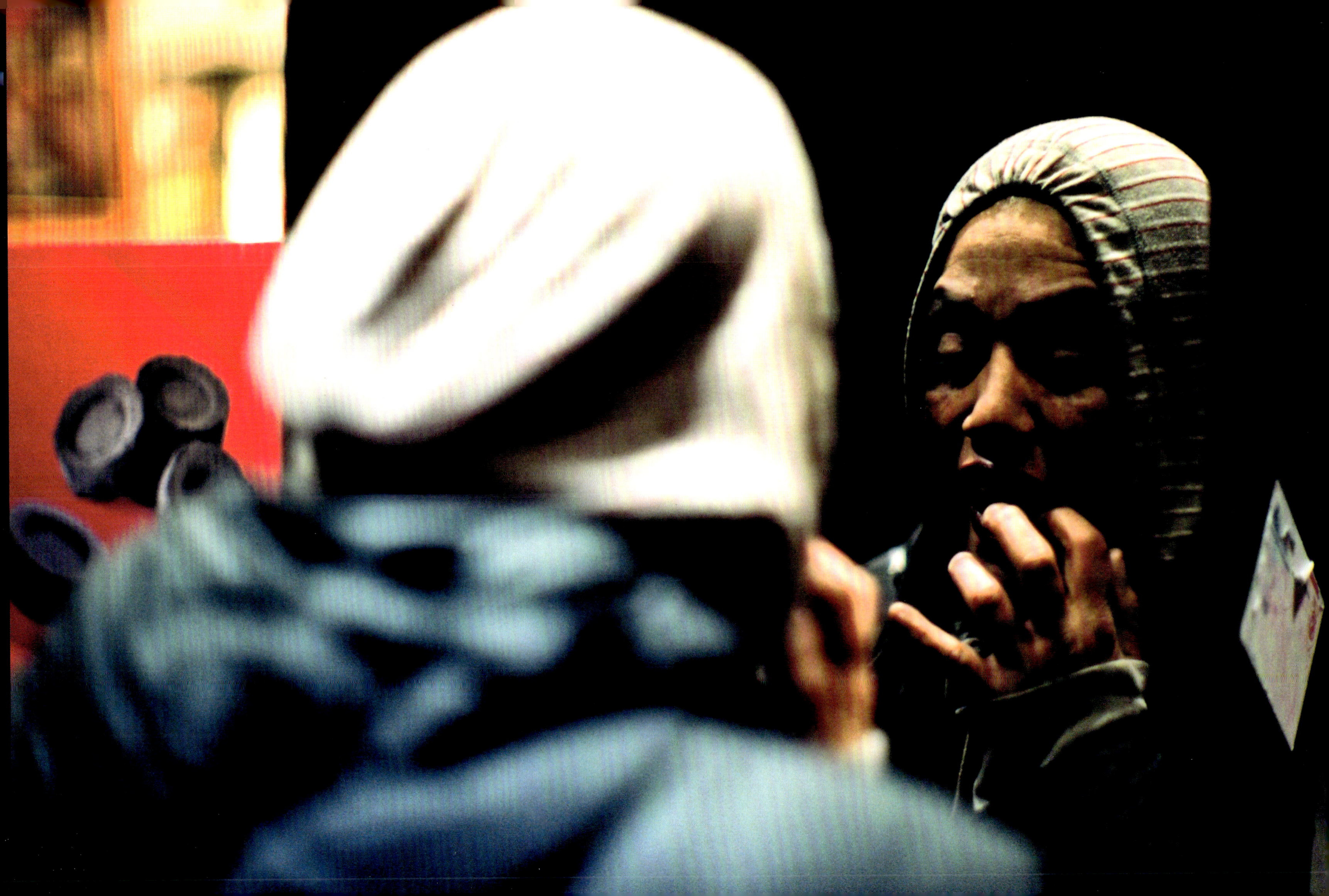

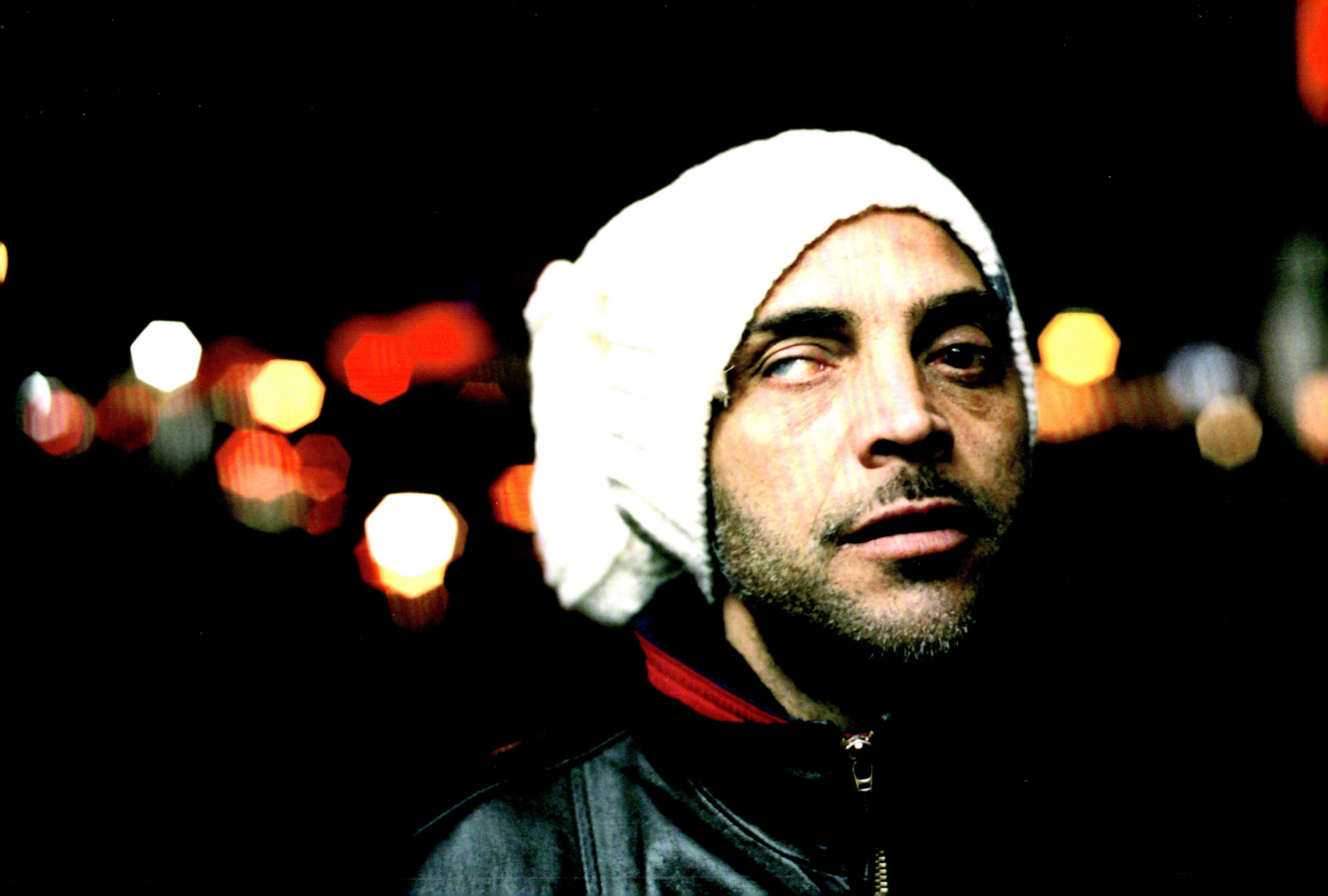

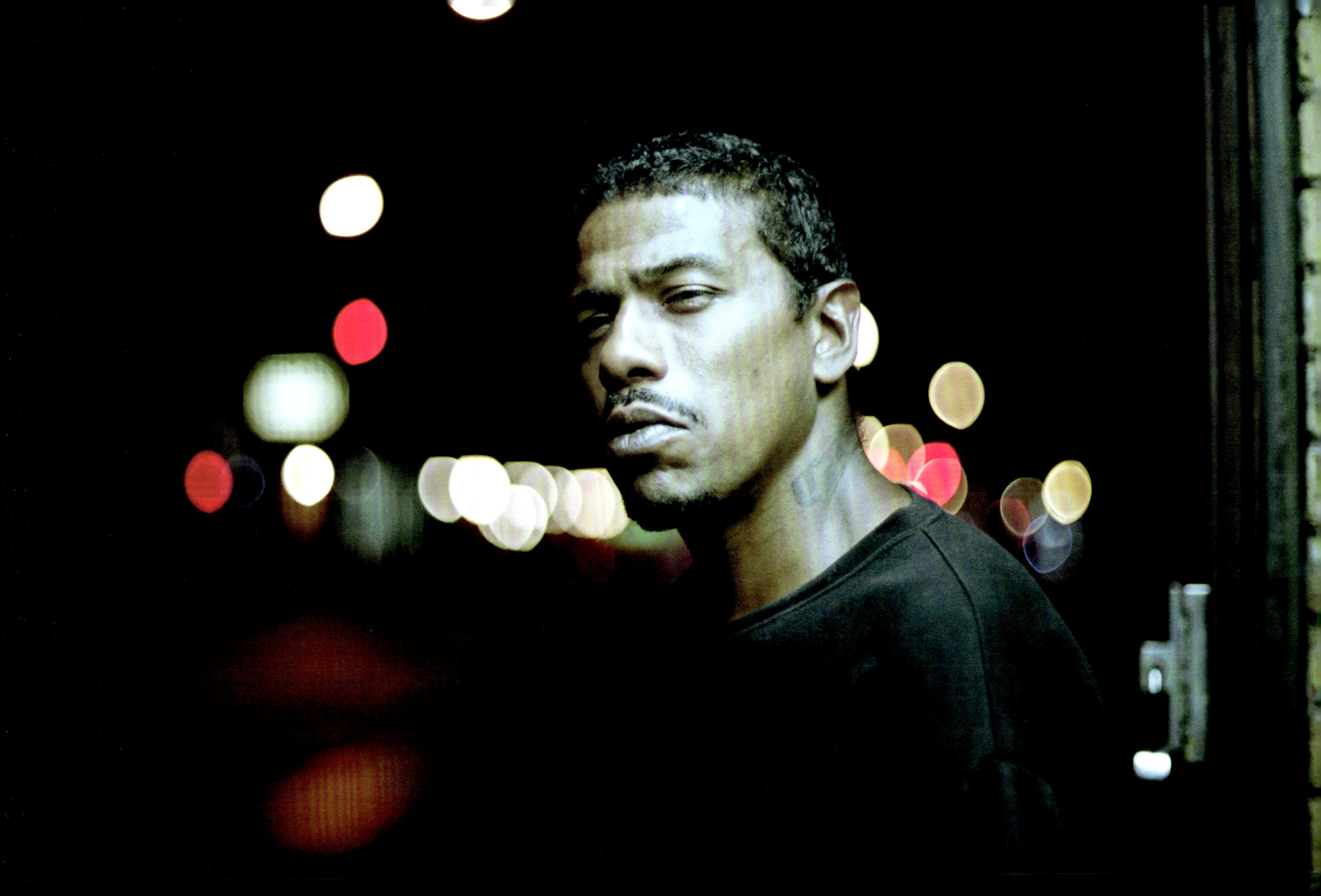

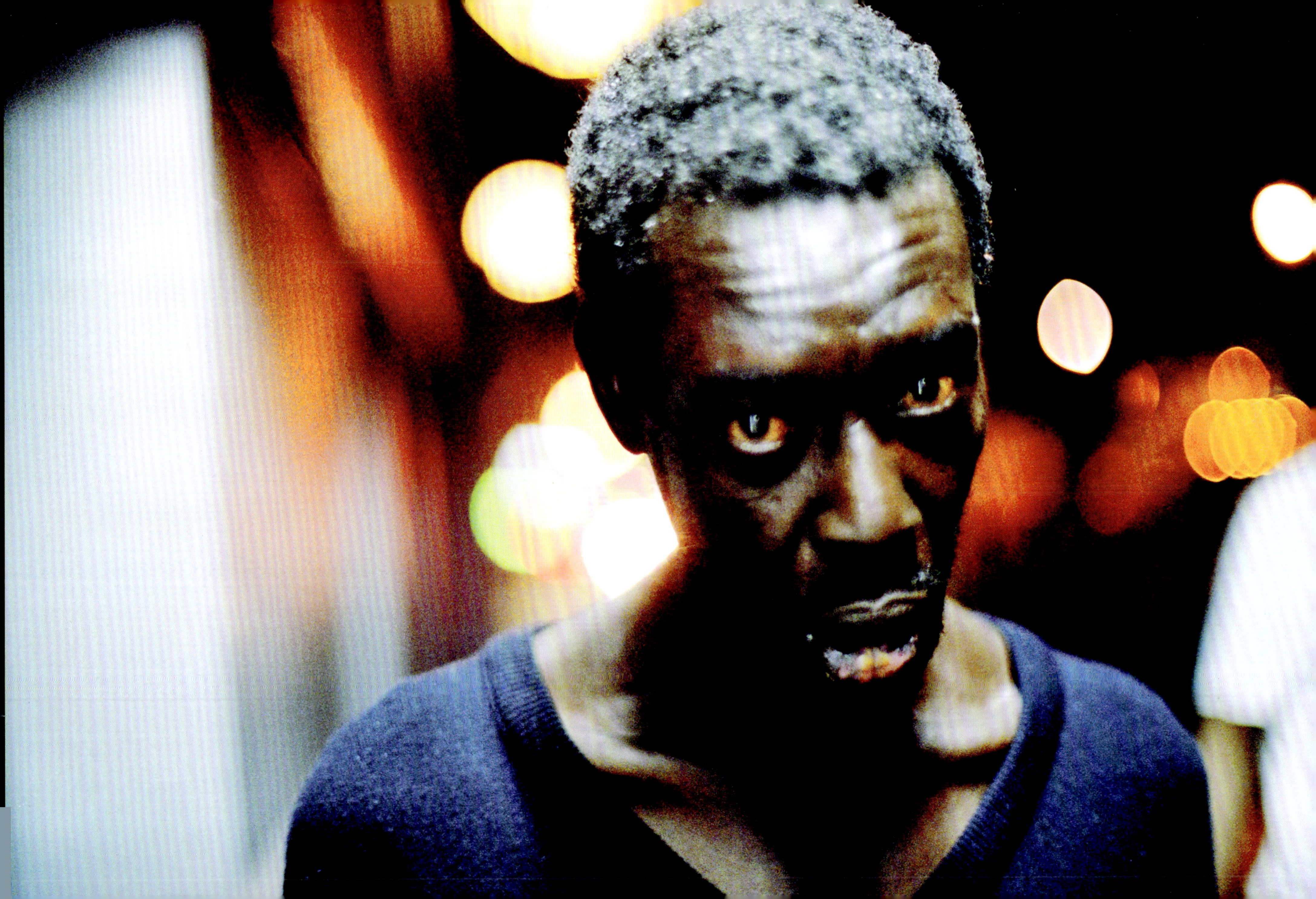

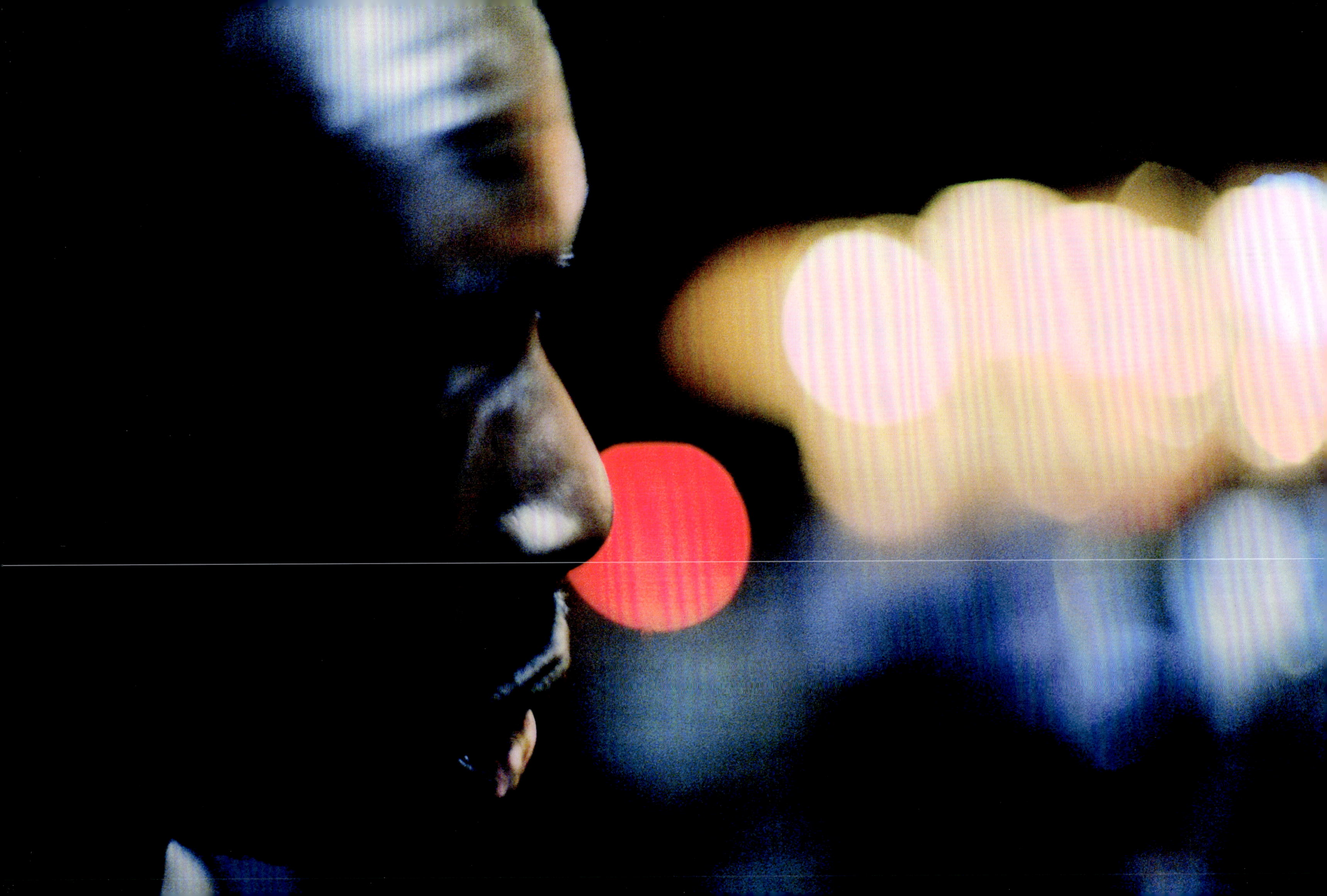

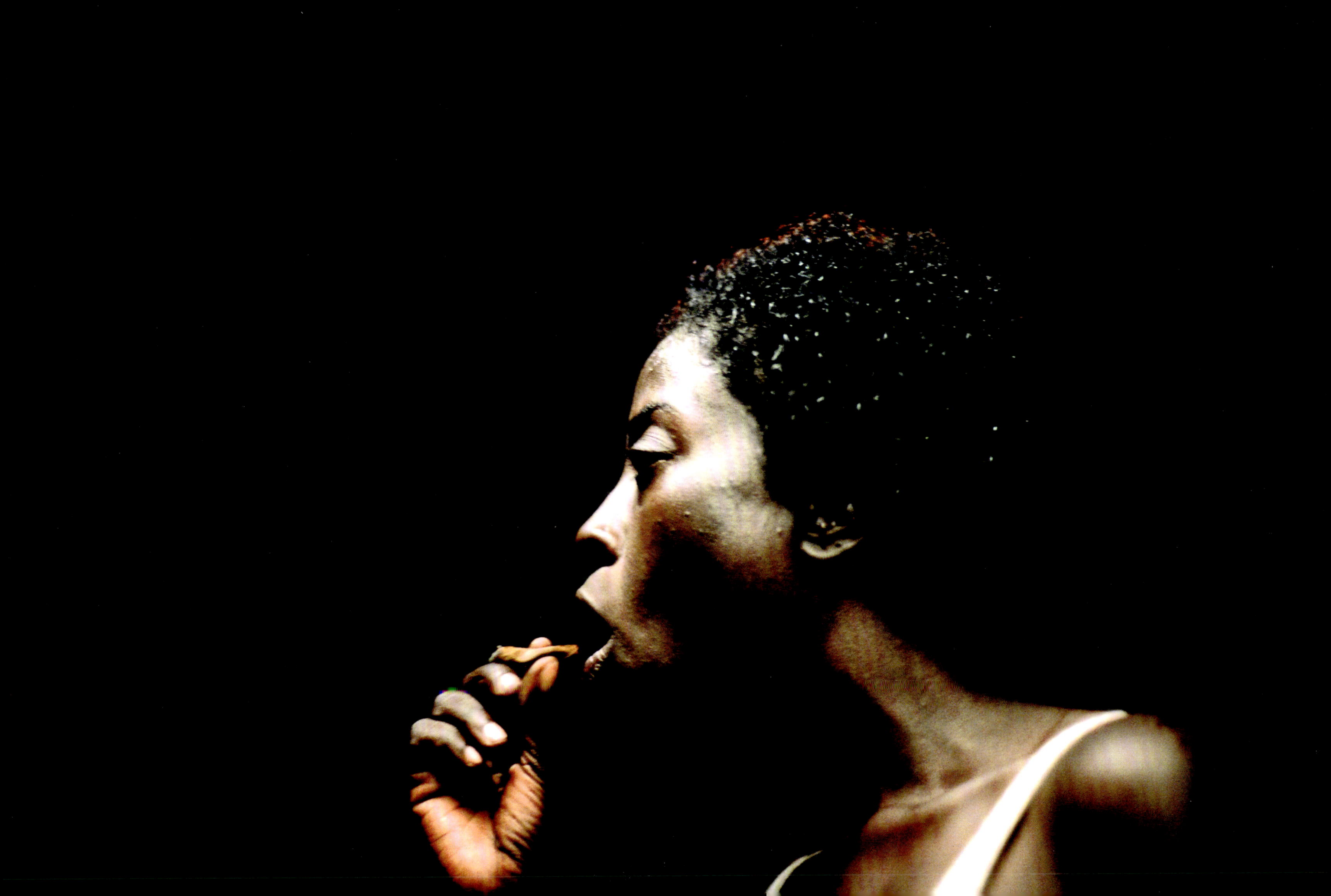

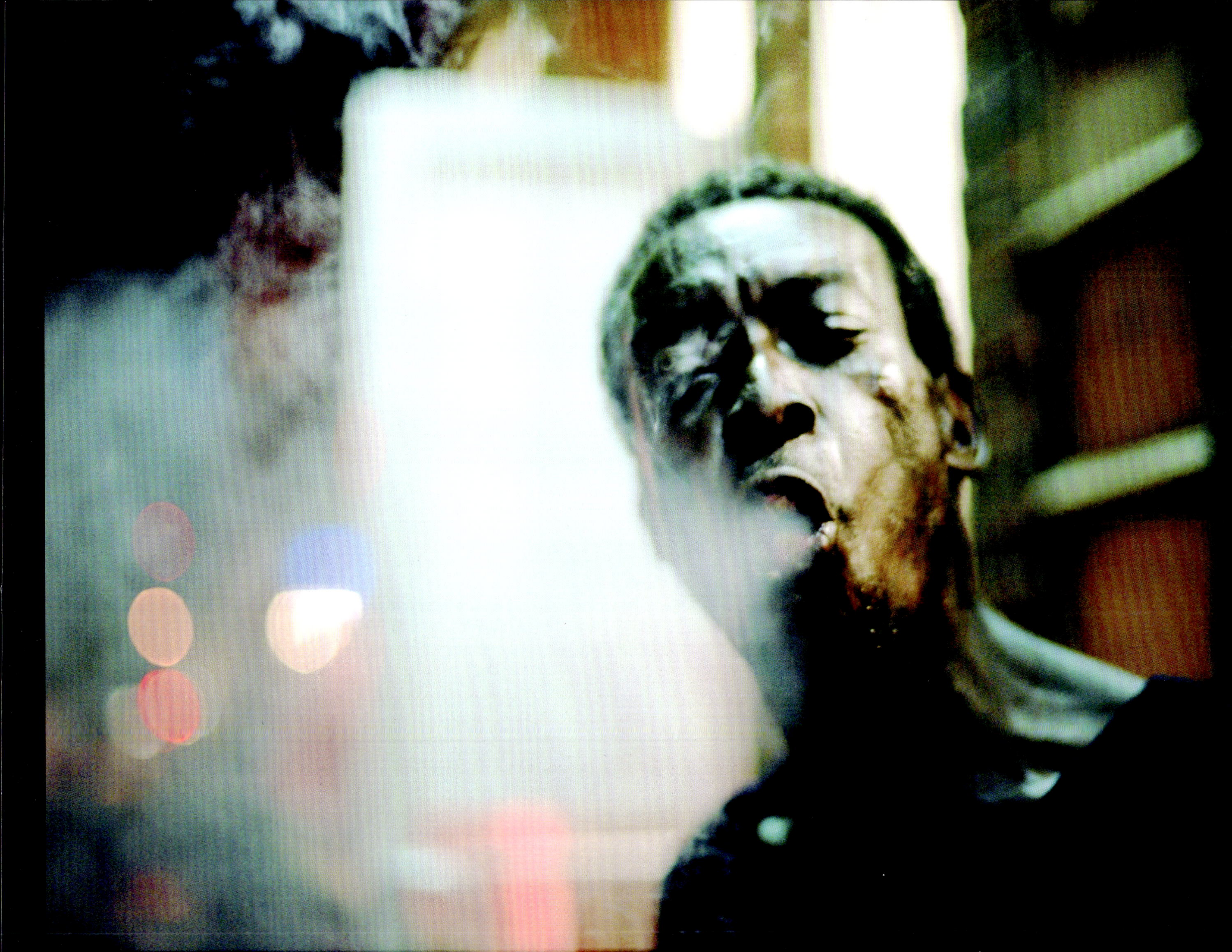

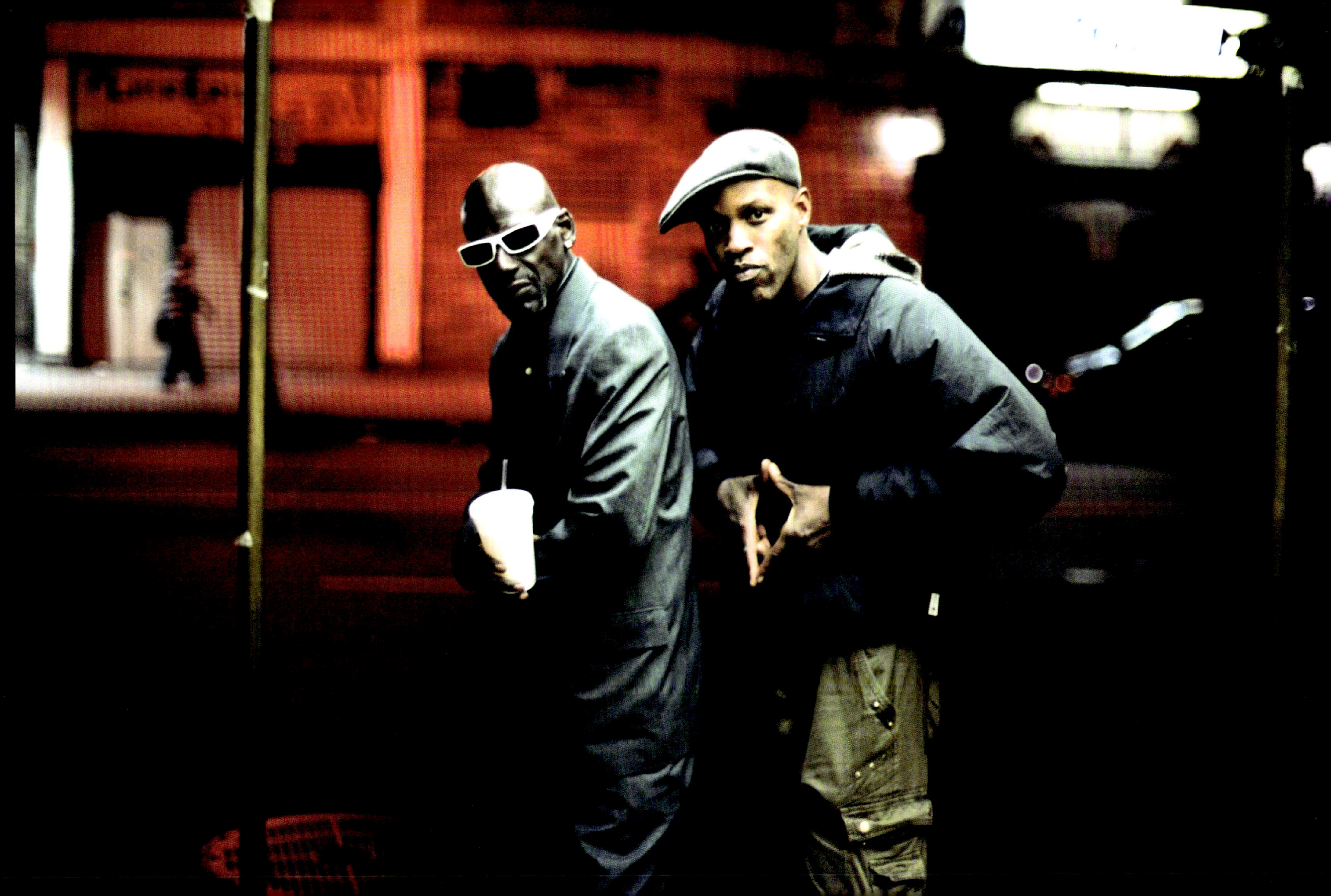

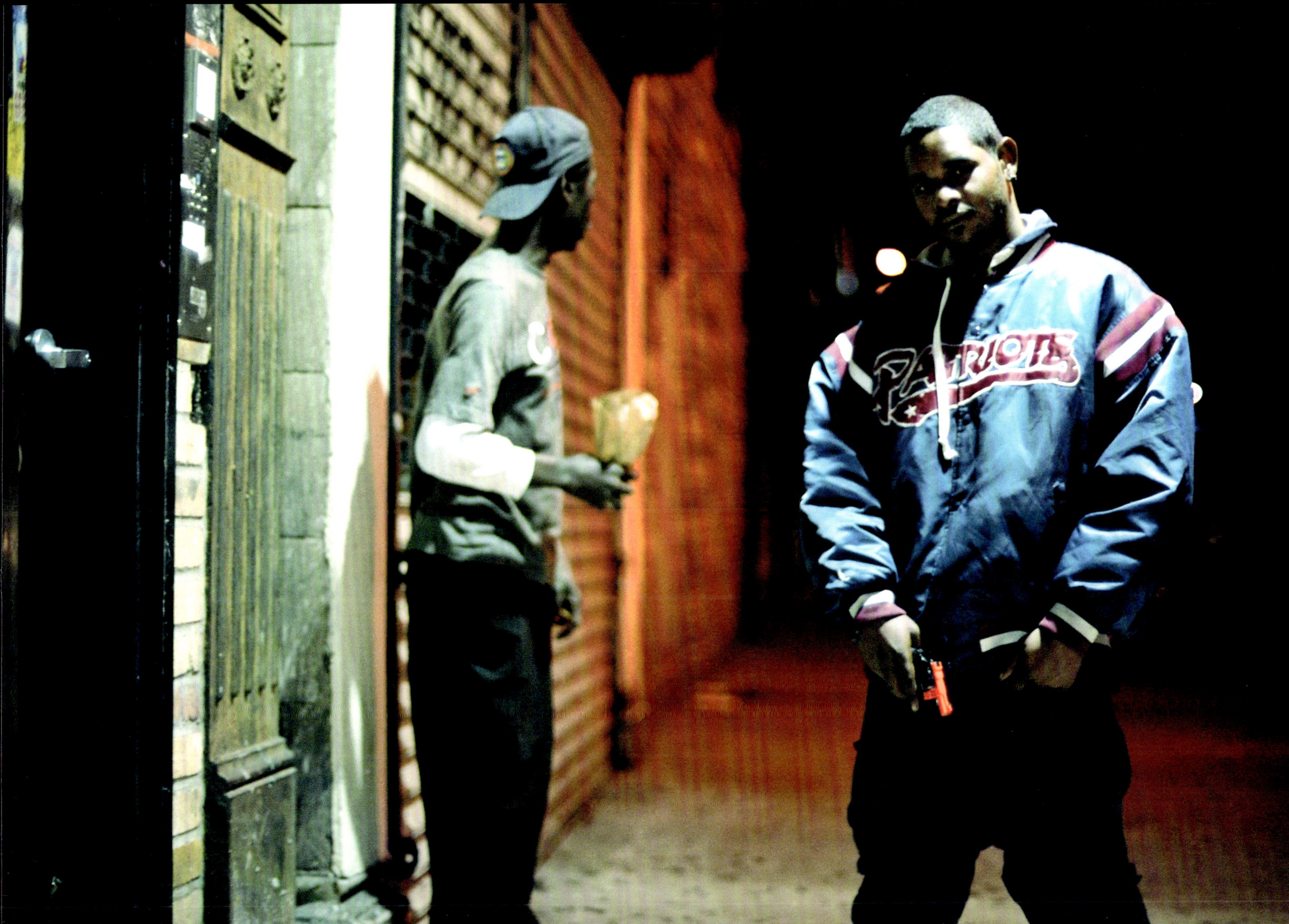
PATRIOTS

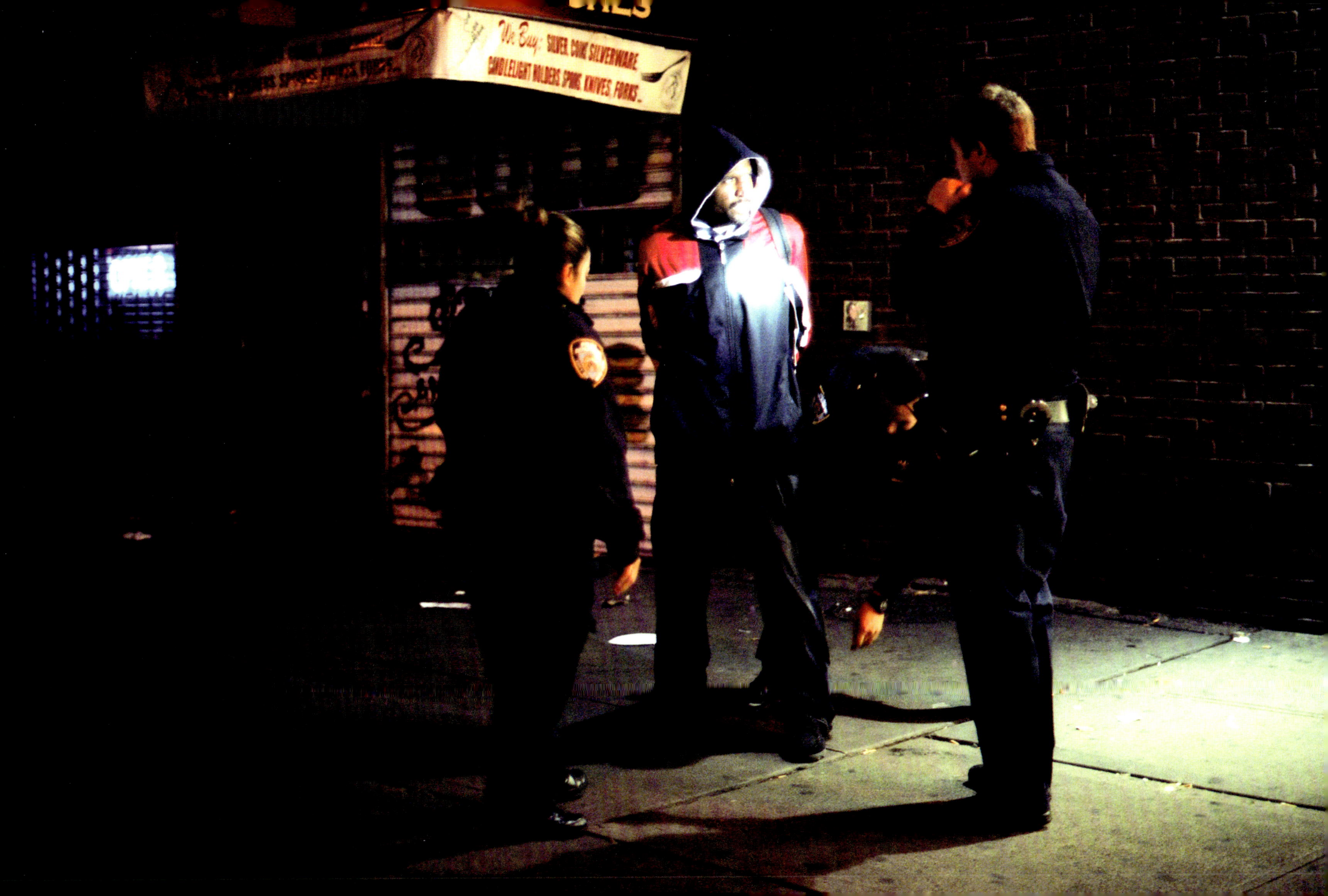
We Buy: SILVER, COINS SILVERWARE
CANDLELIGHT HOLDERS SPOONS KNIVES, FORKS...

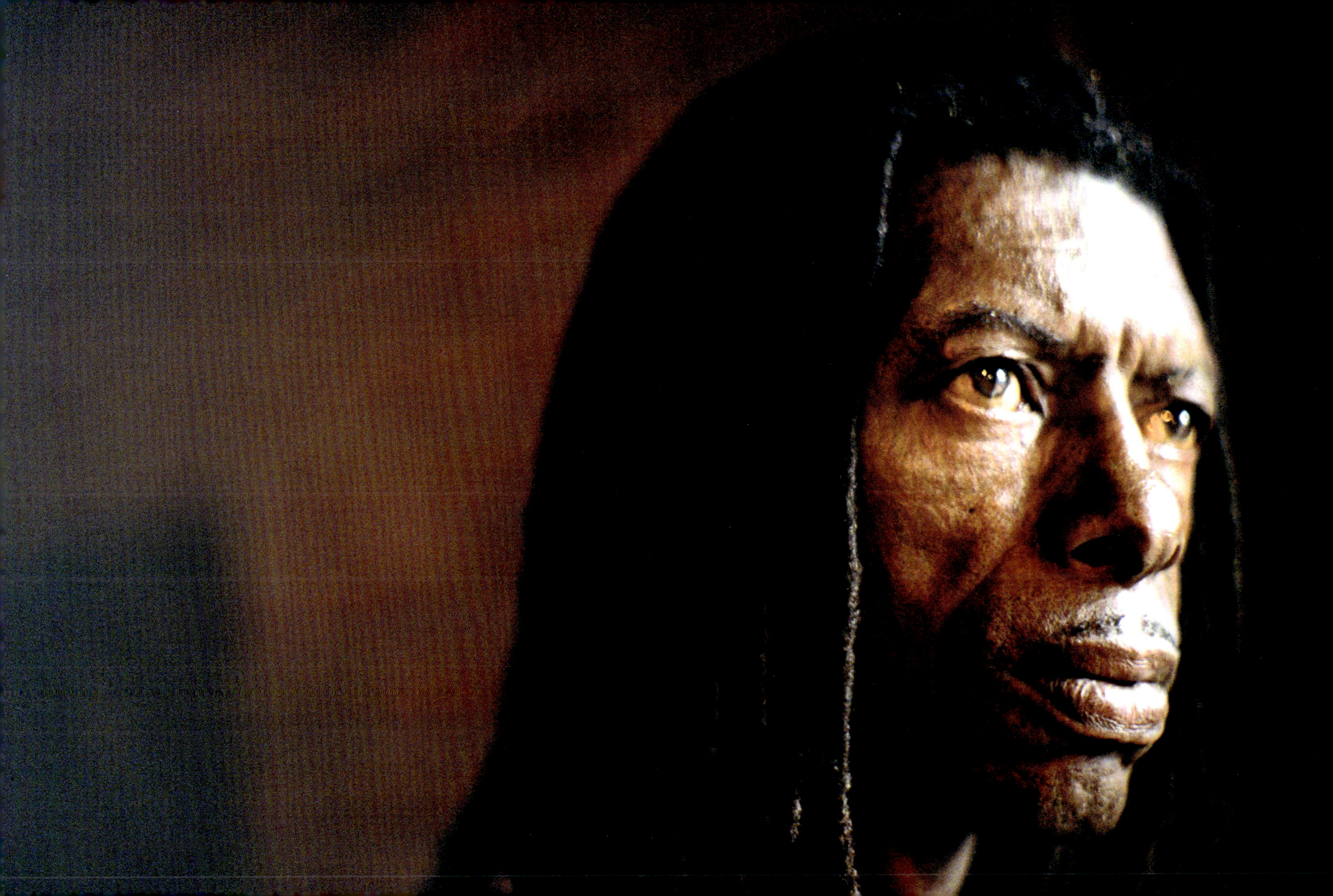

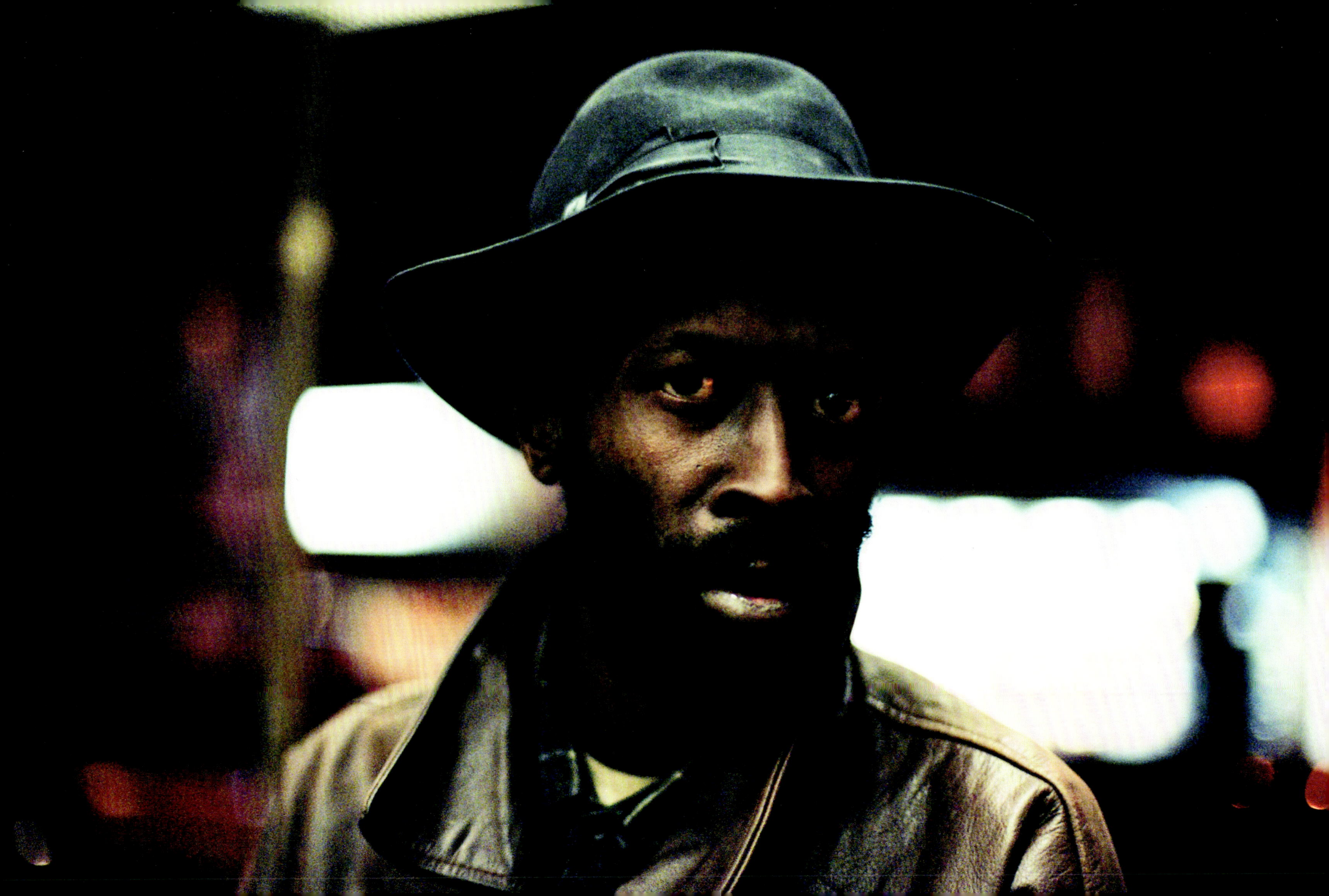

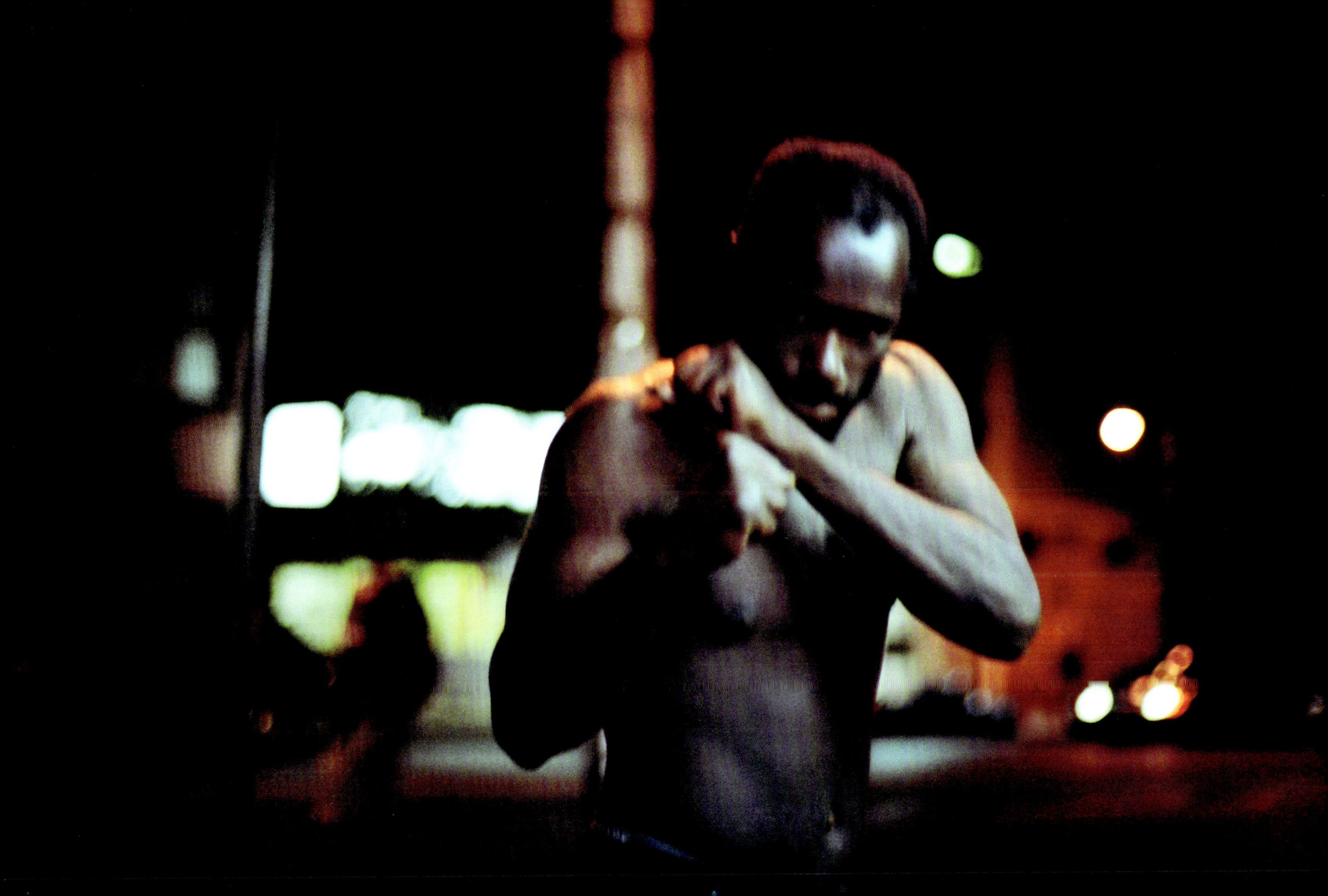

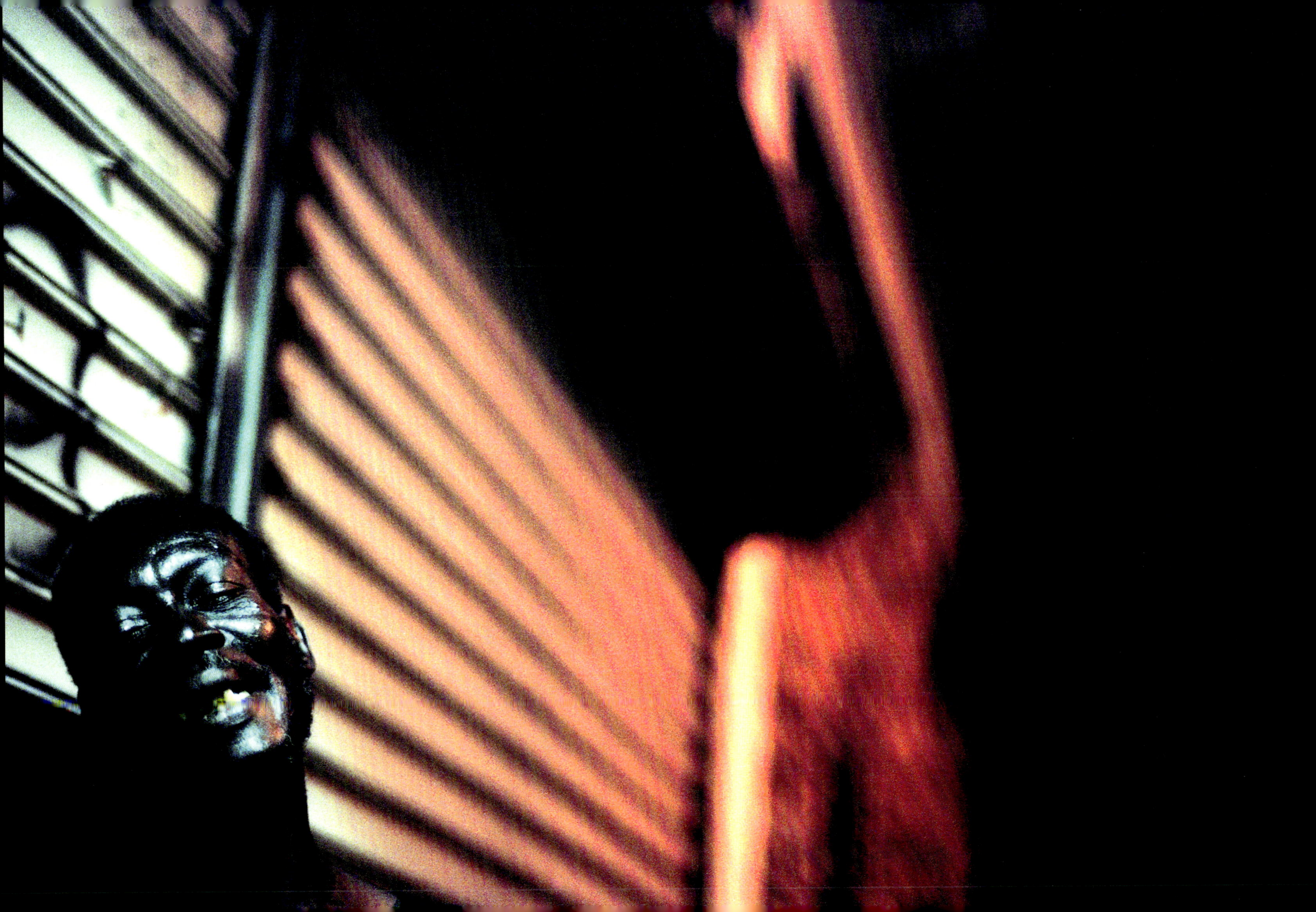

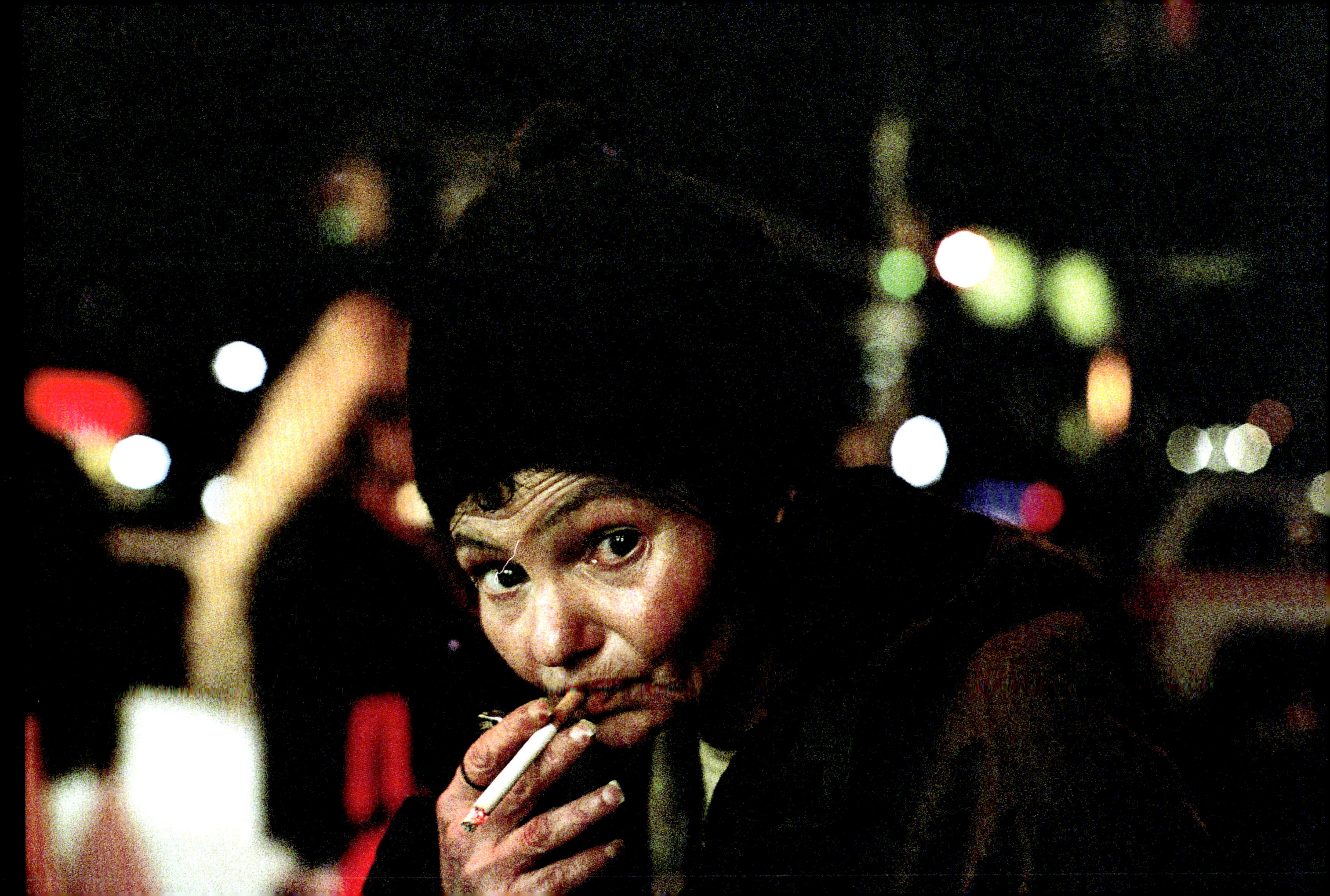

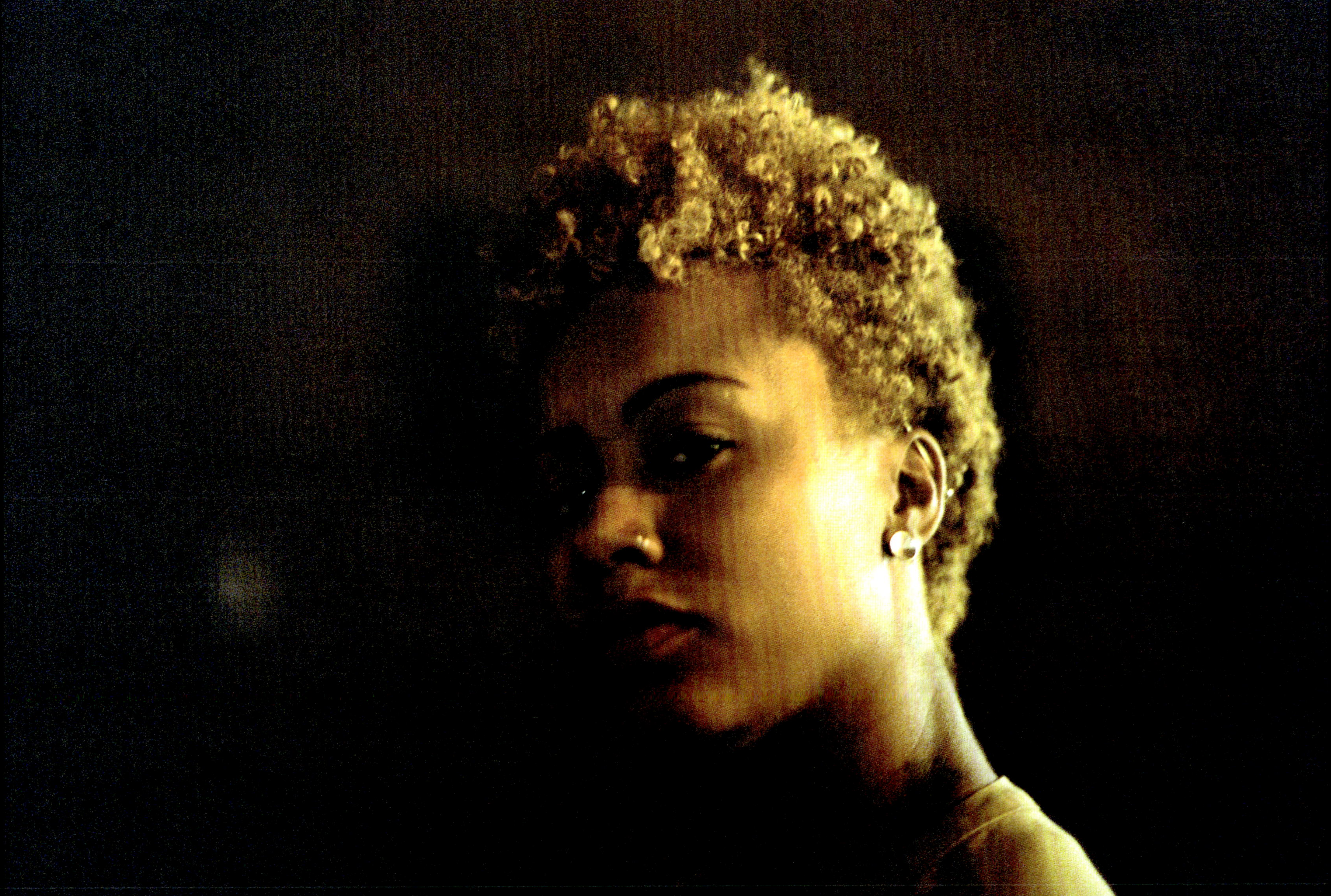

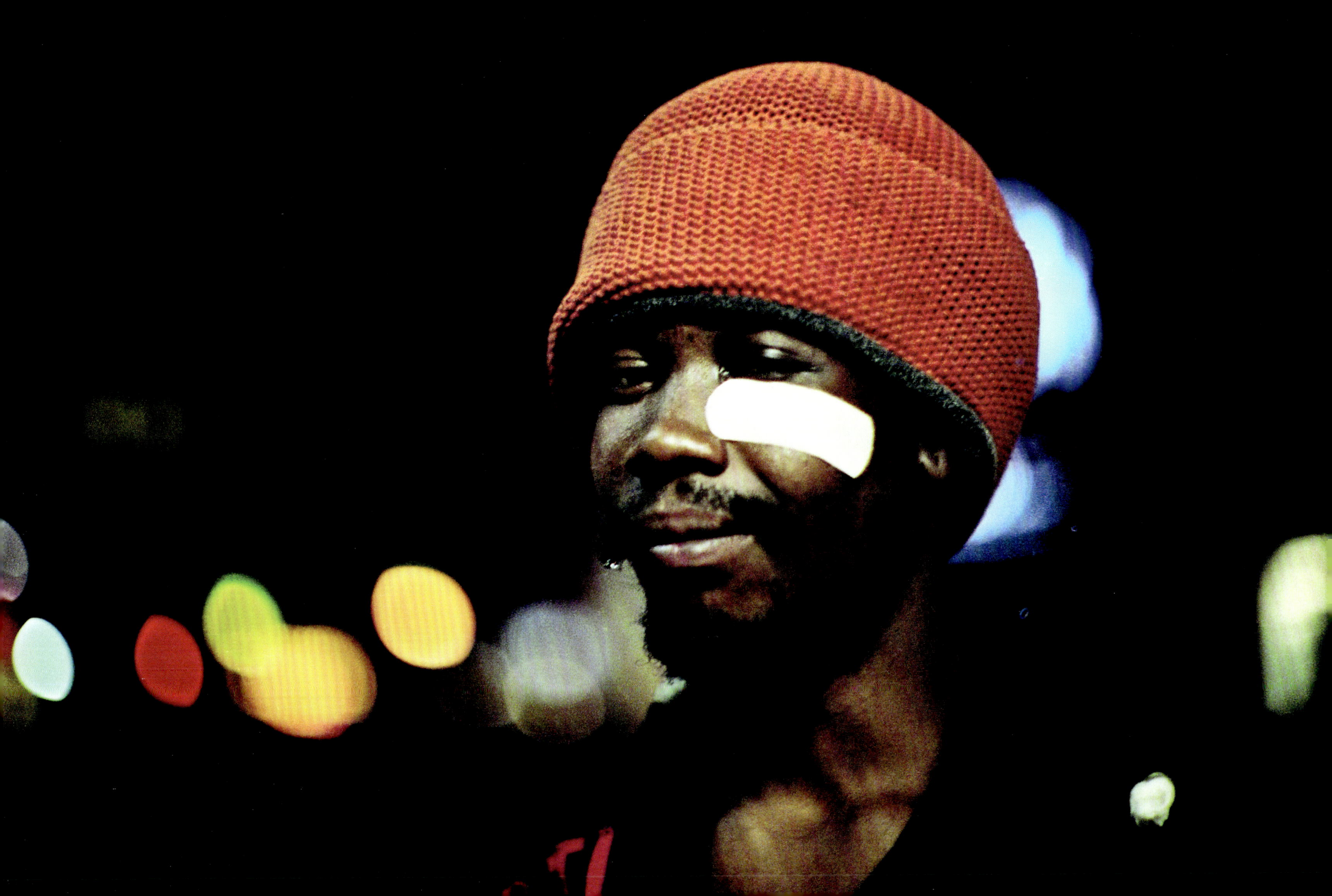

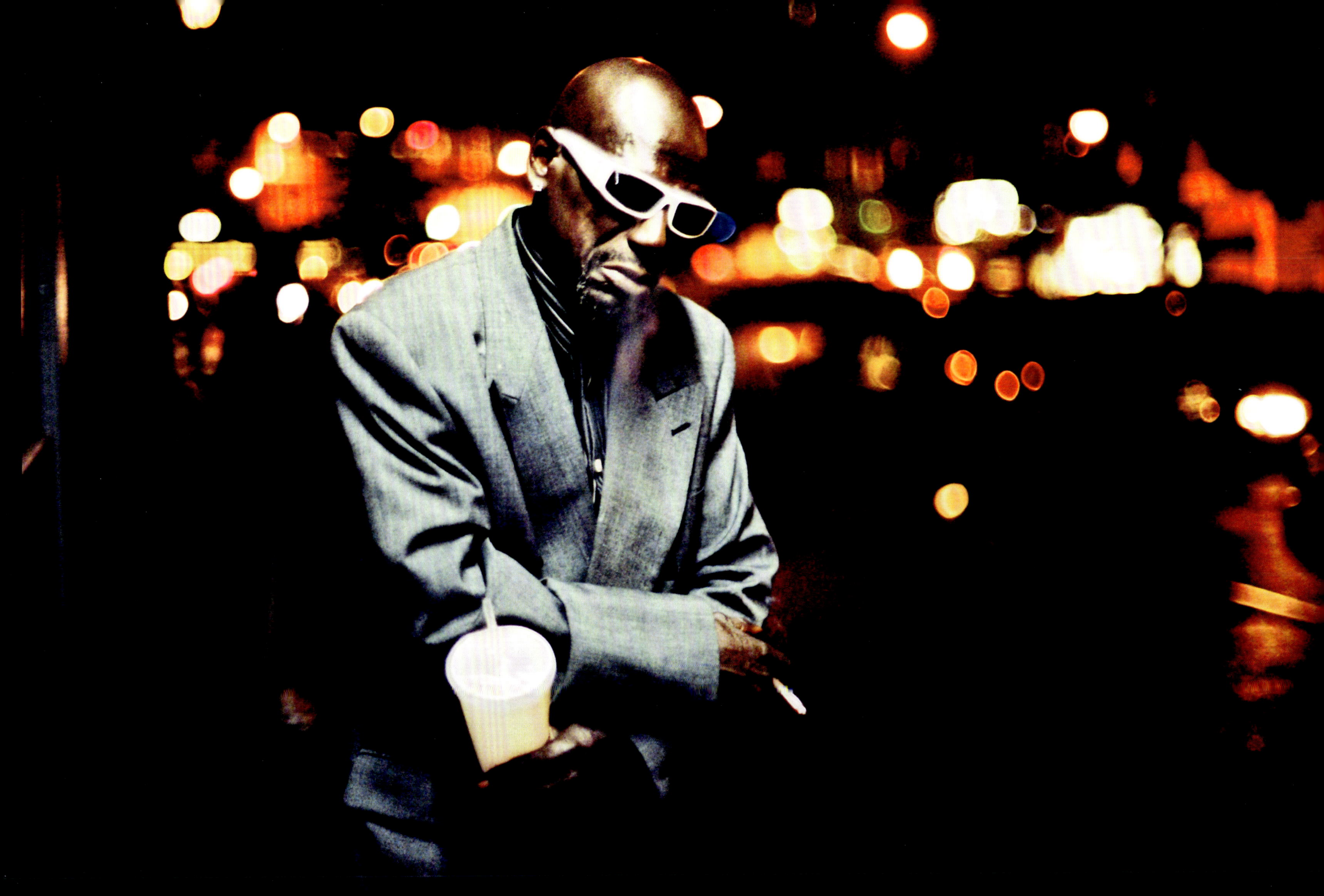

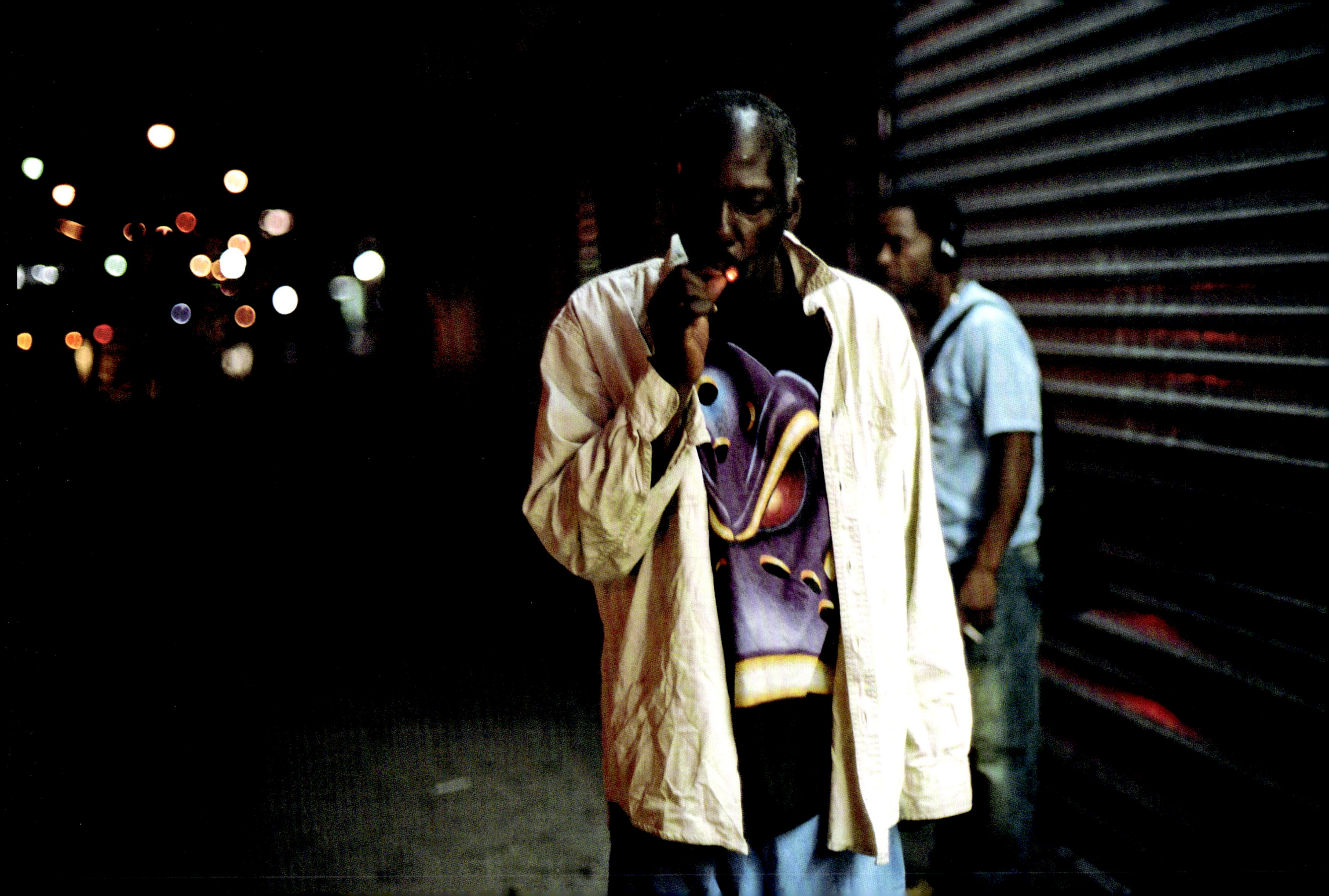

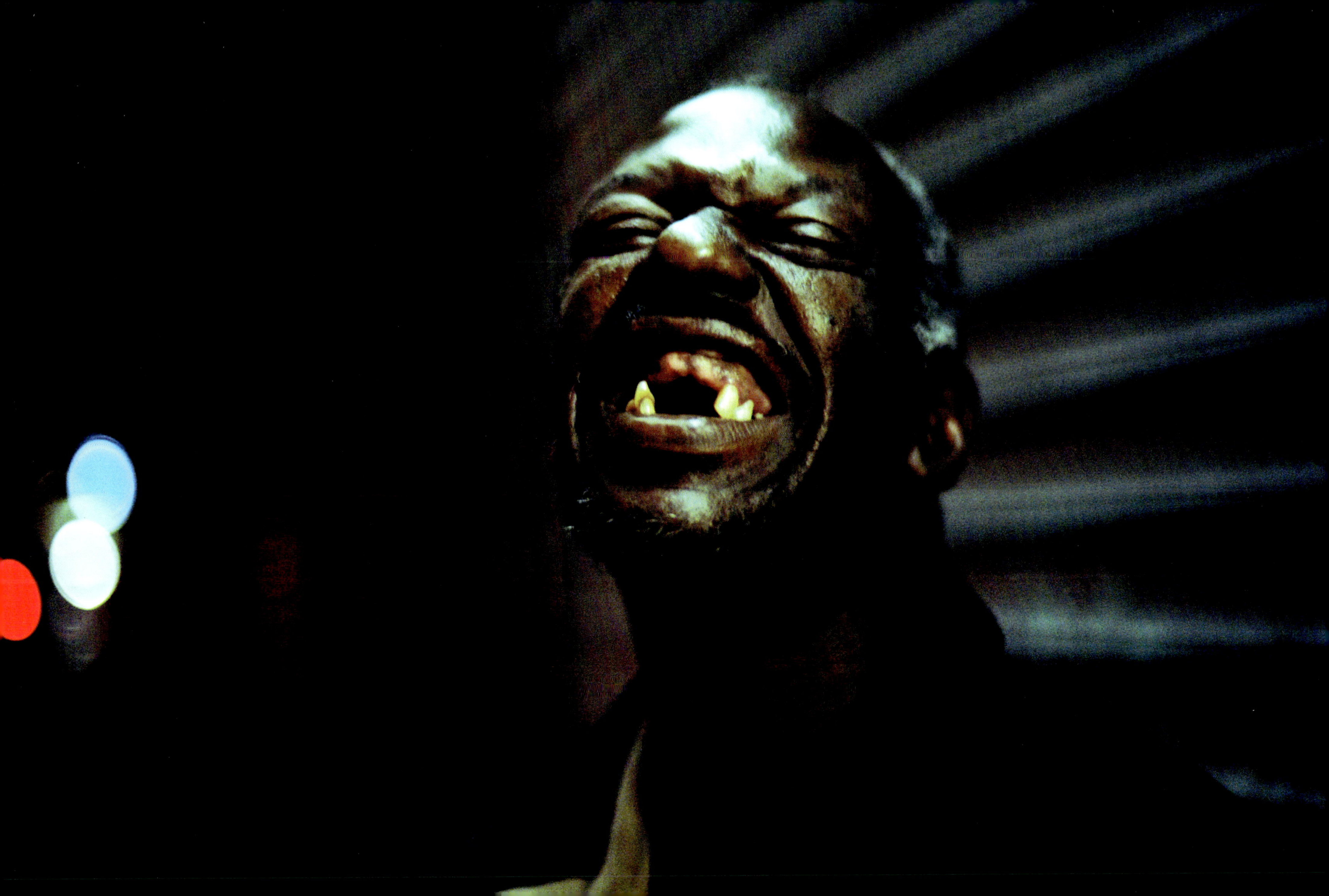

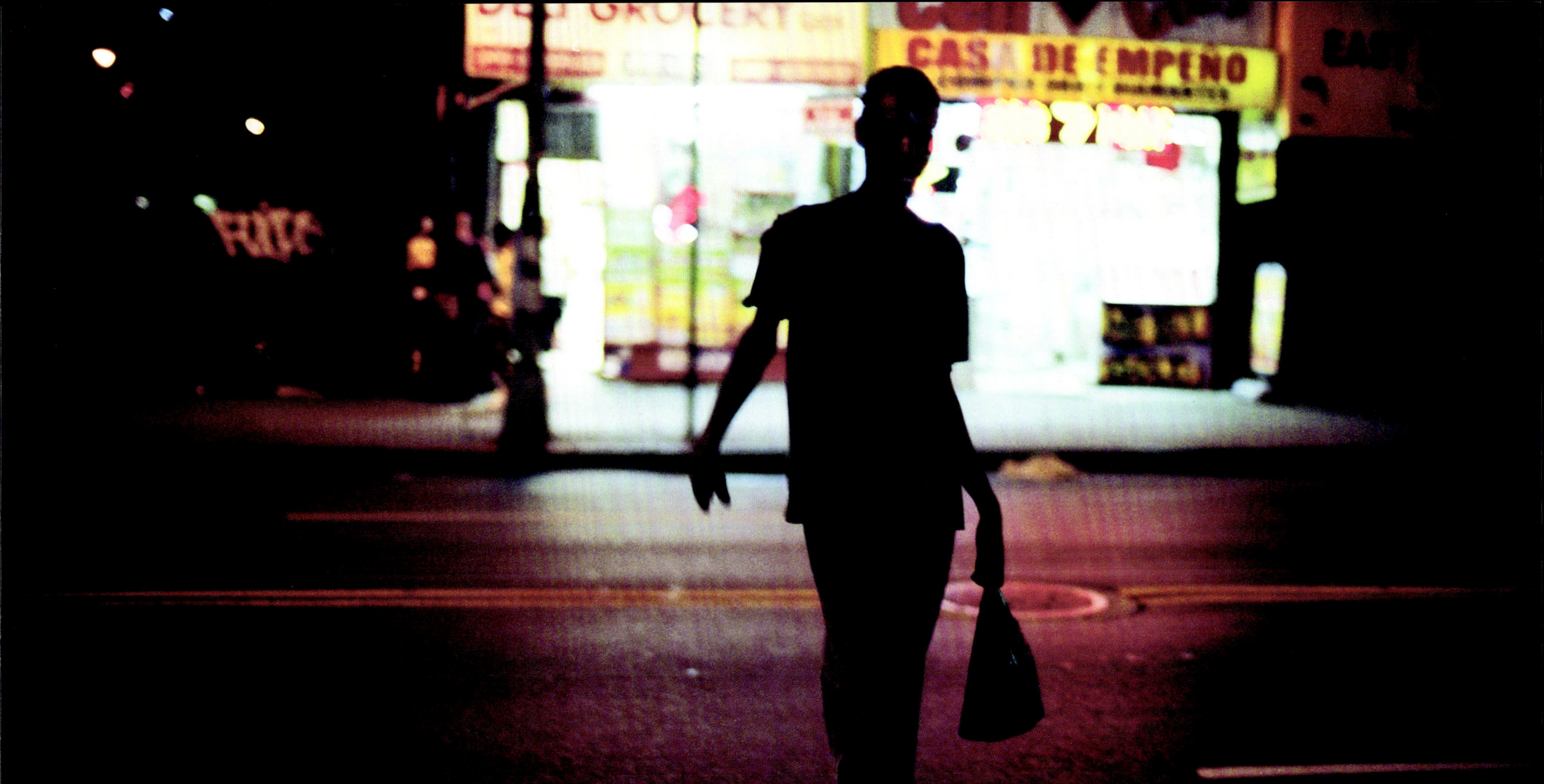
GROCERY
DE EMPENO

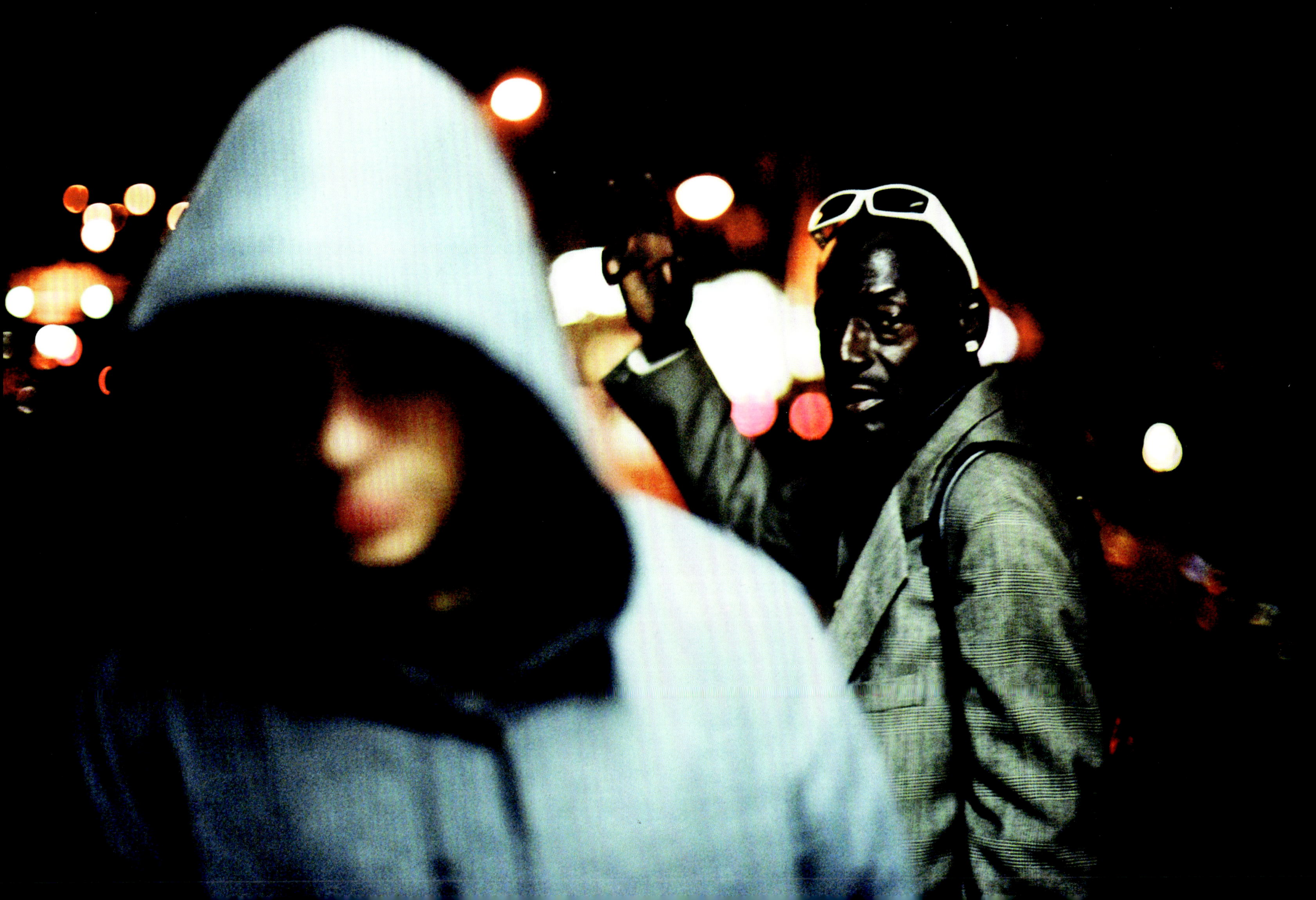

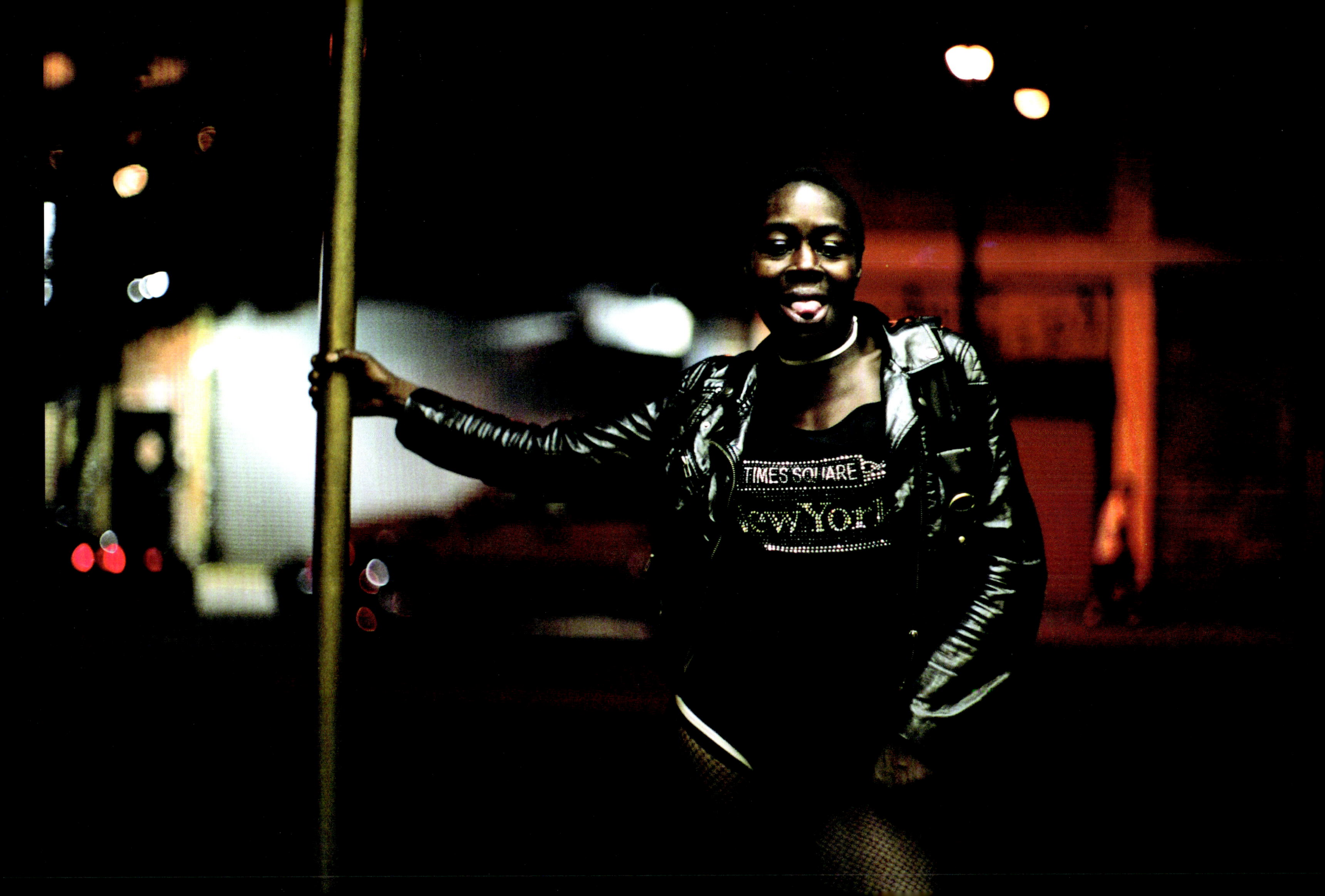
TIMES SQUARE

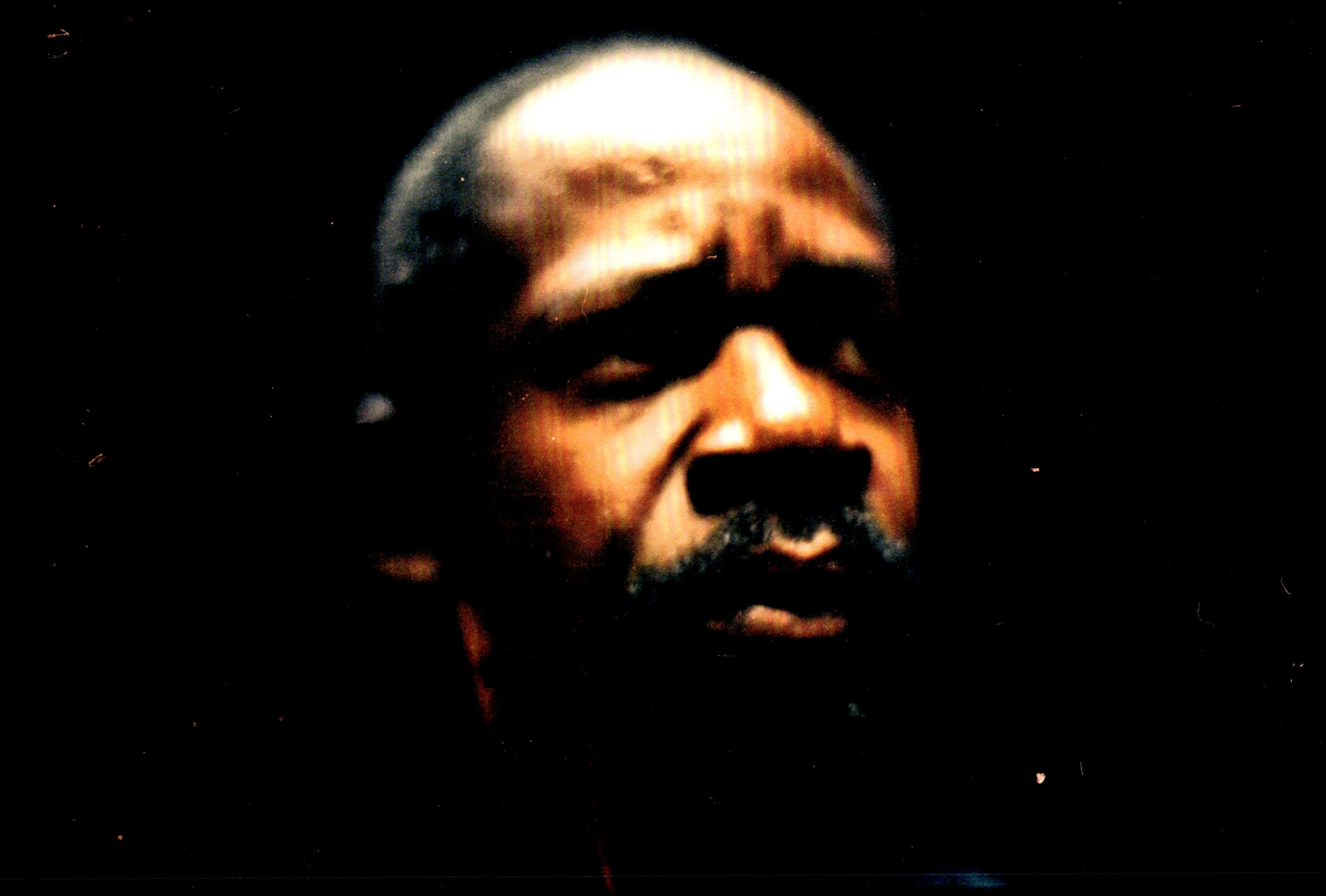

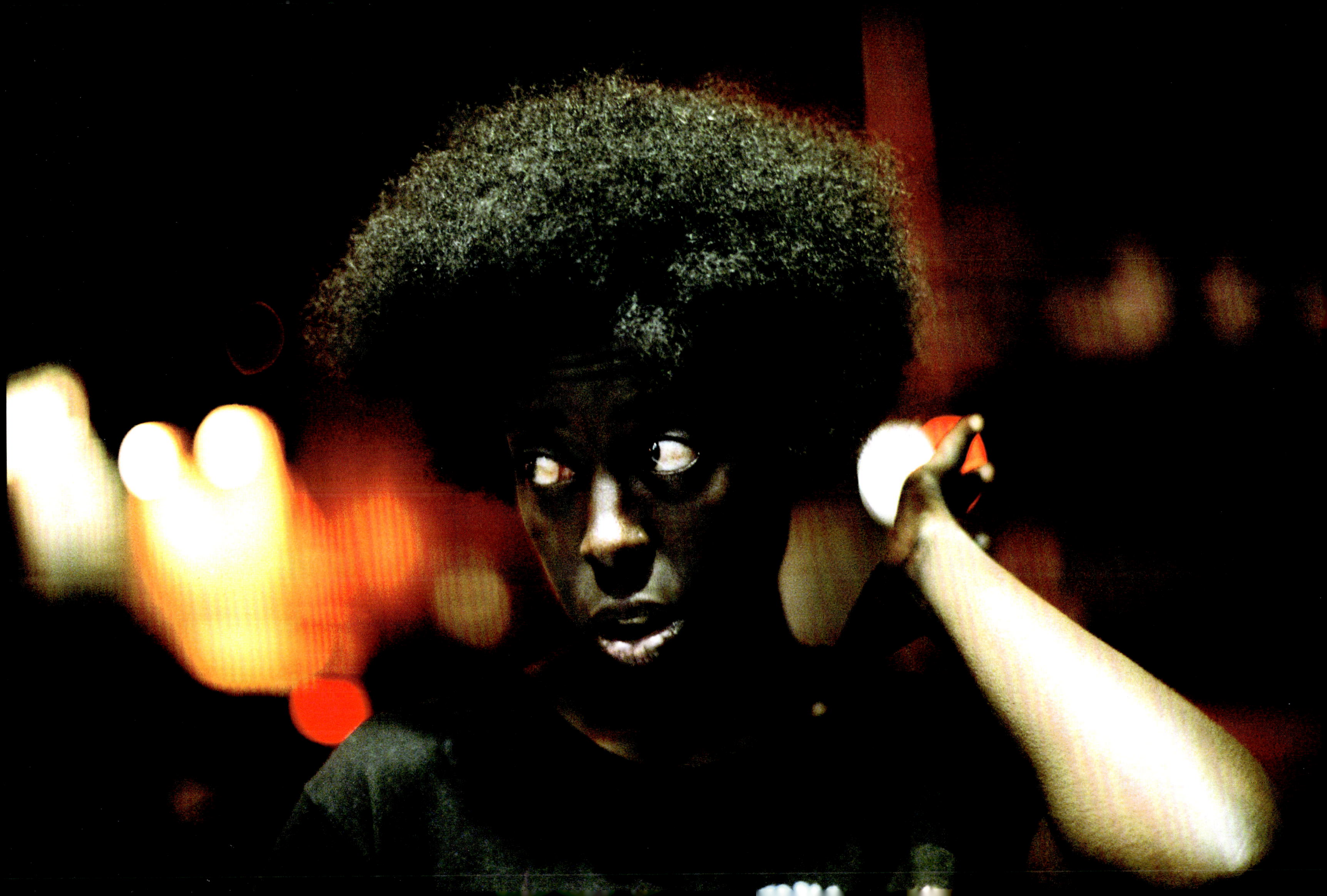

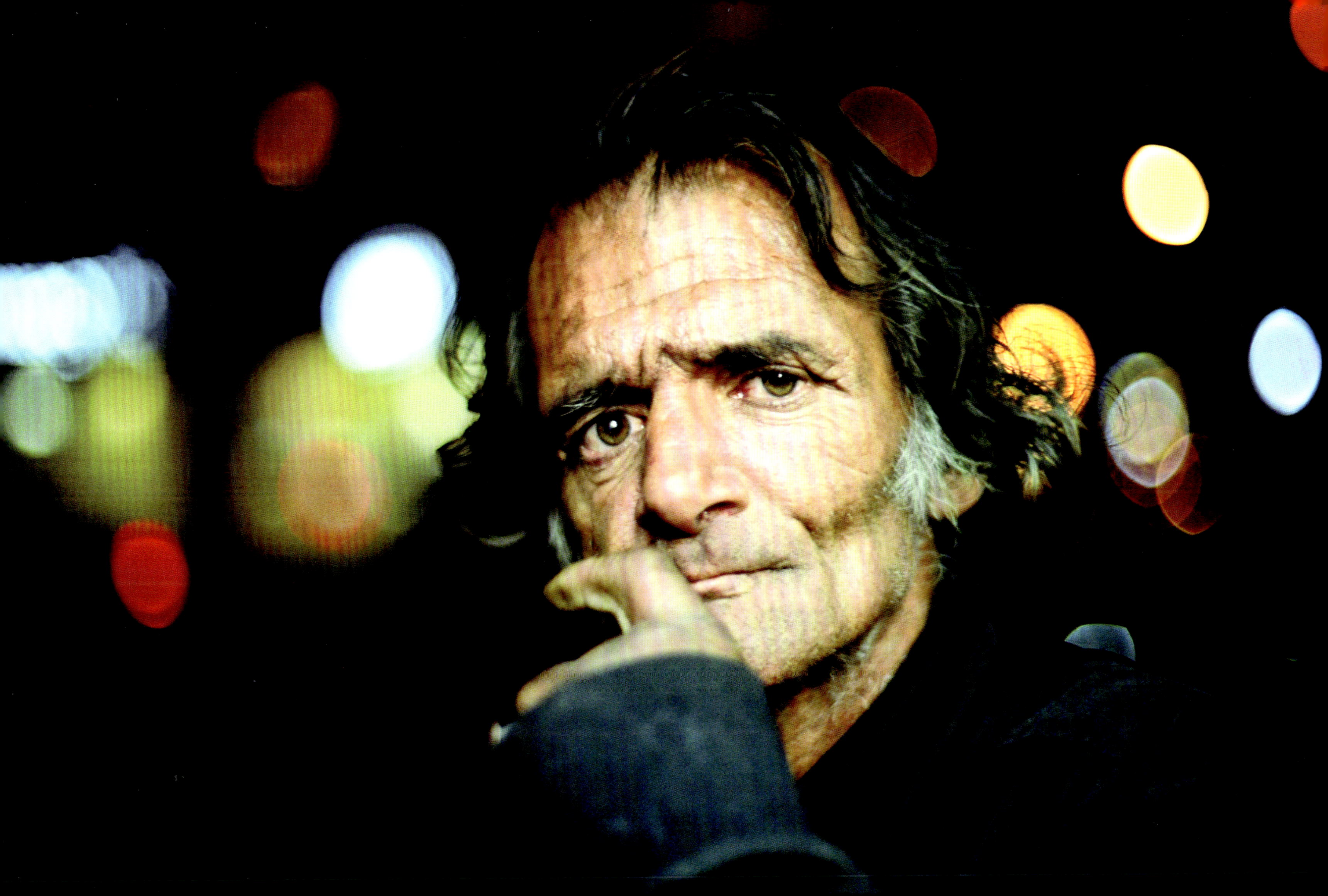

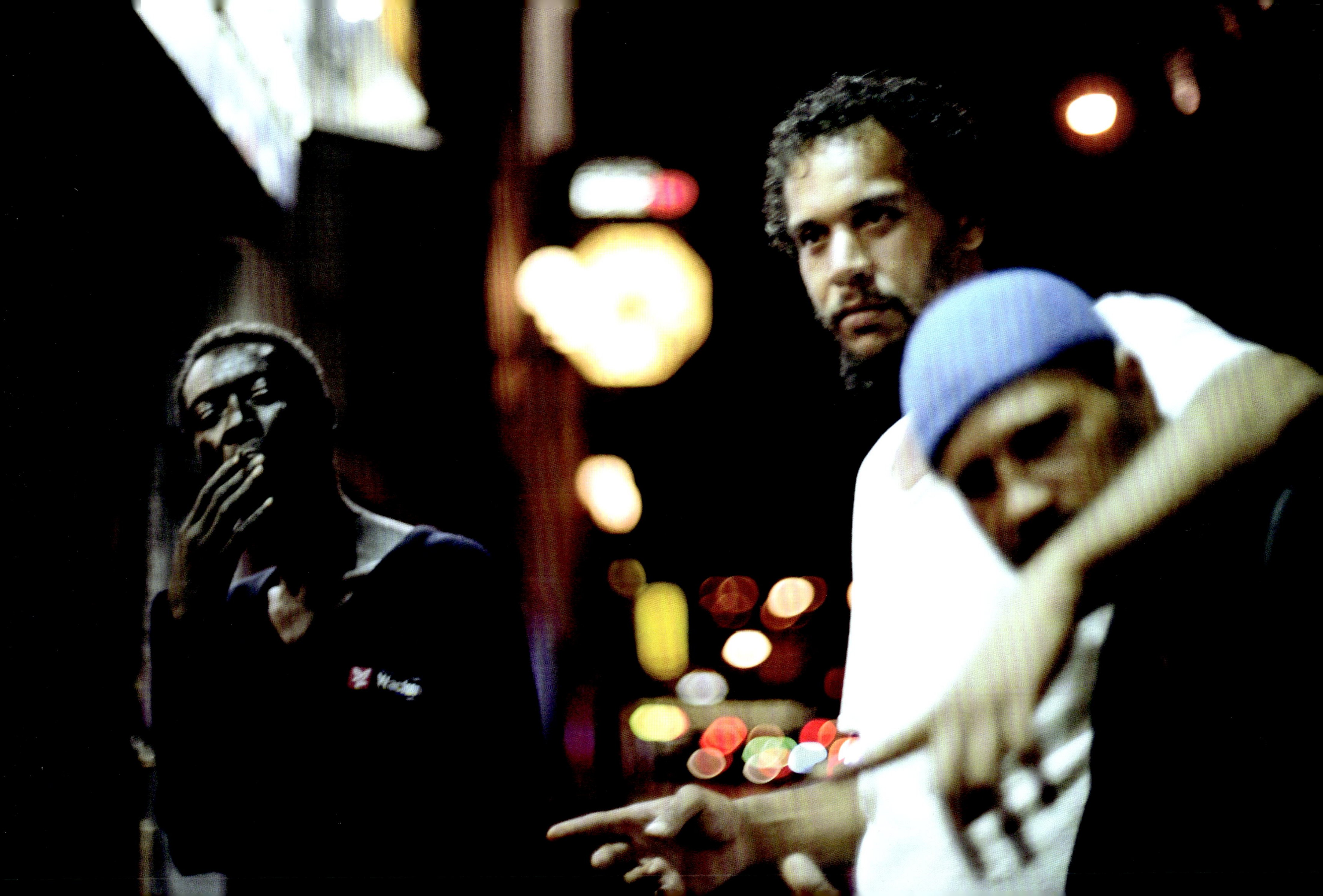

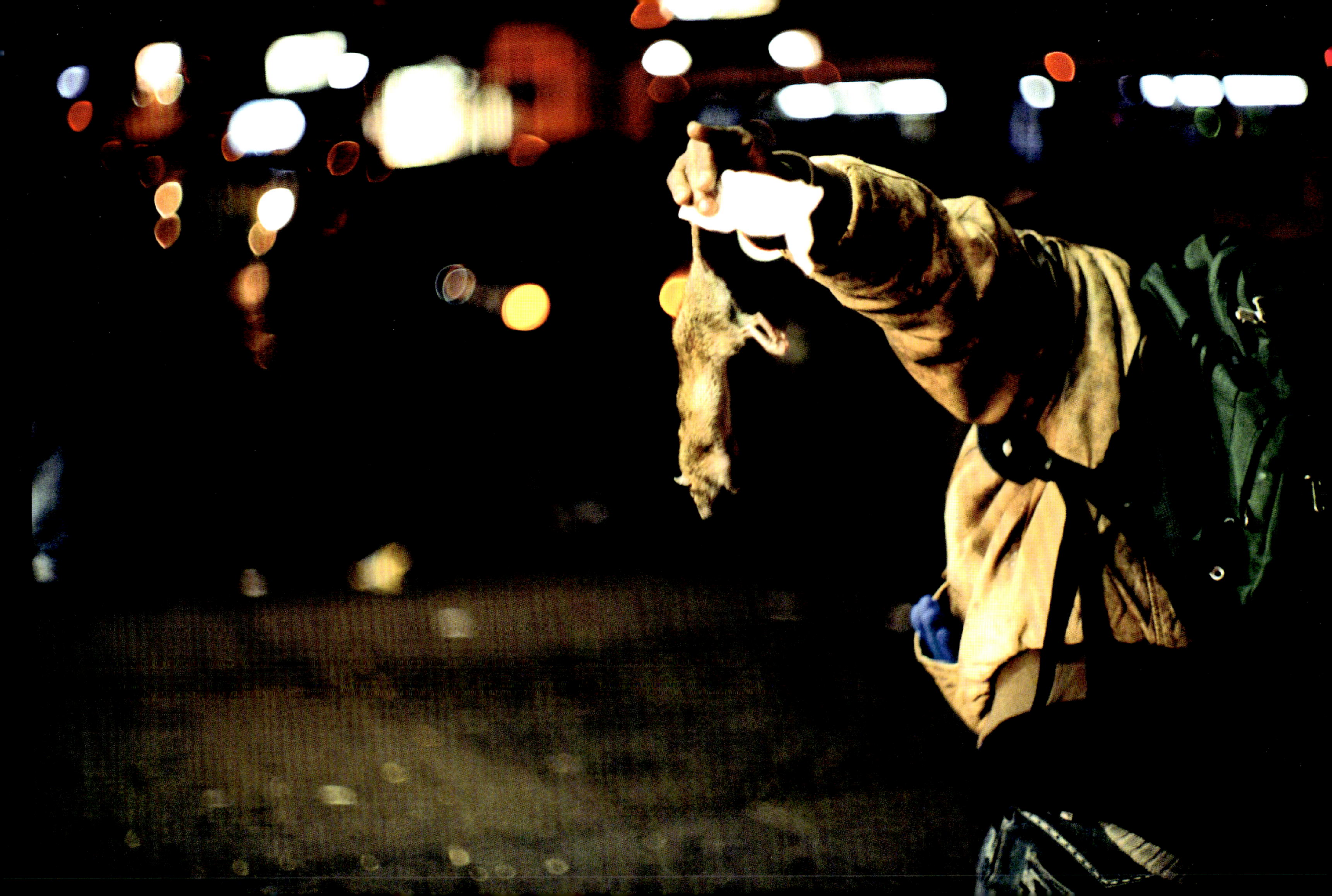

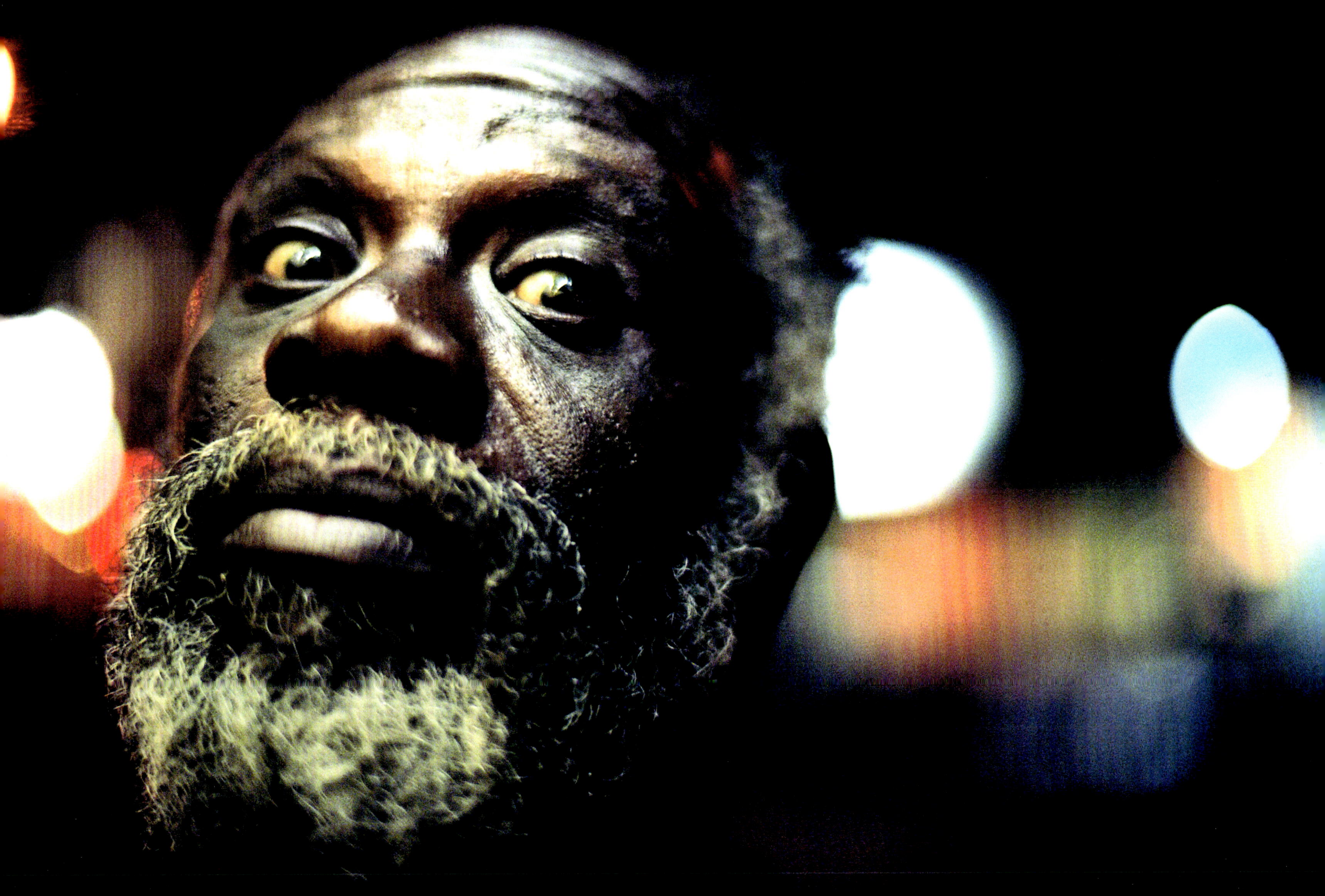

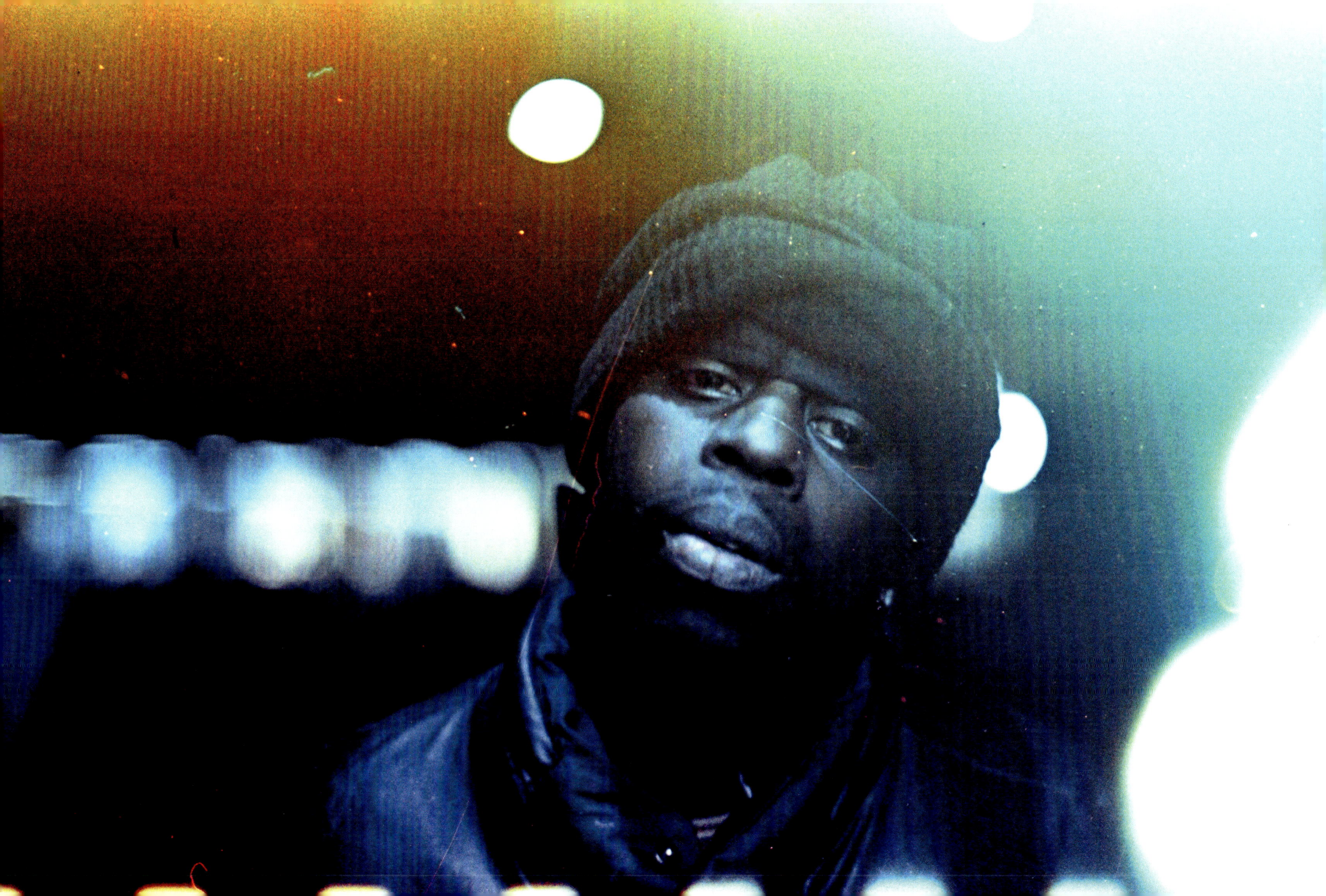

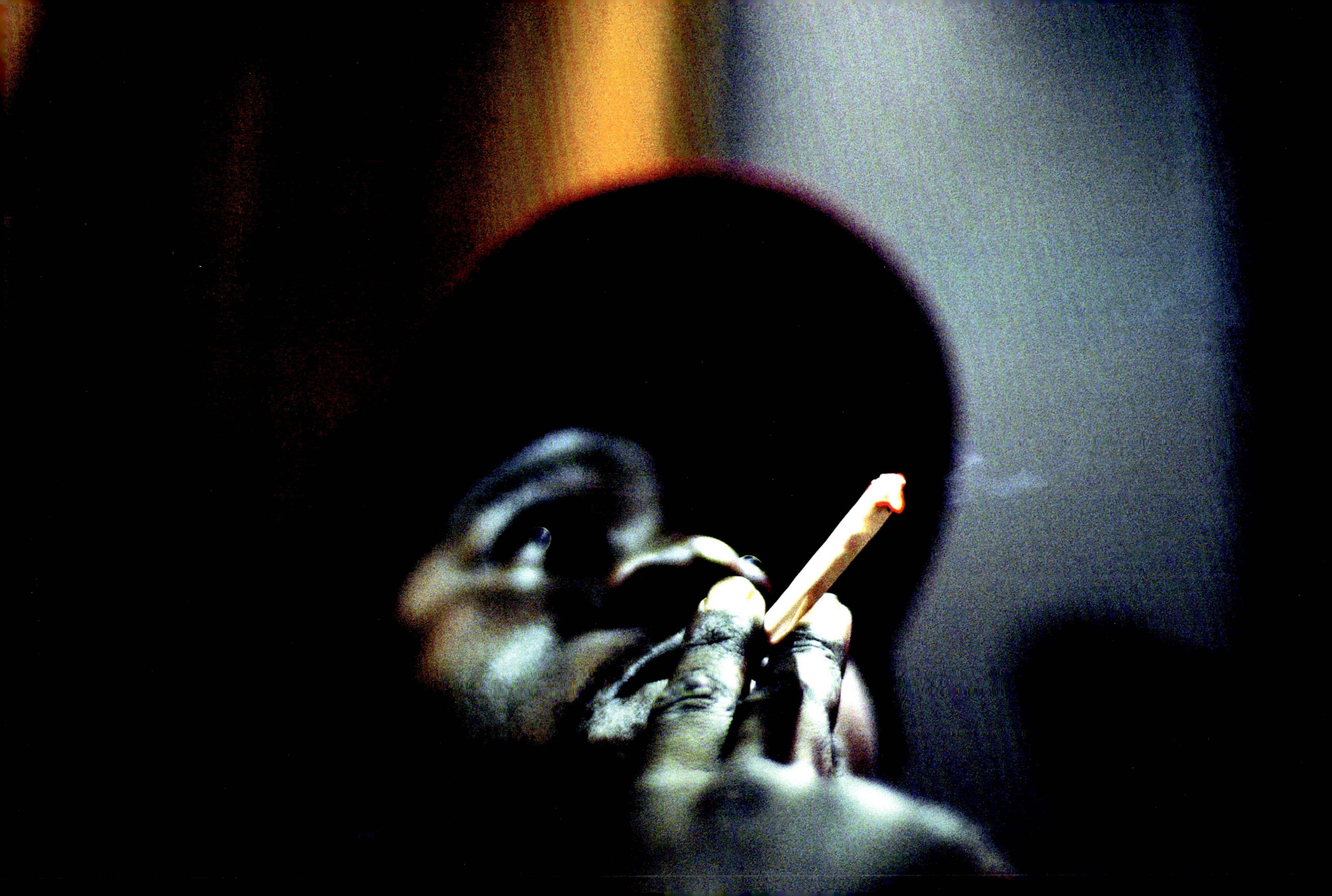

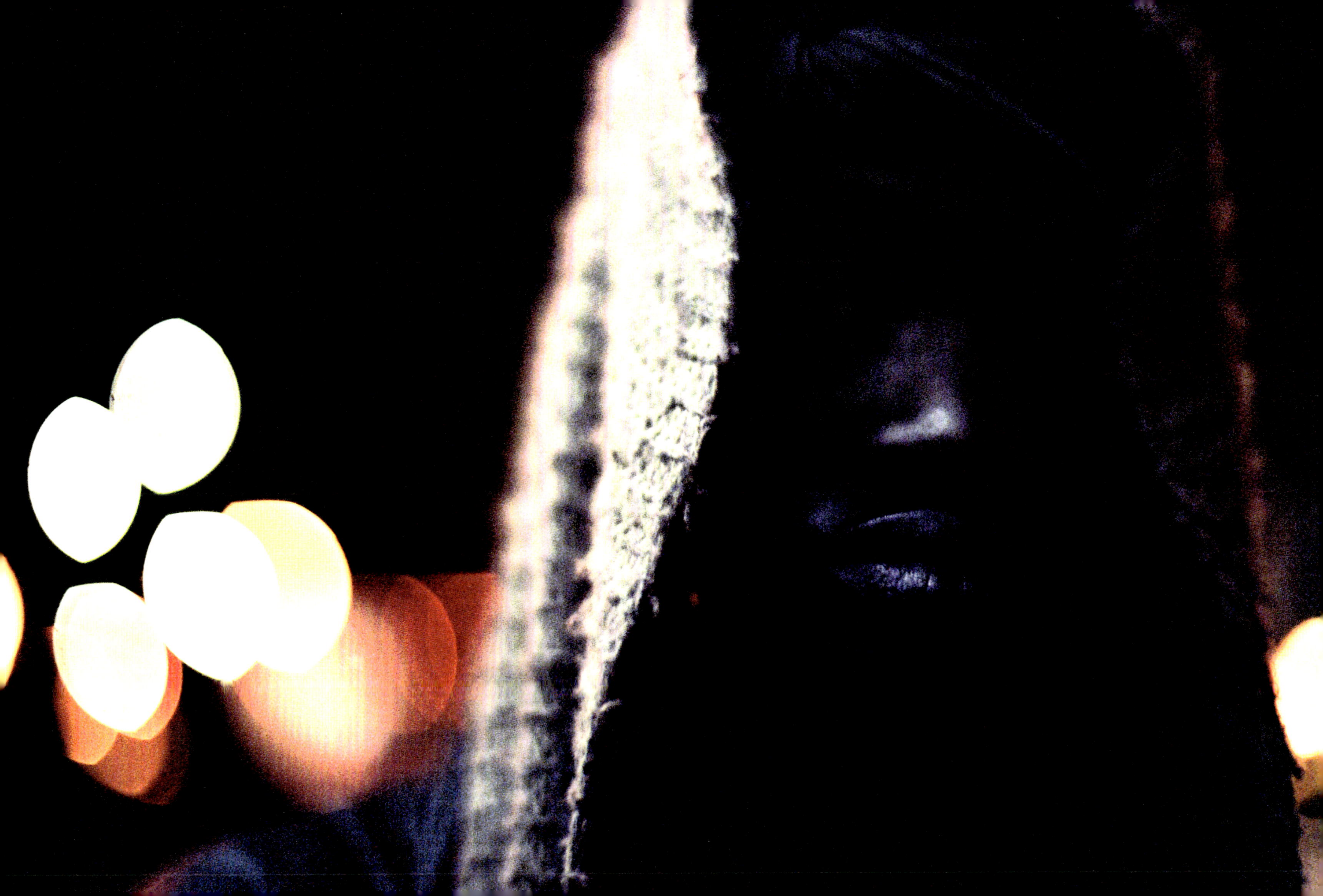

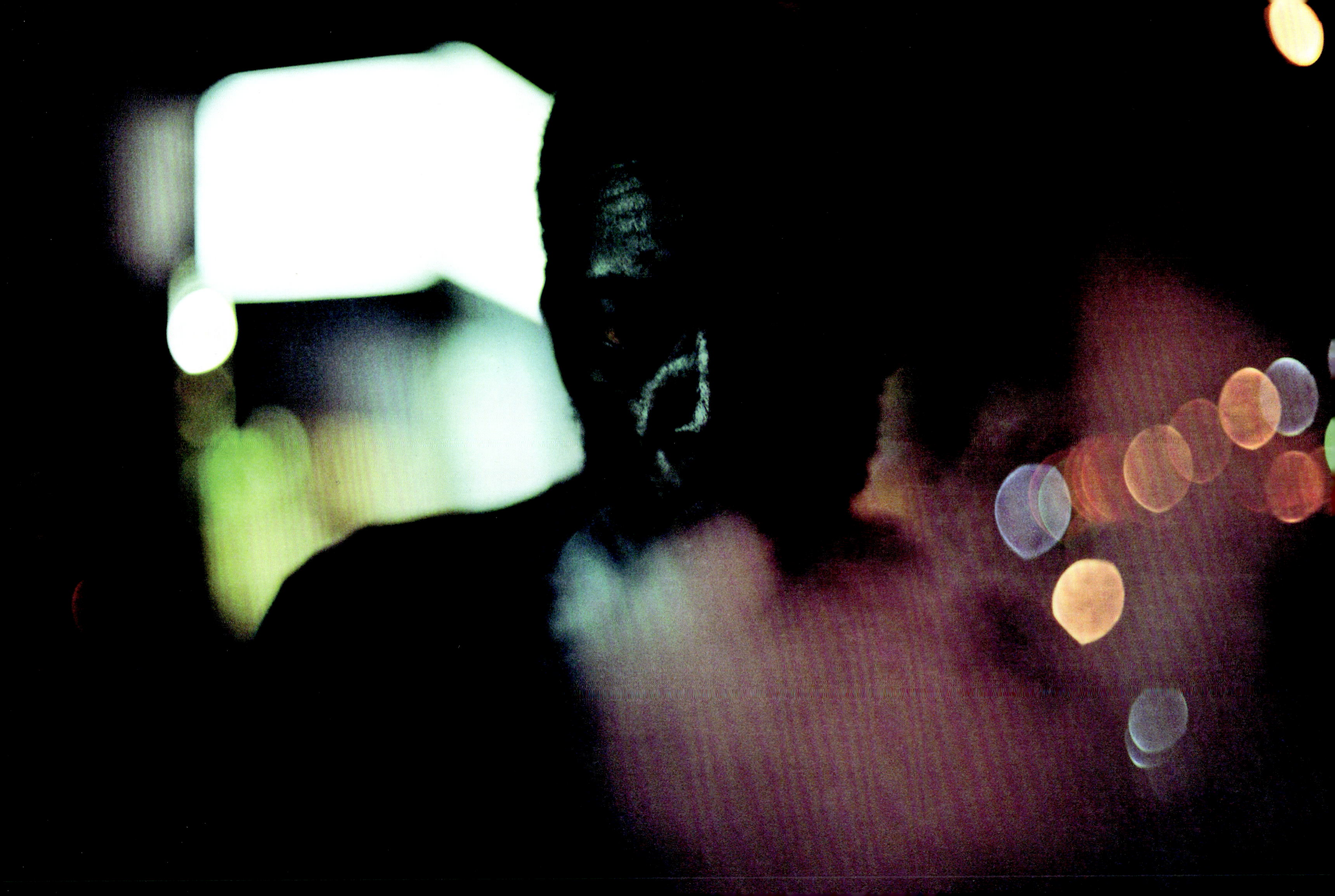

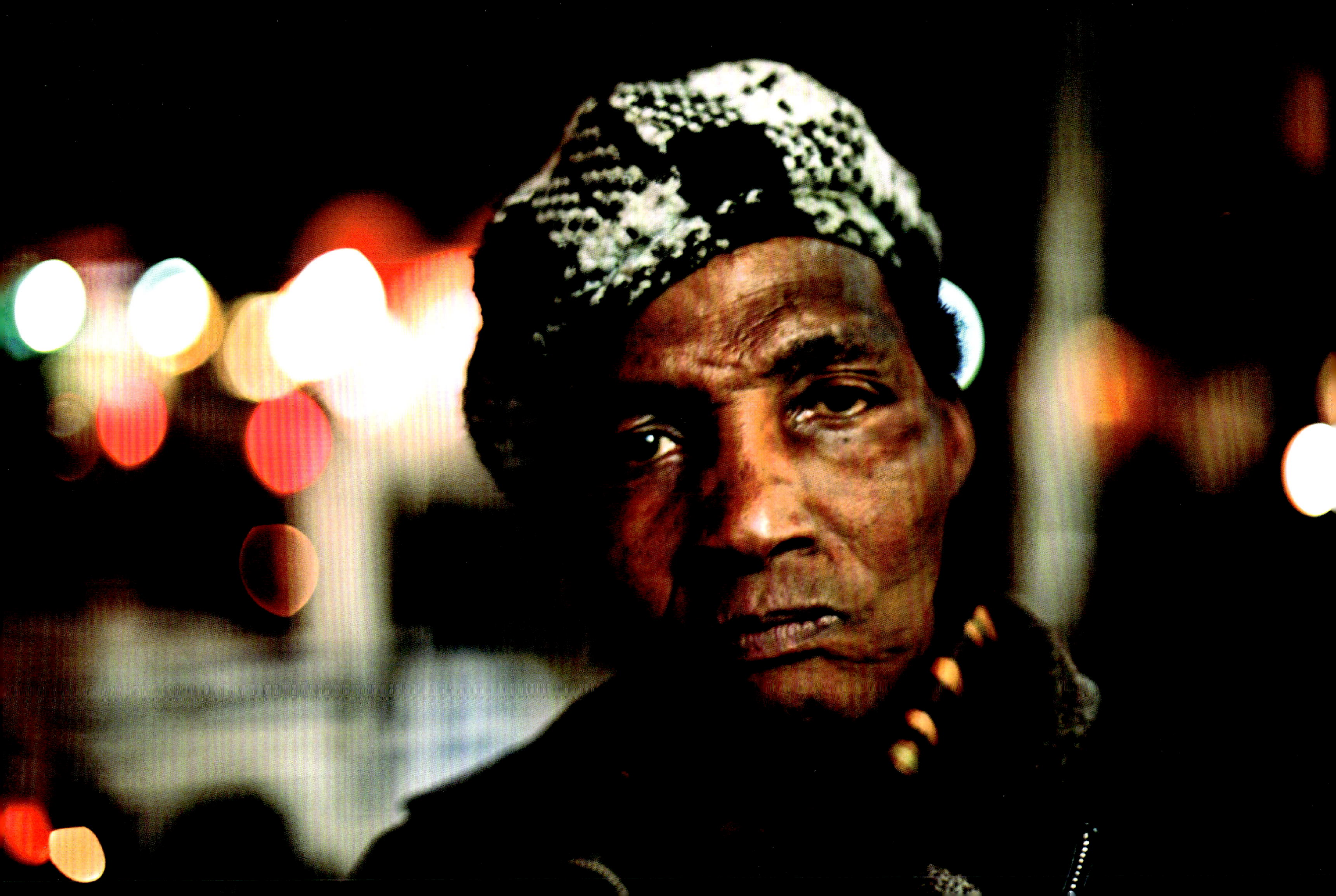

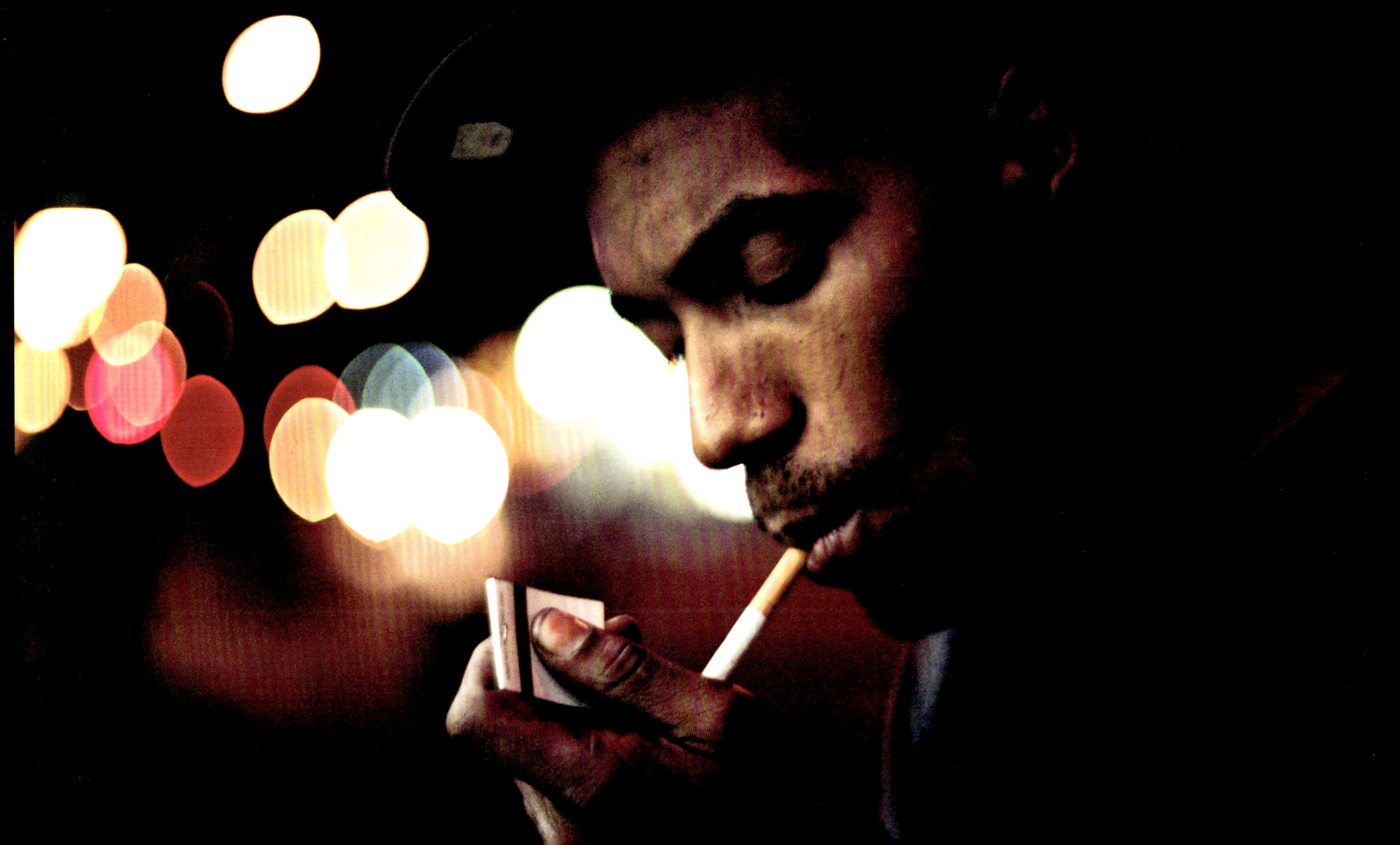

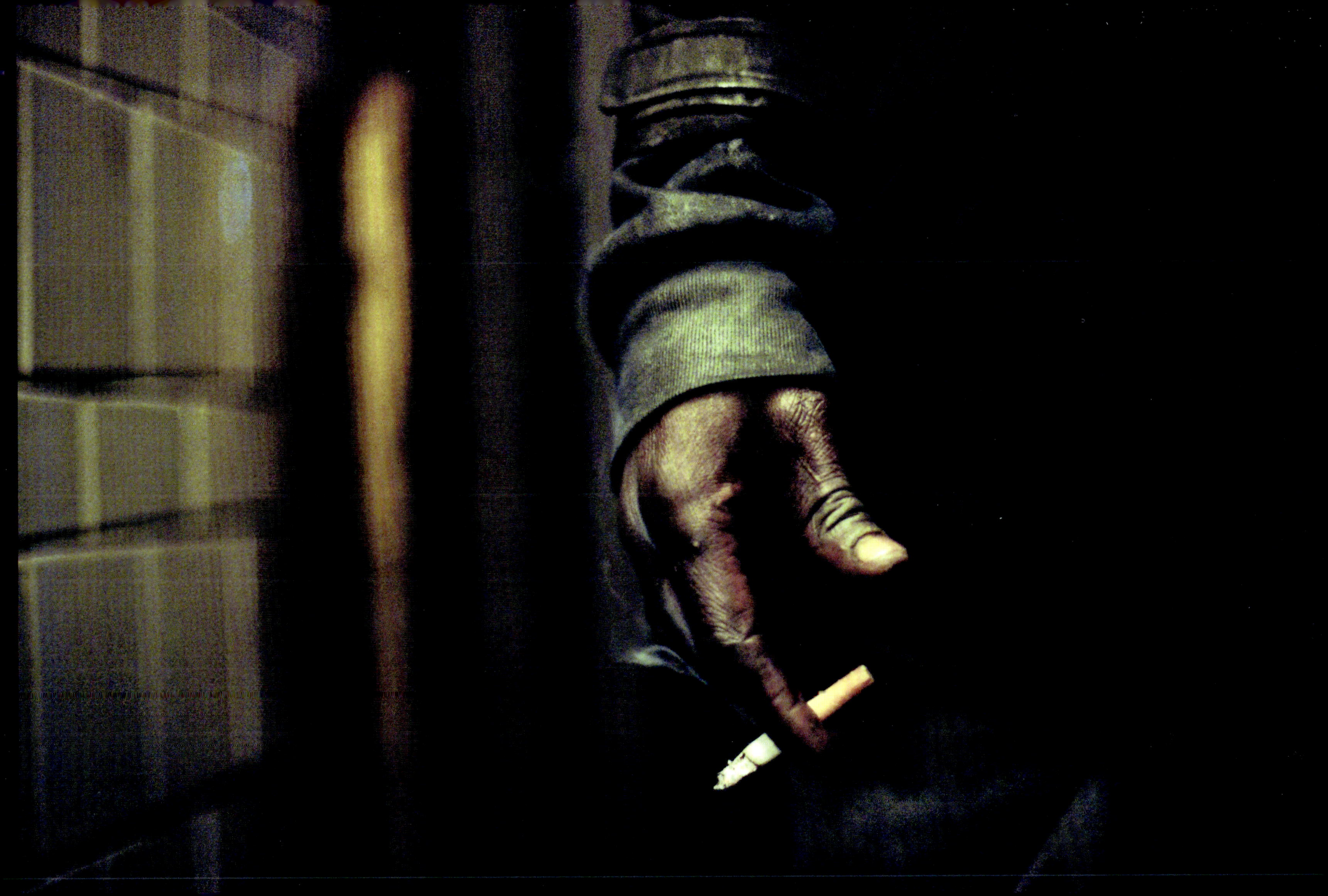

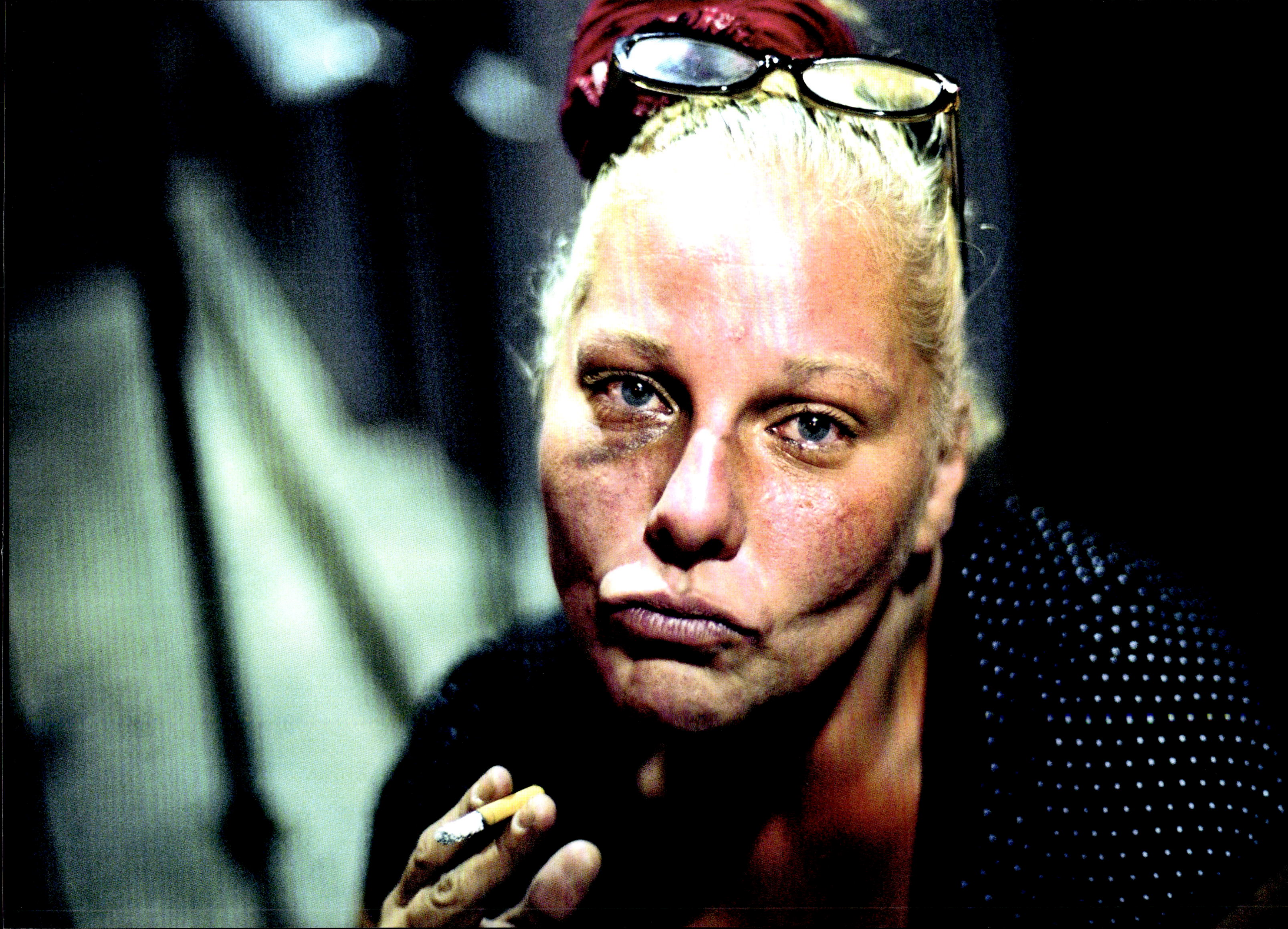

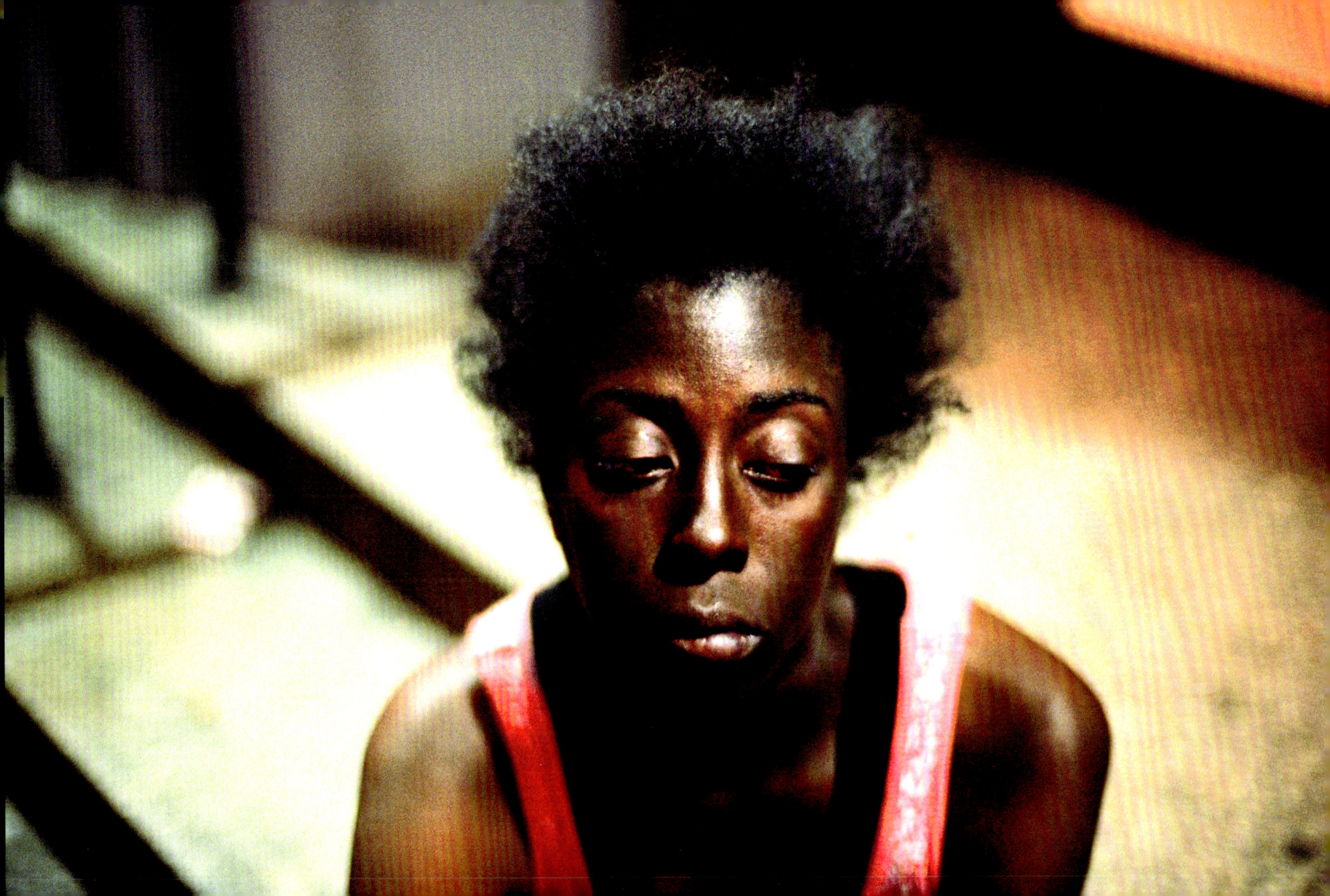

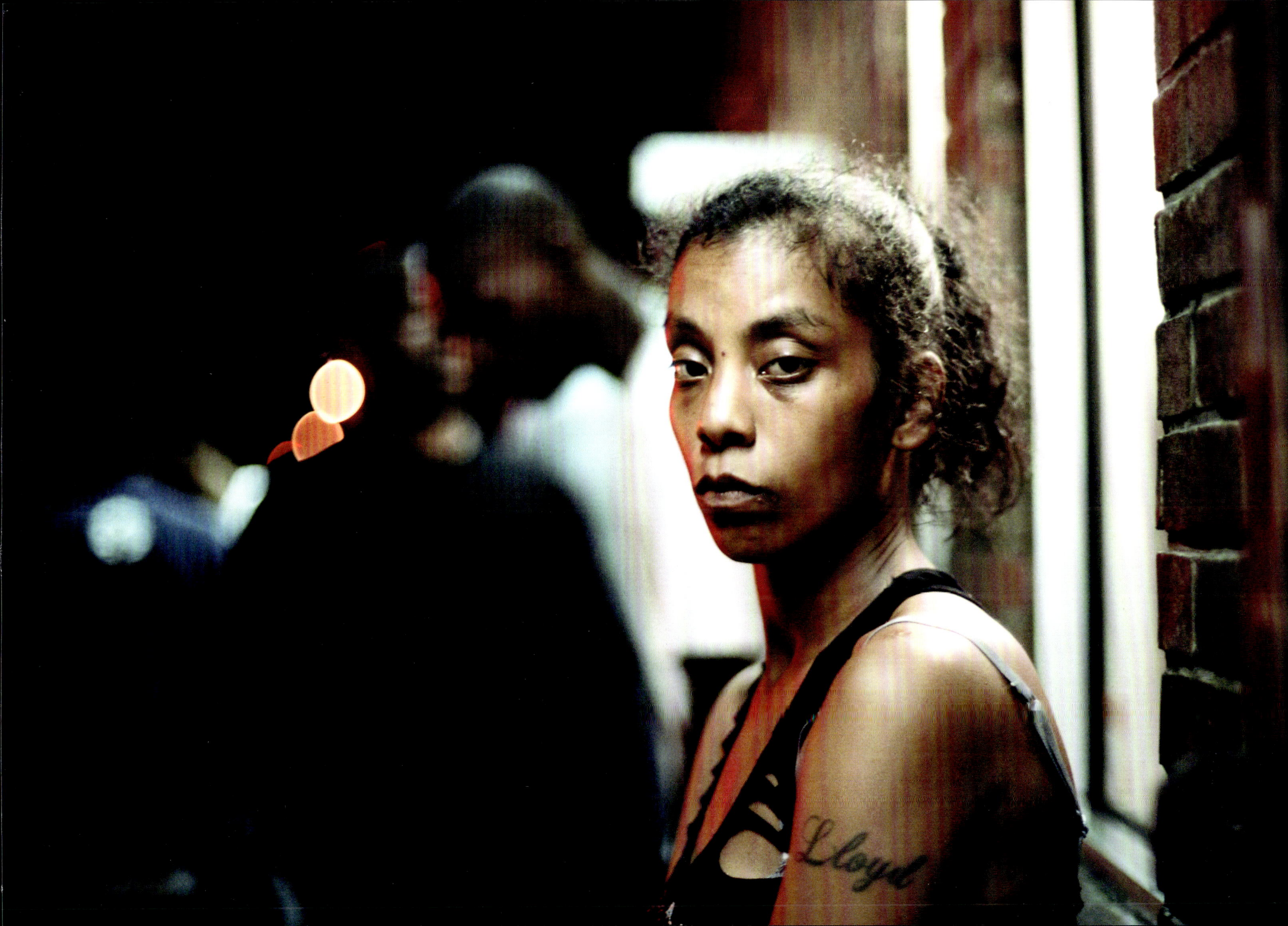
Lloyd

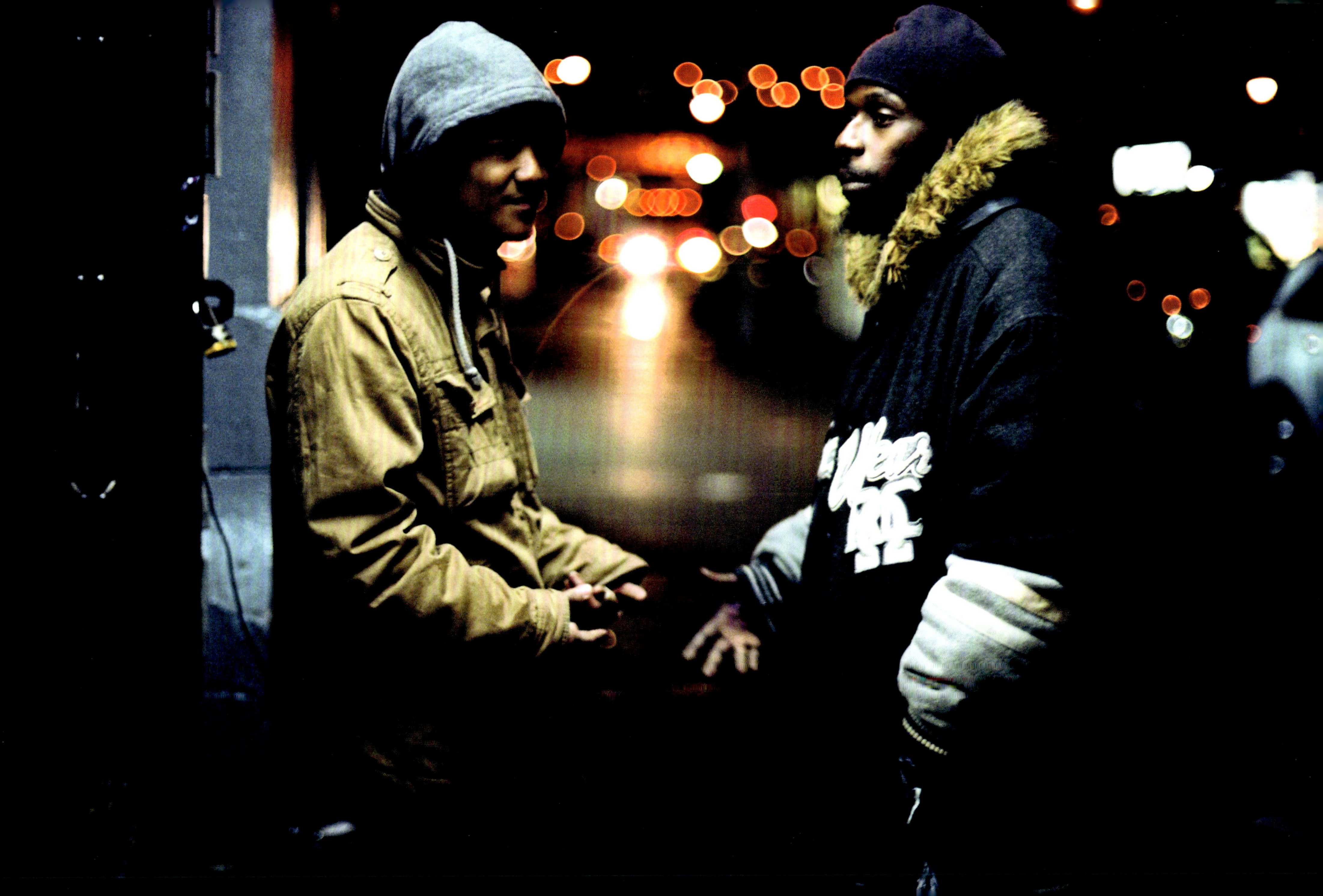

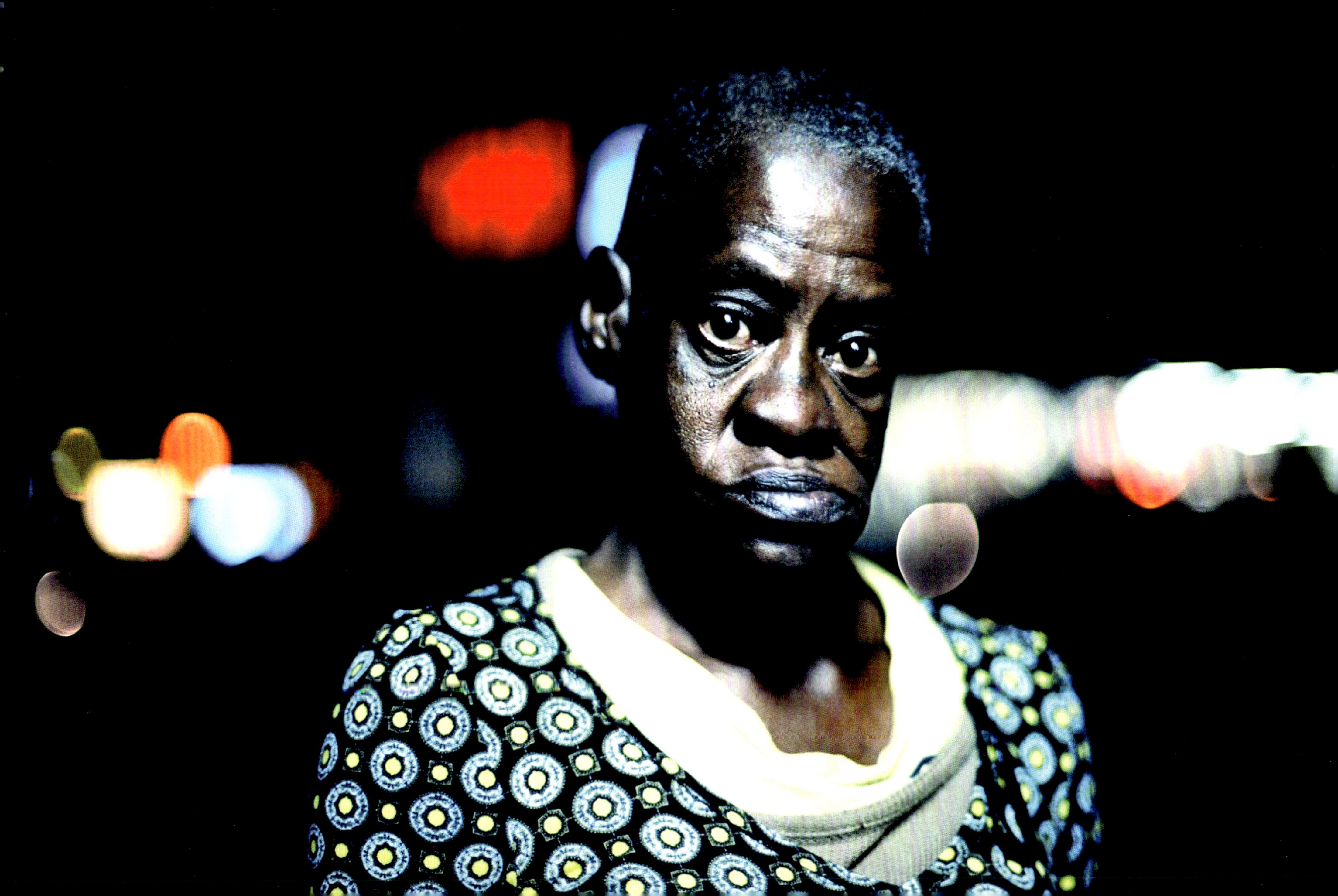

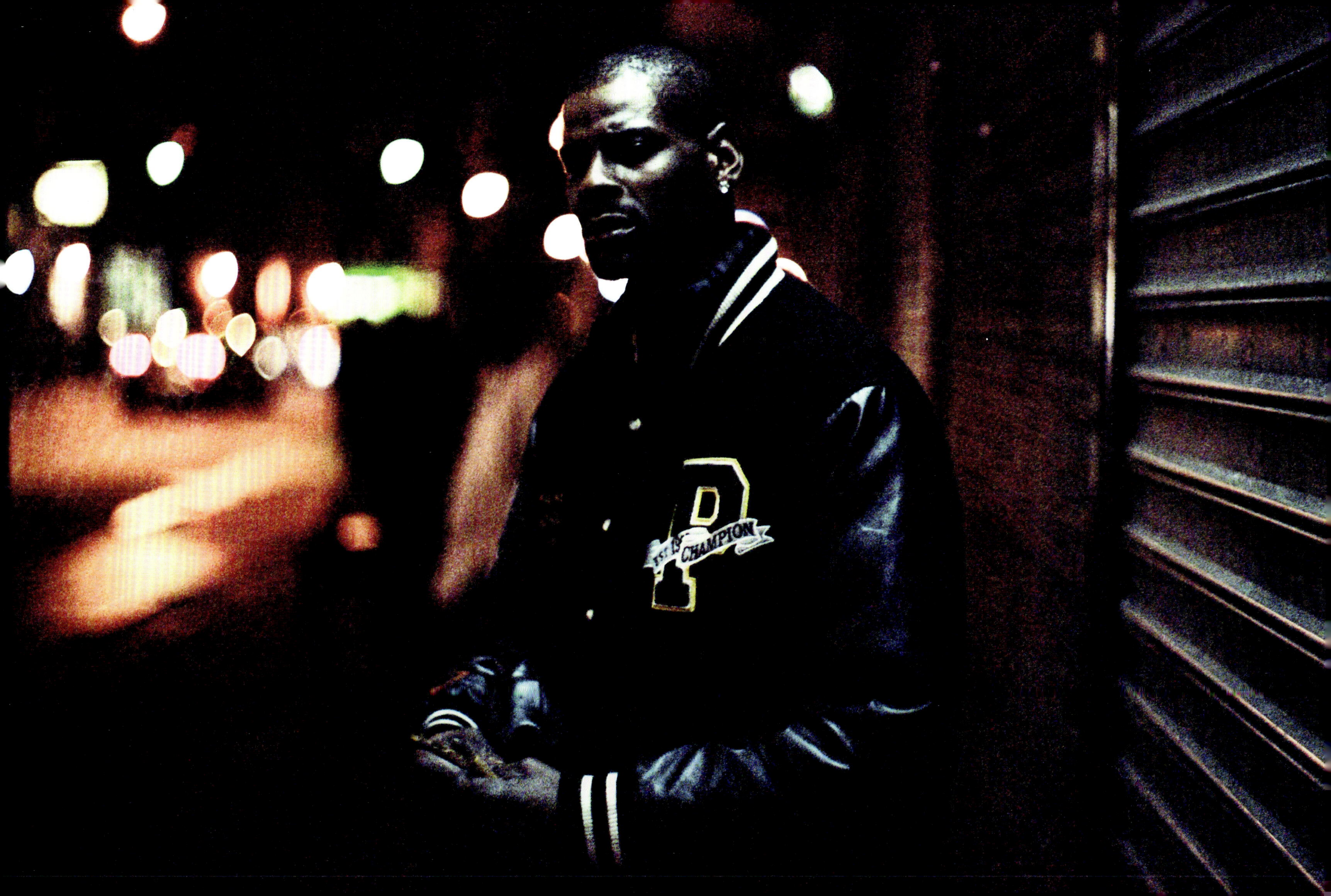
CHAMPION

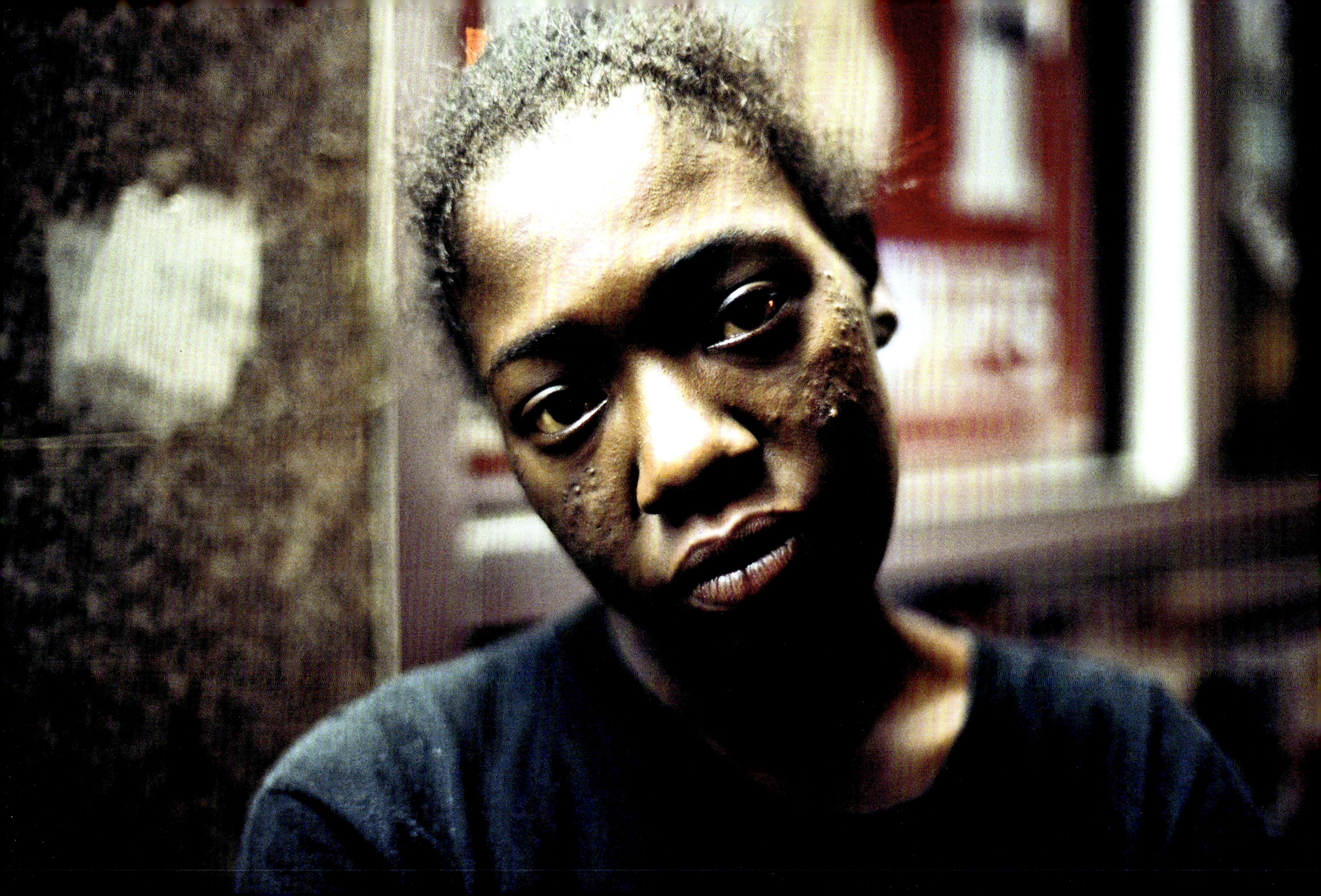

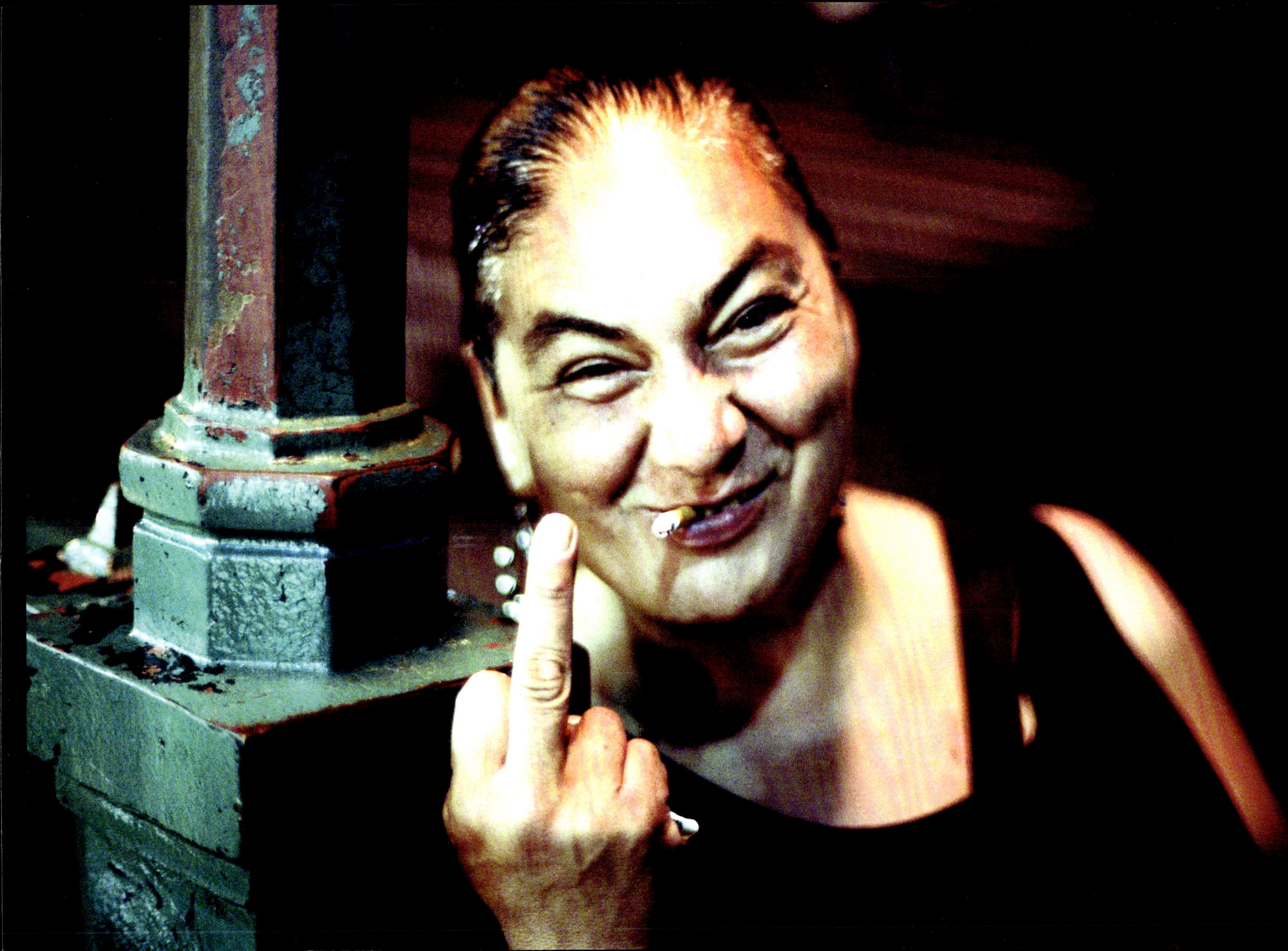

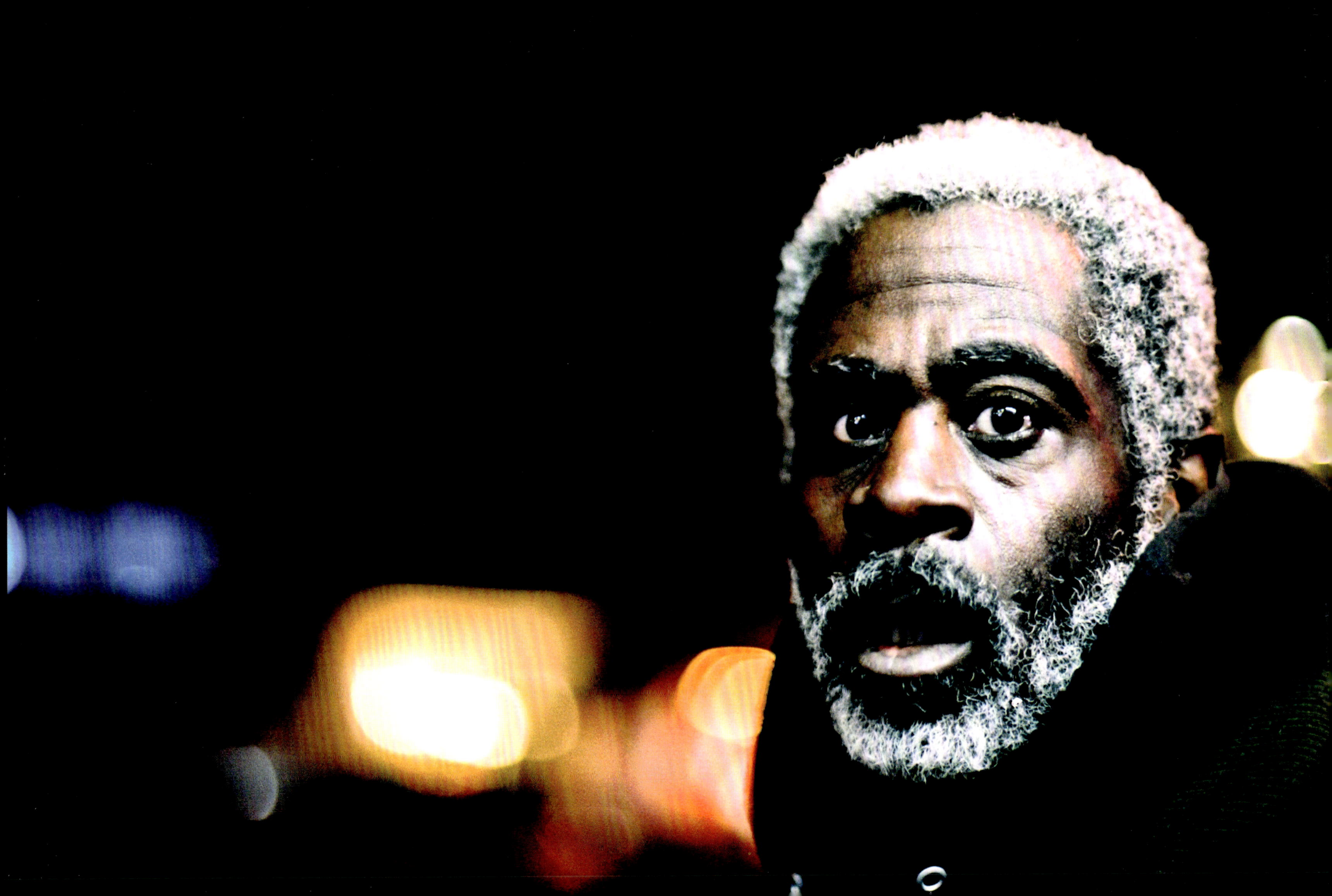

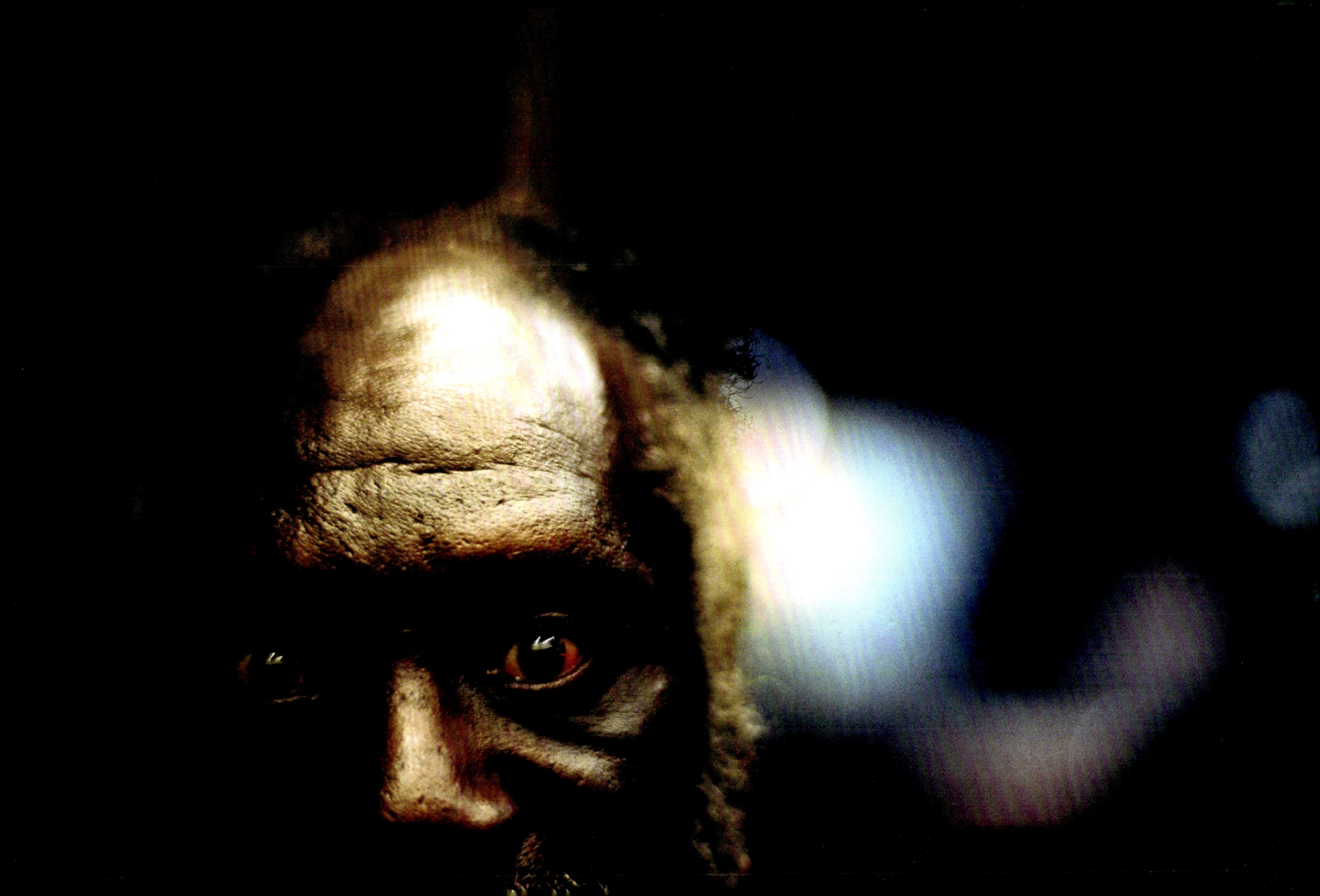

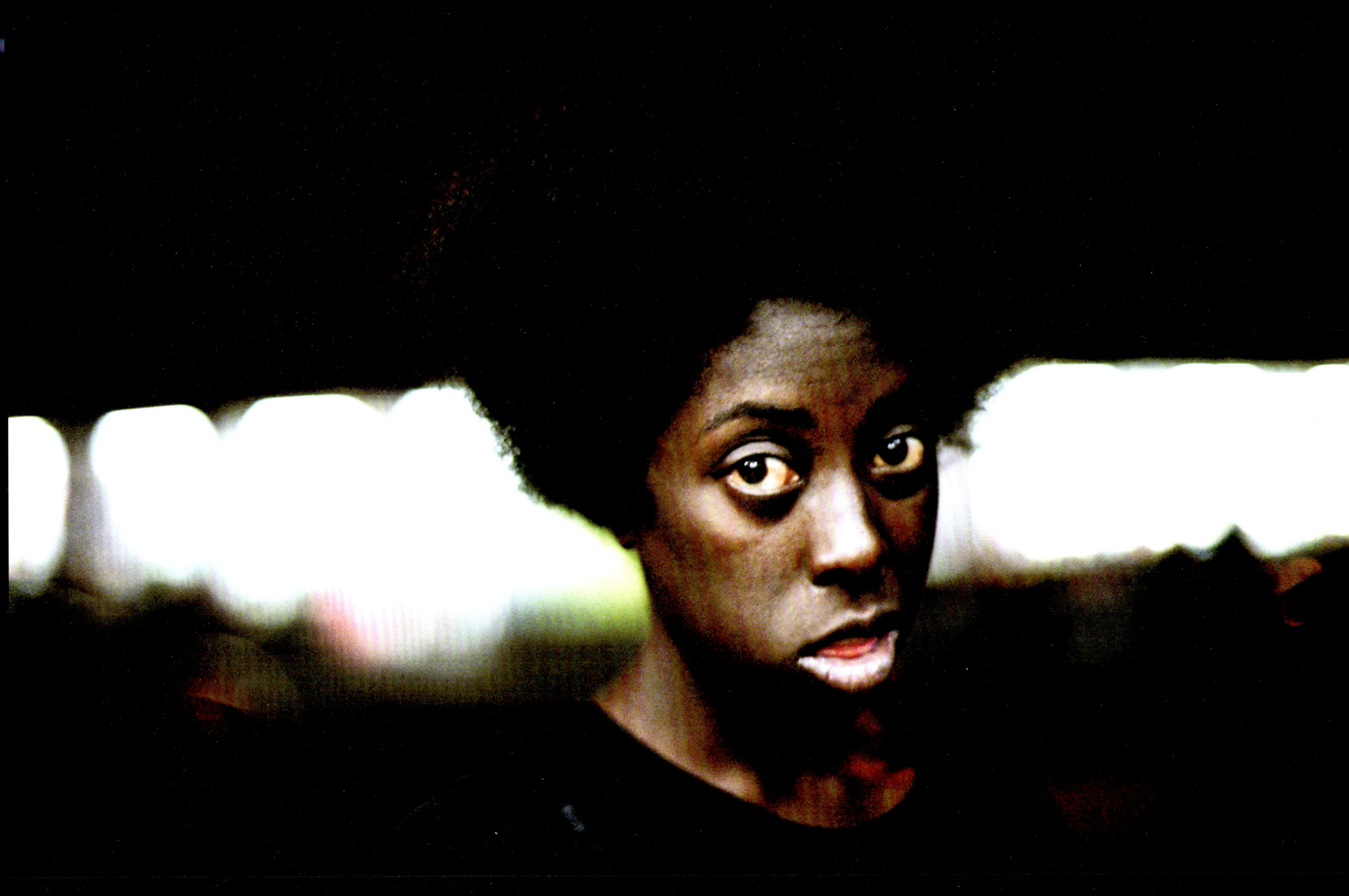

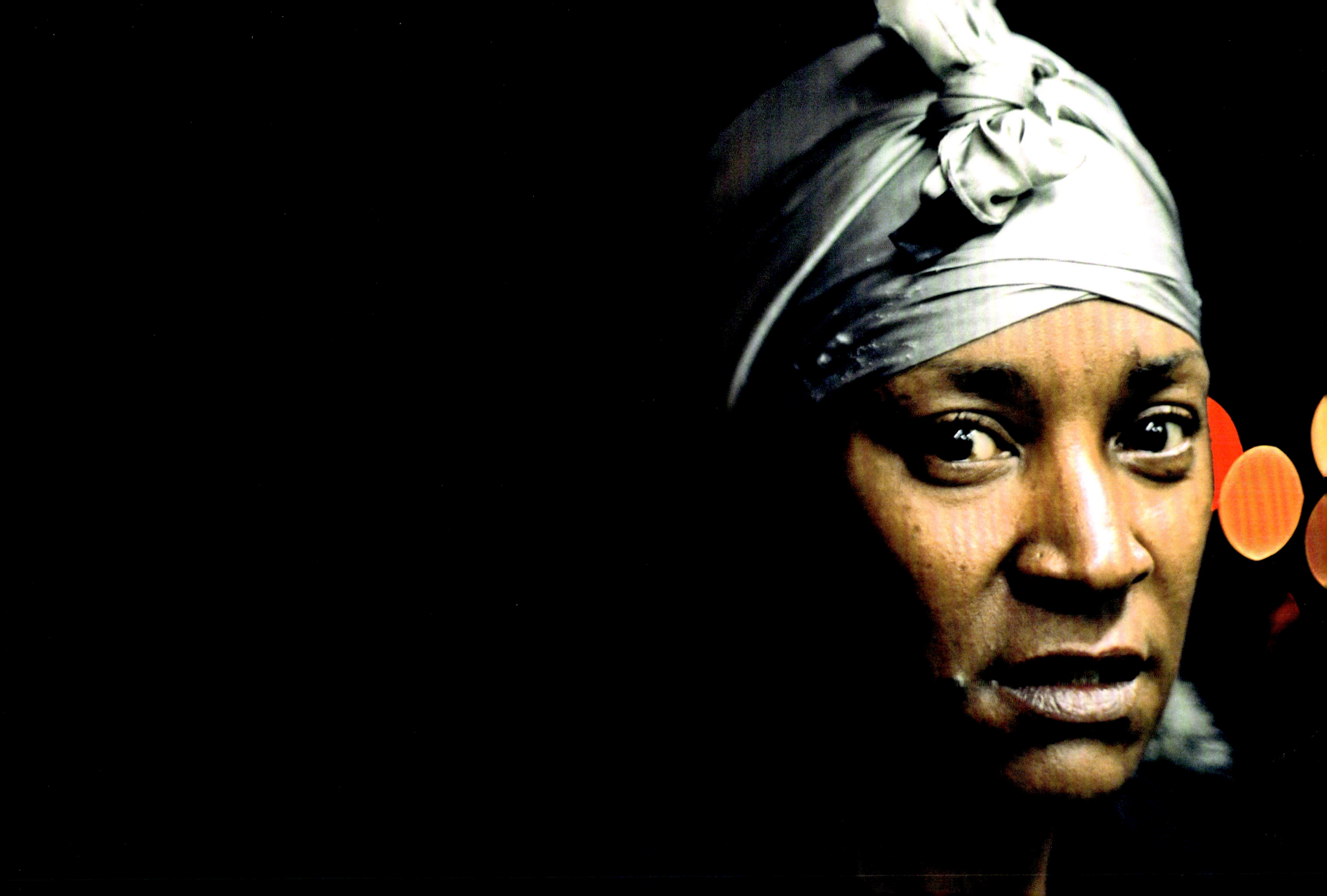

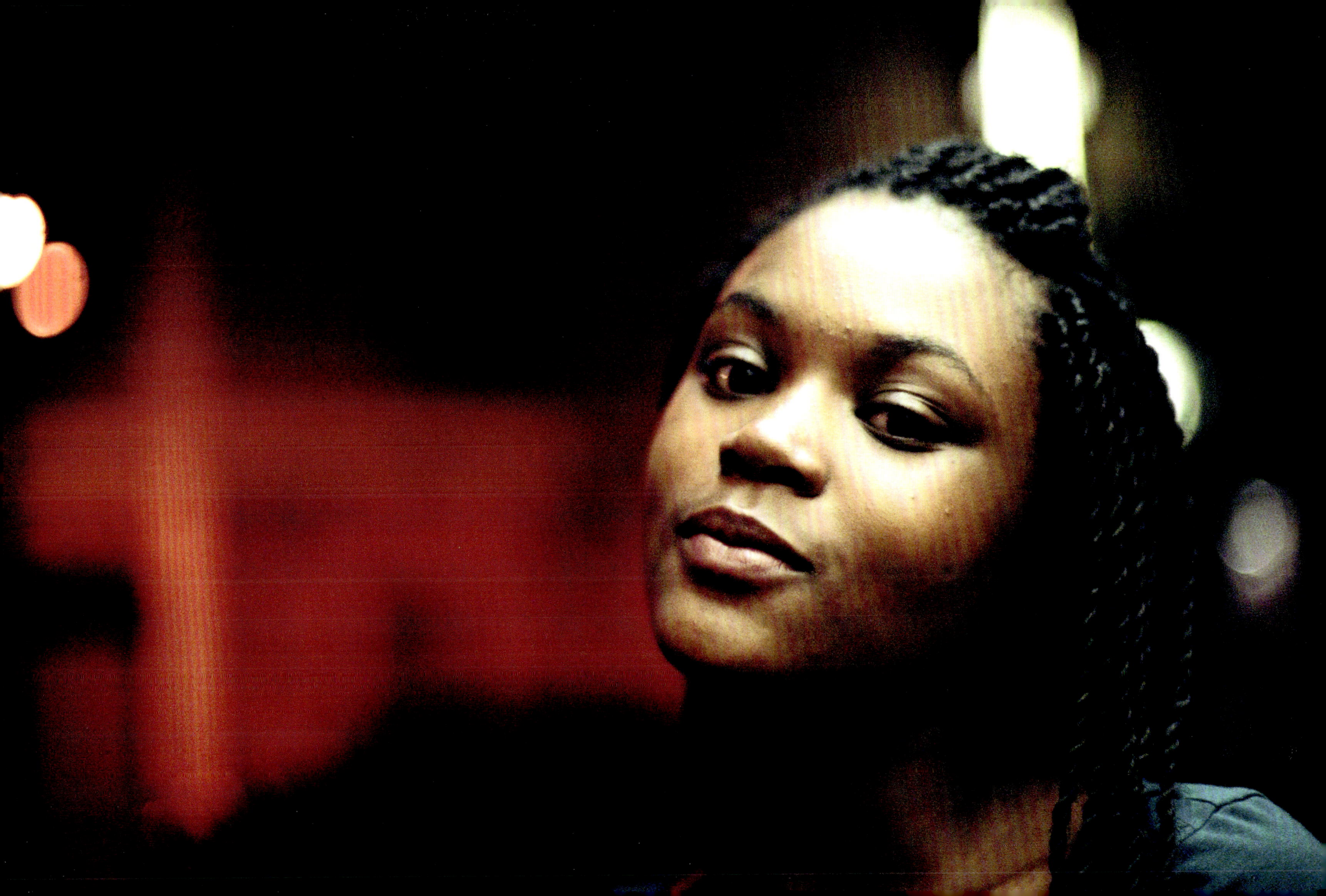

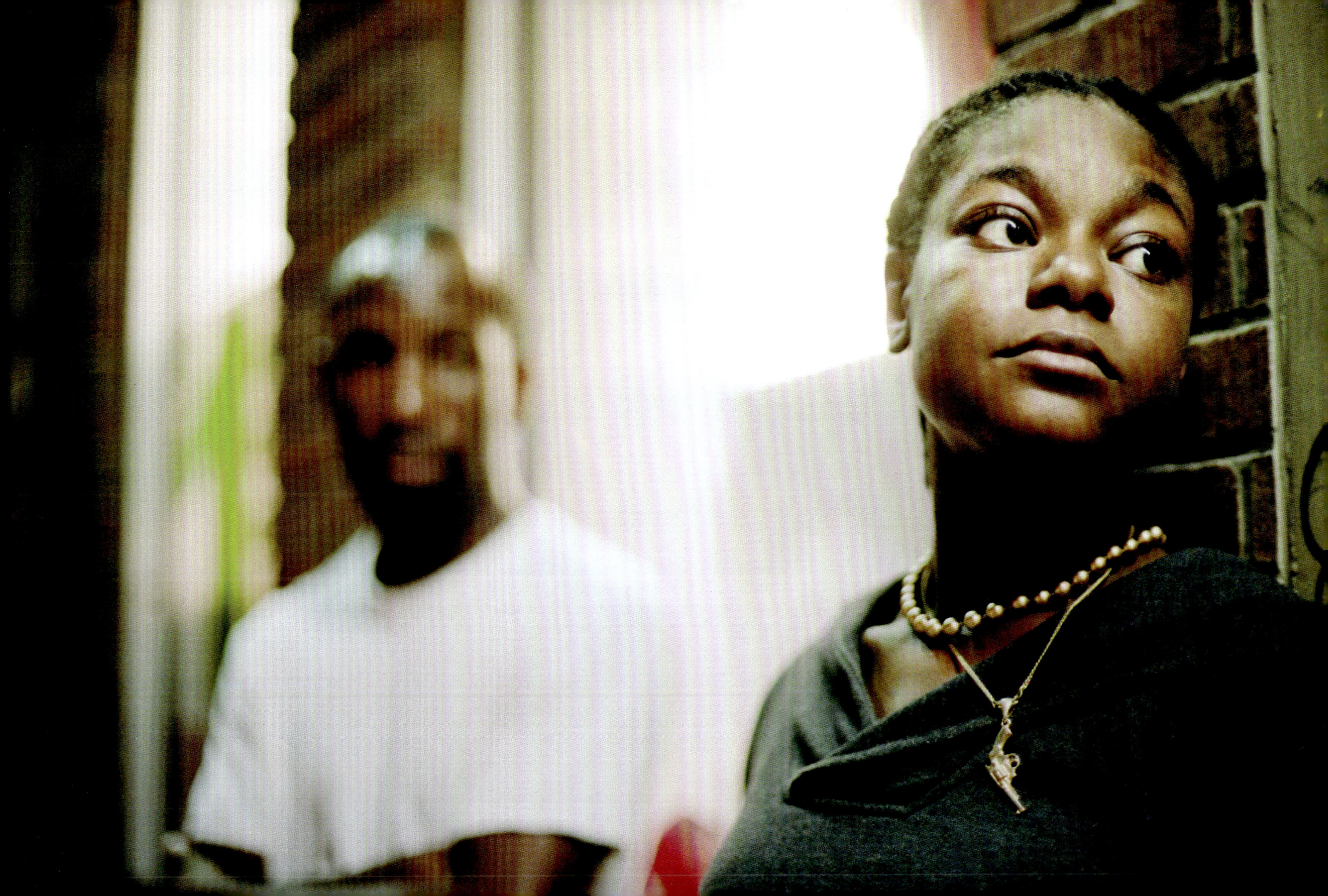

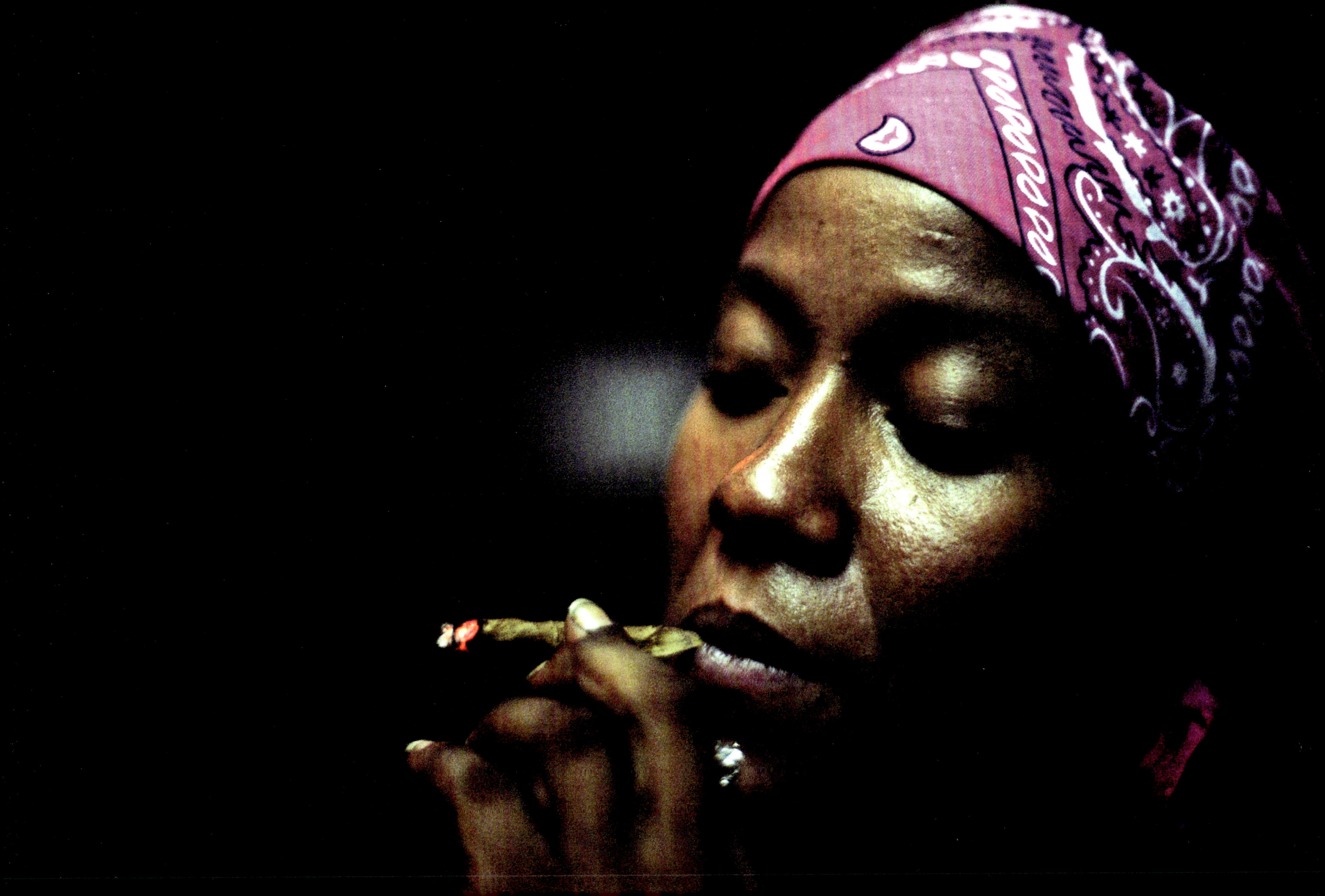

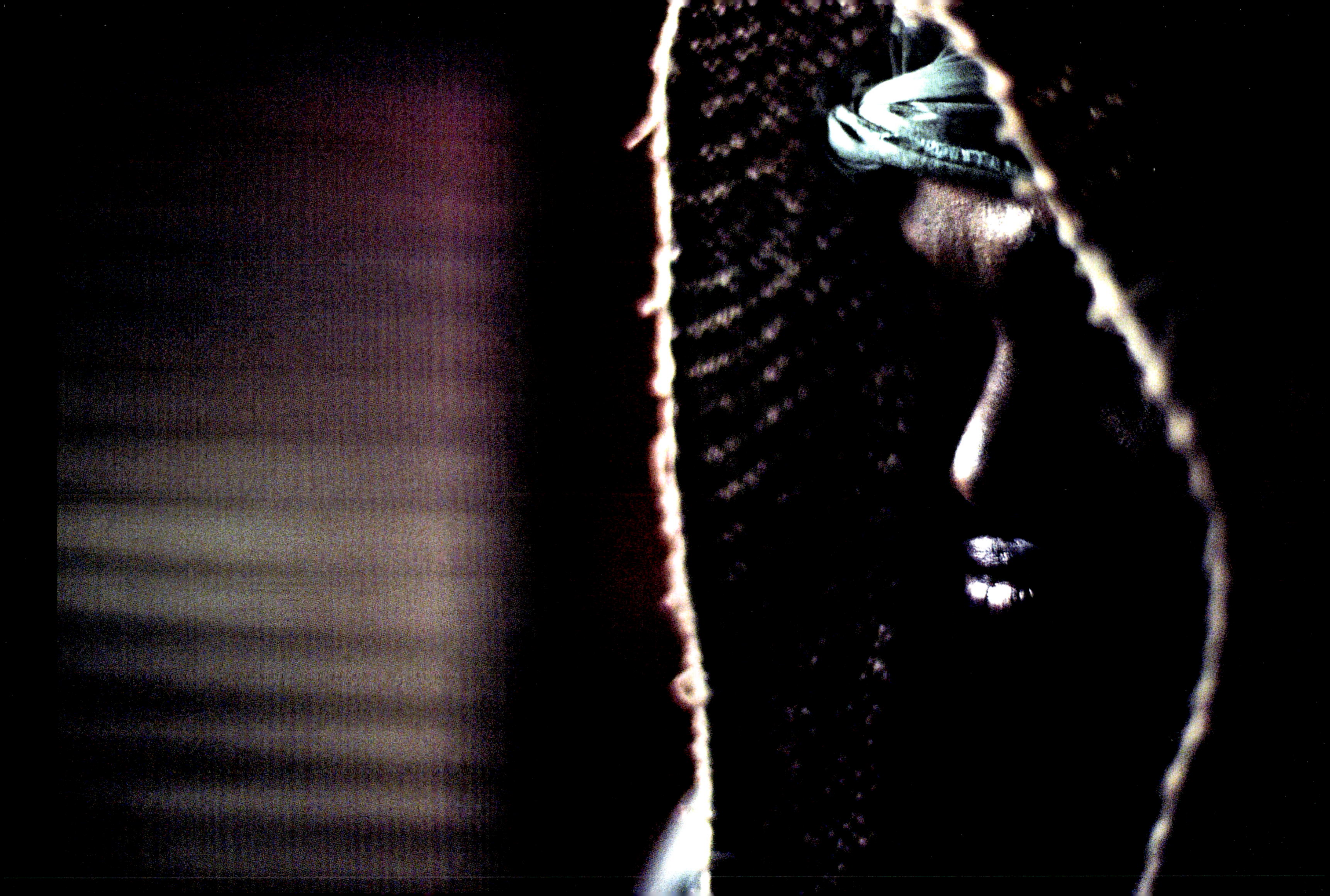

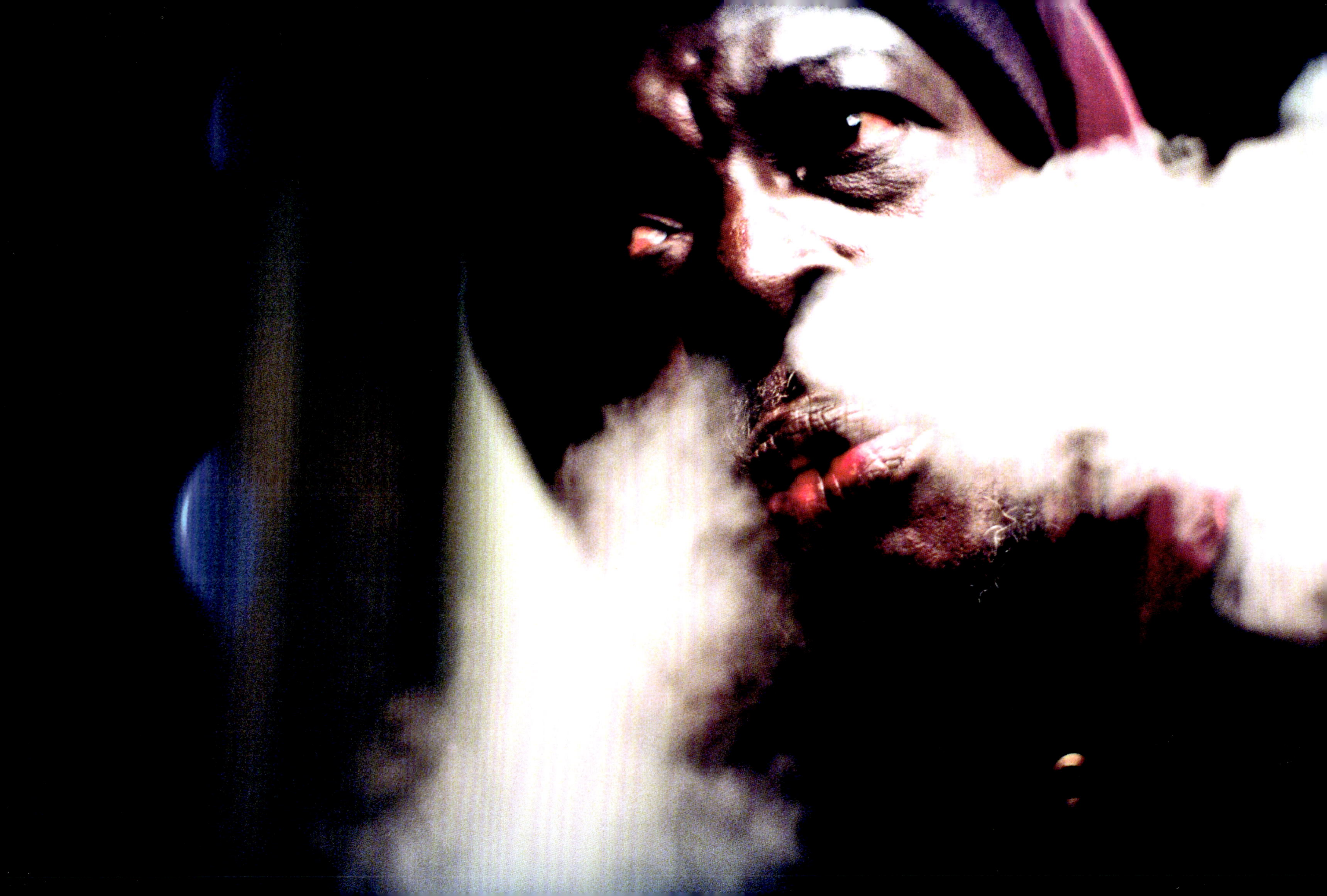

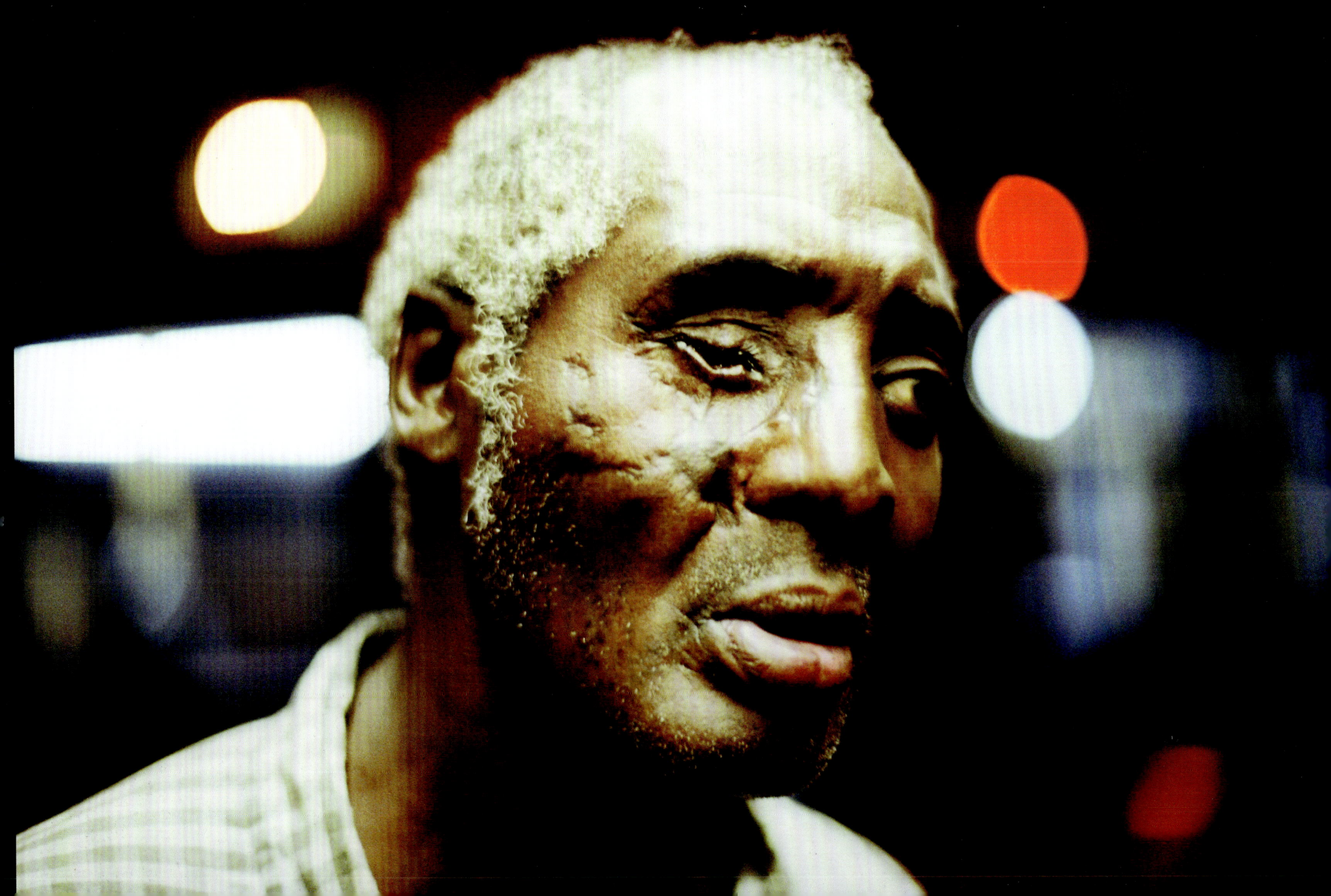

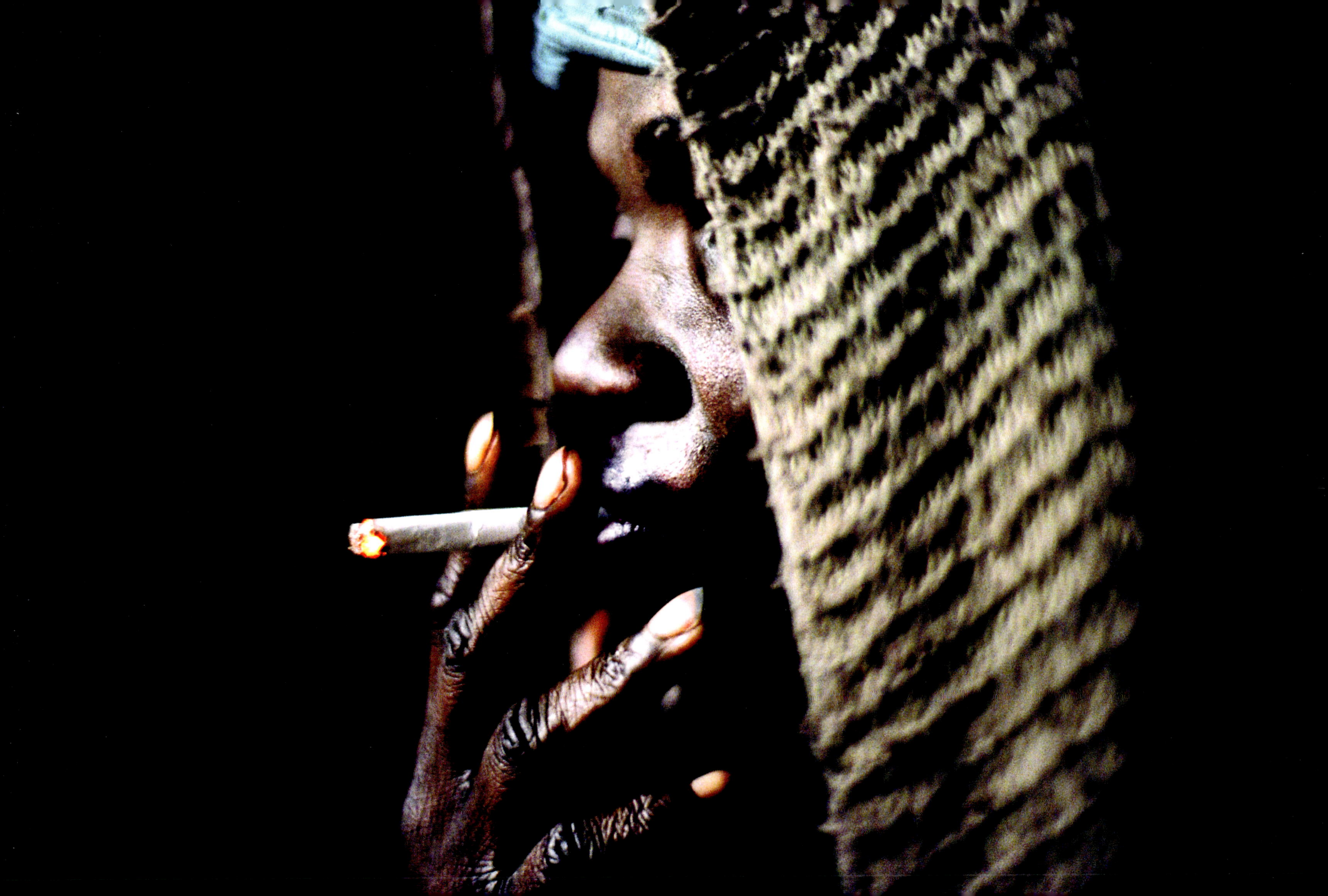

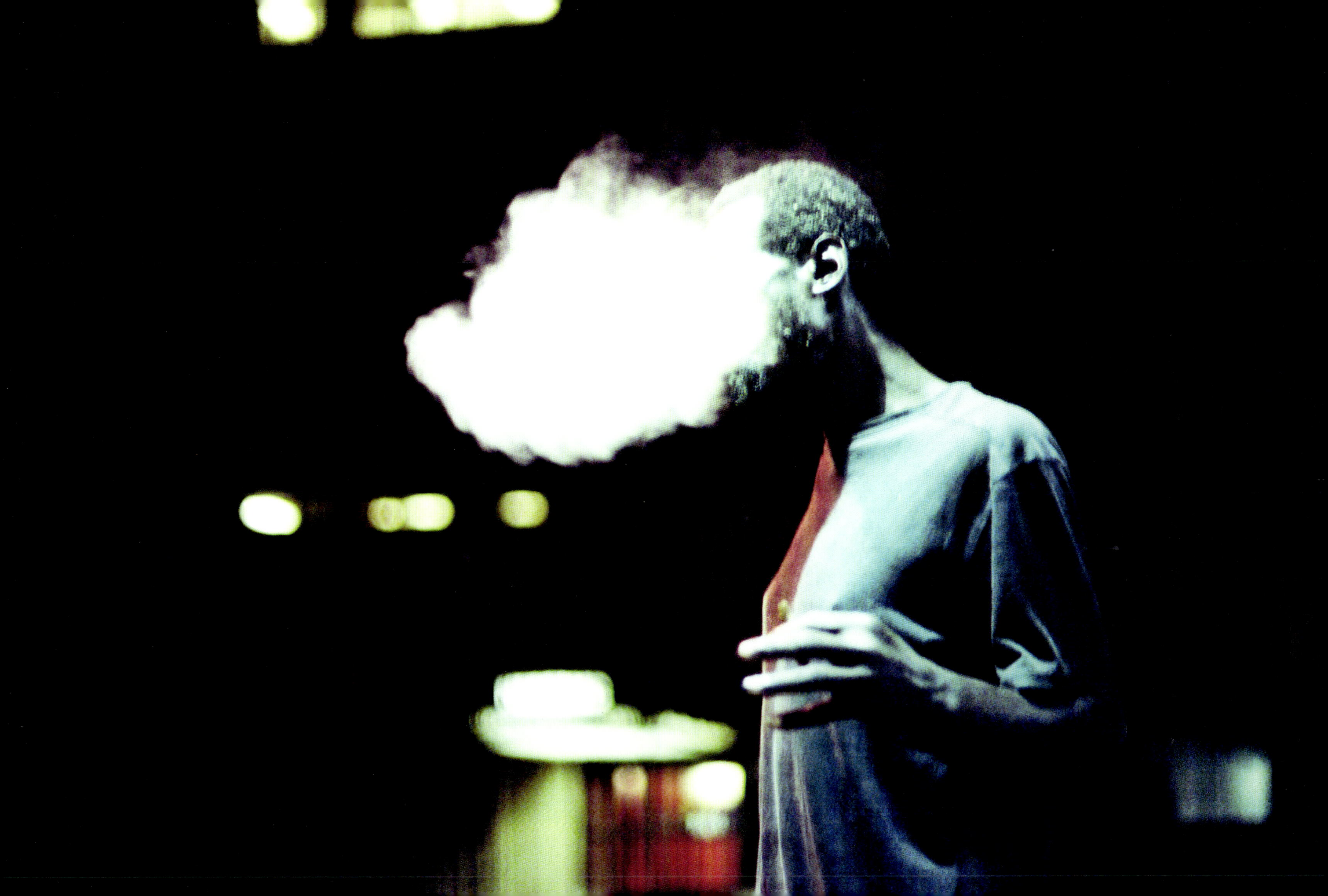

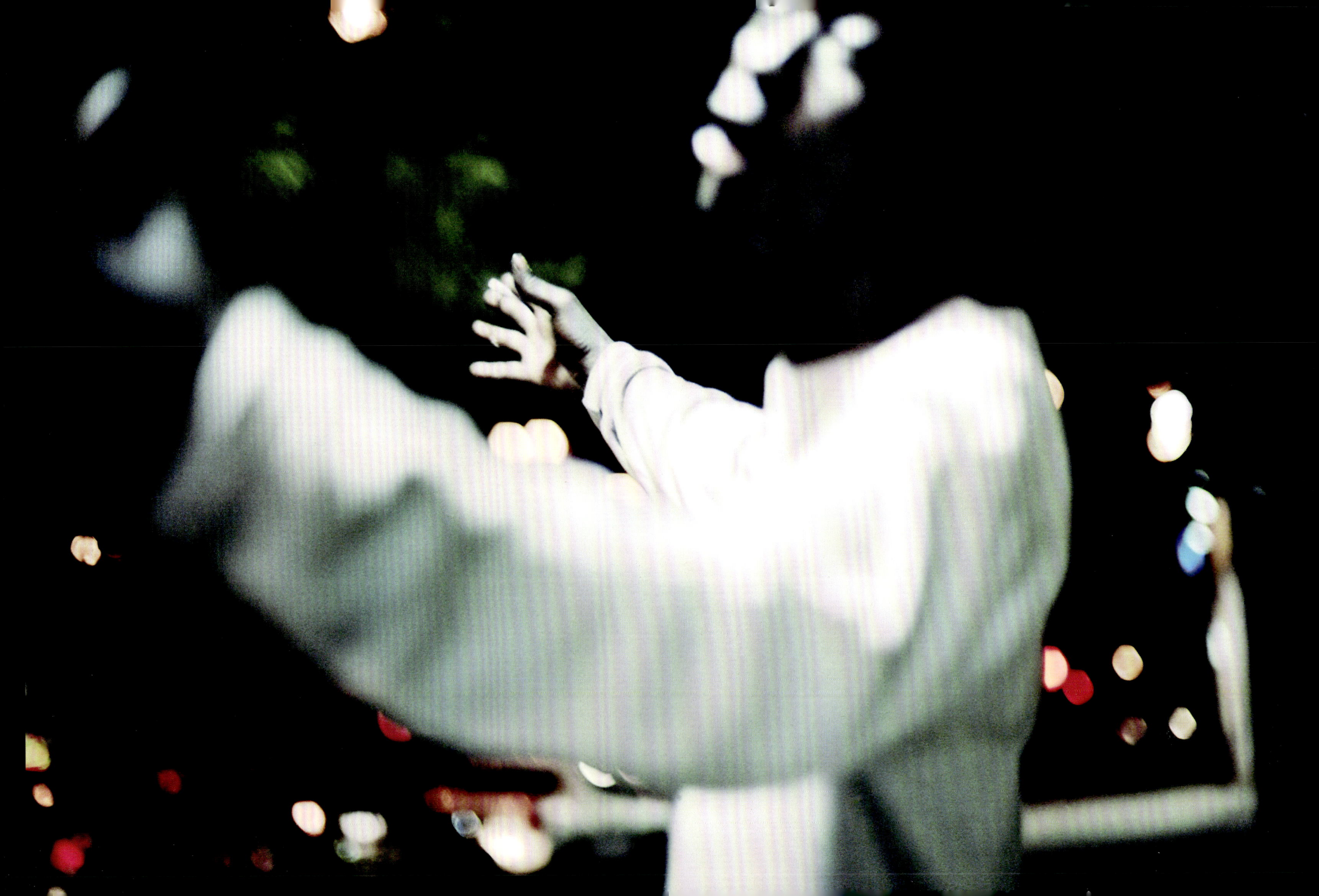

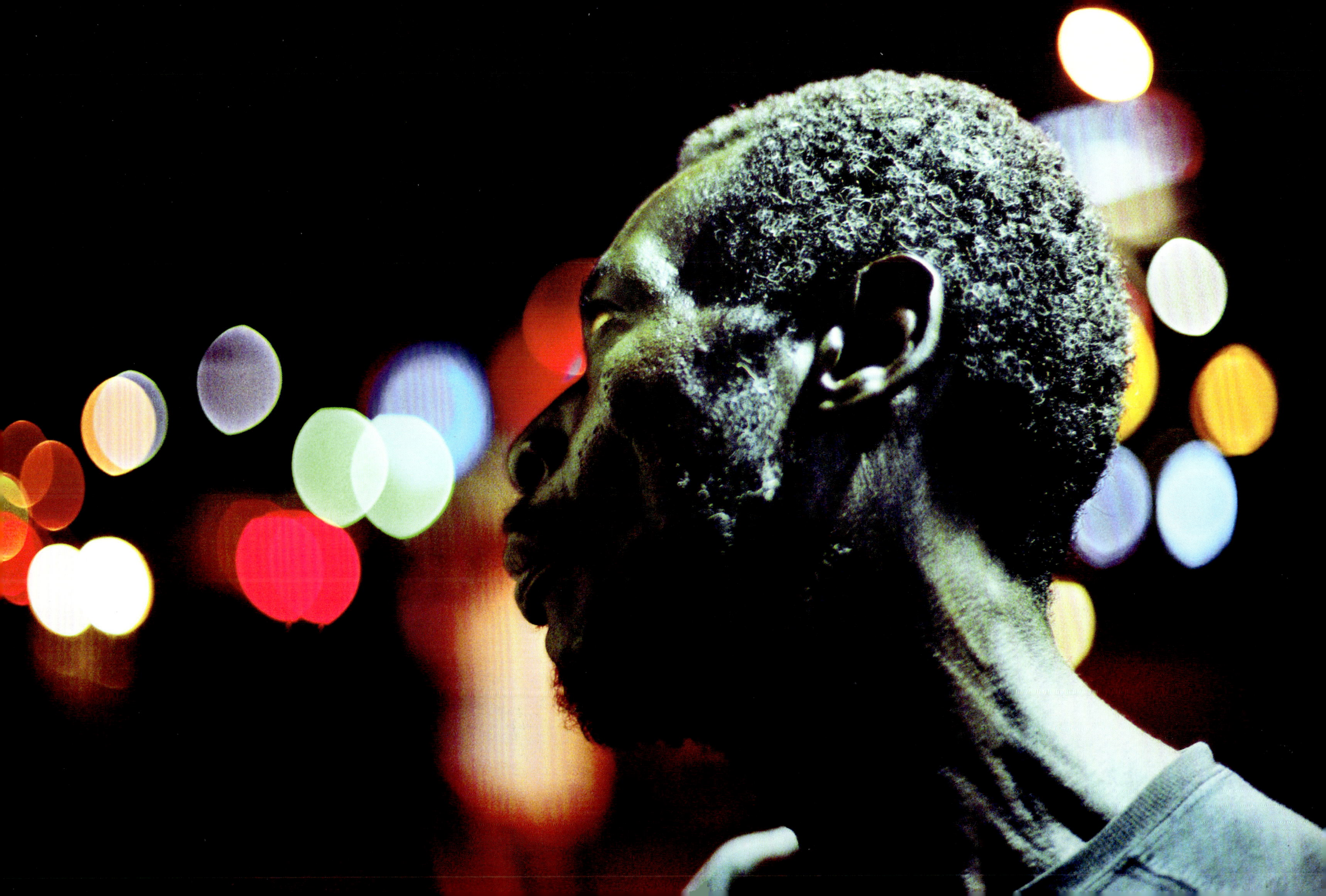

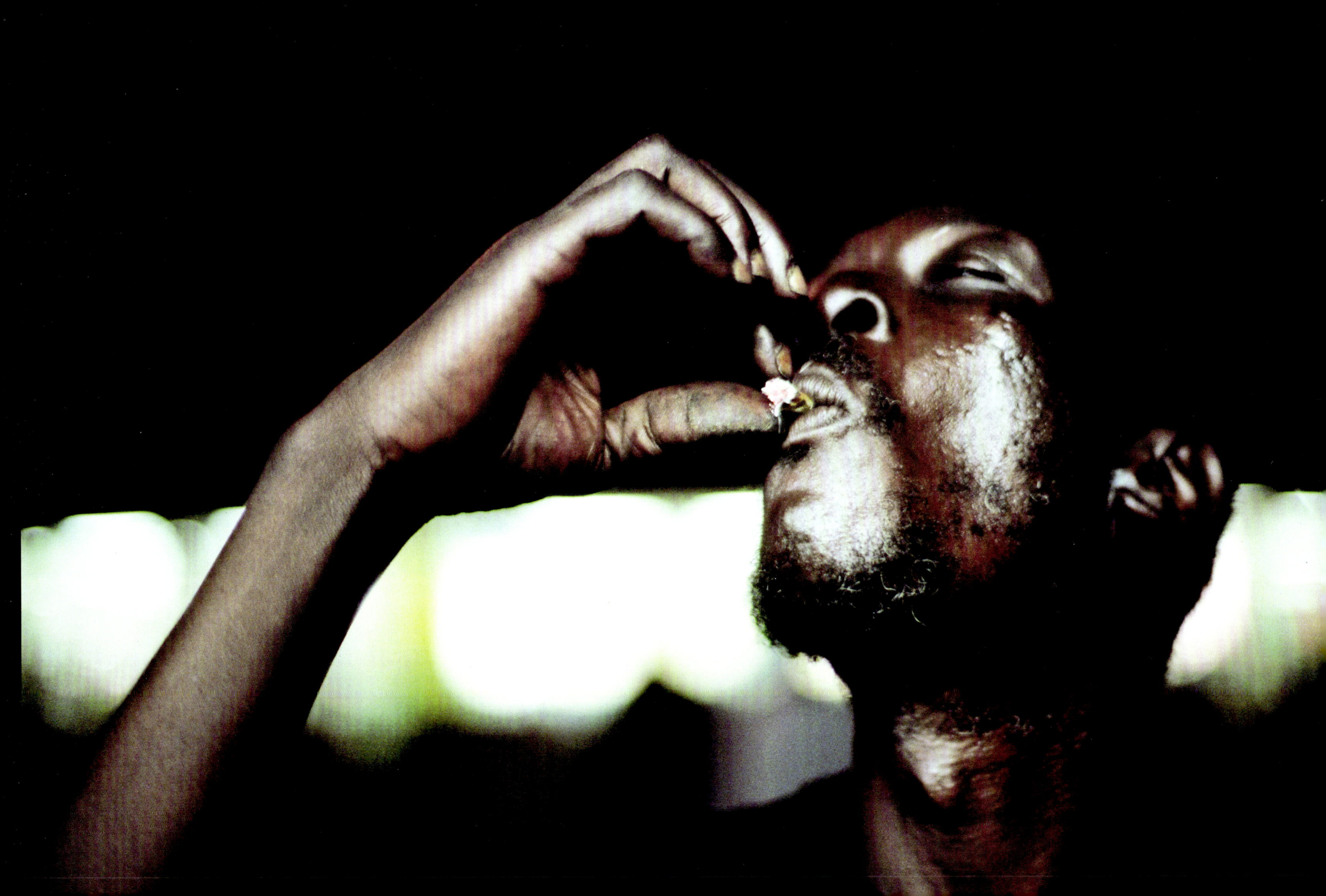

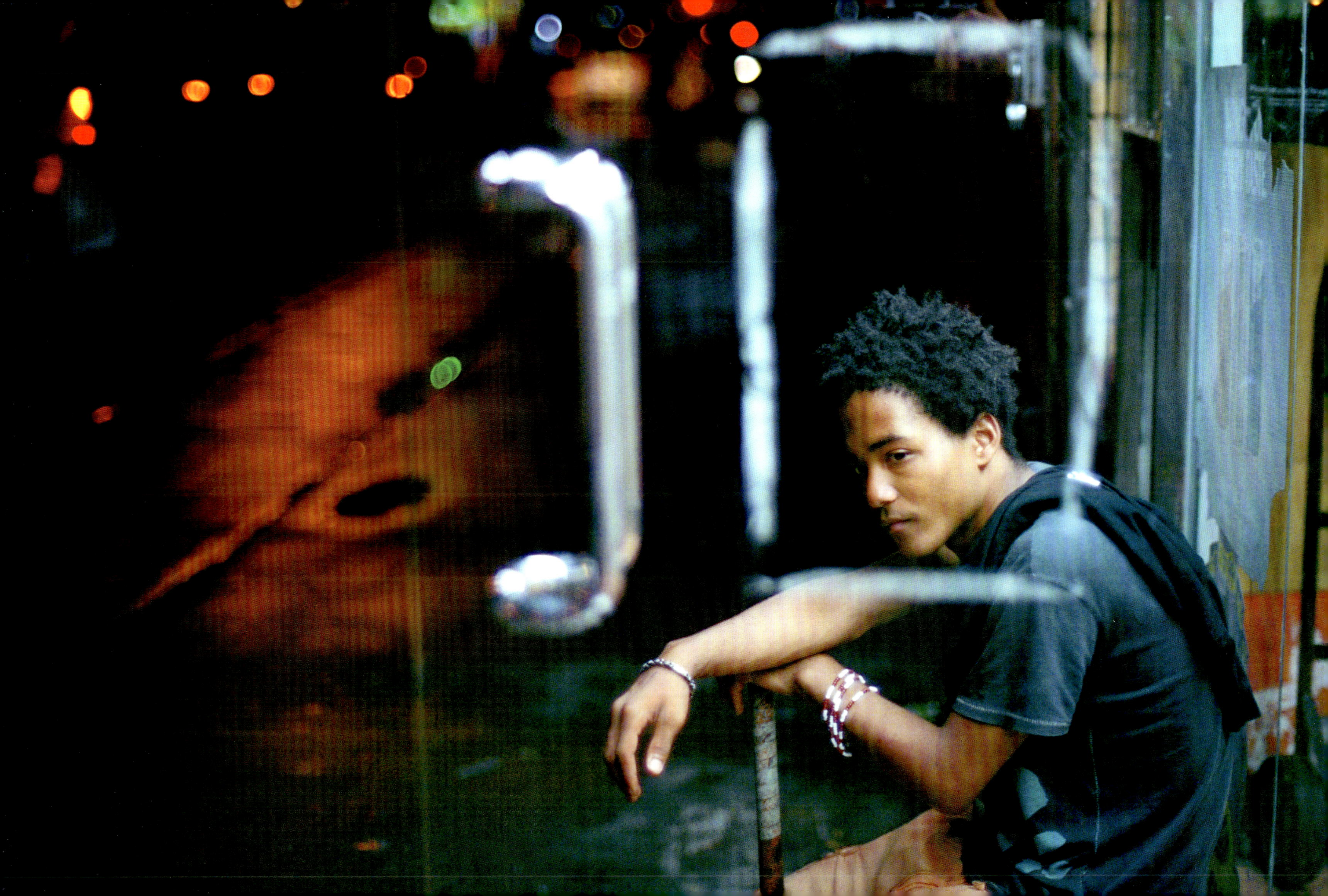

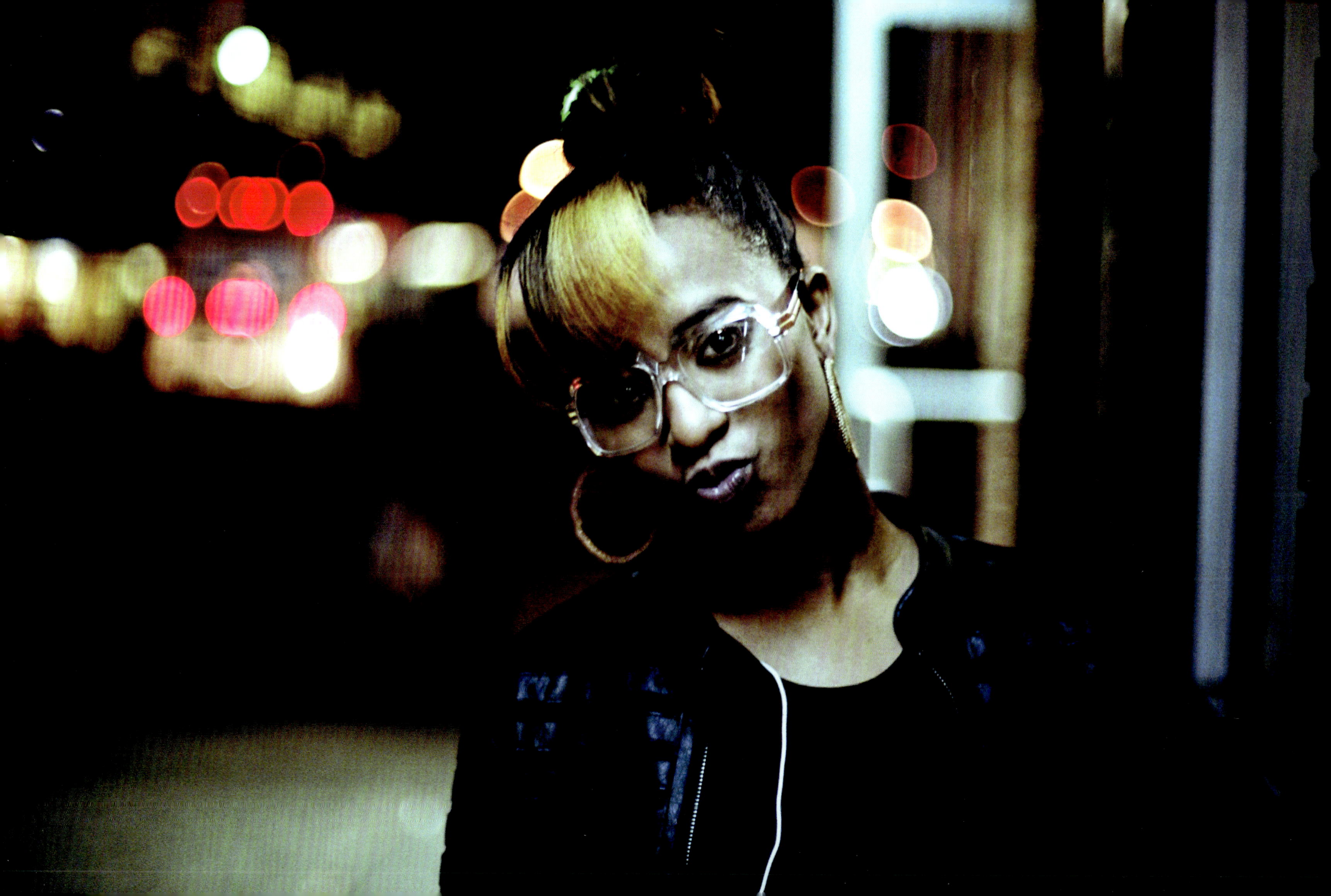

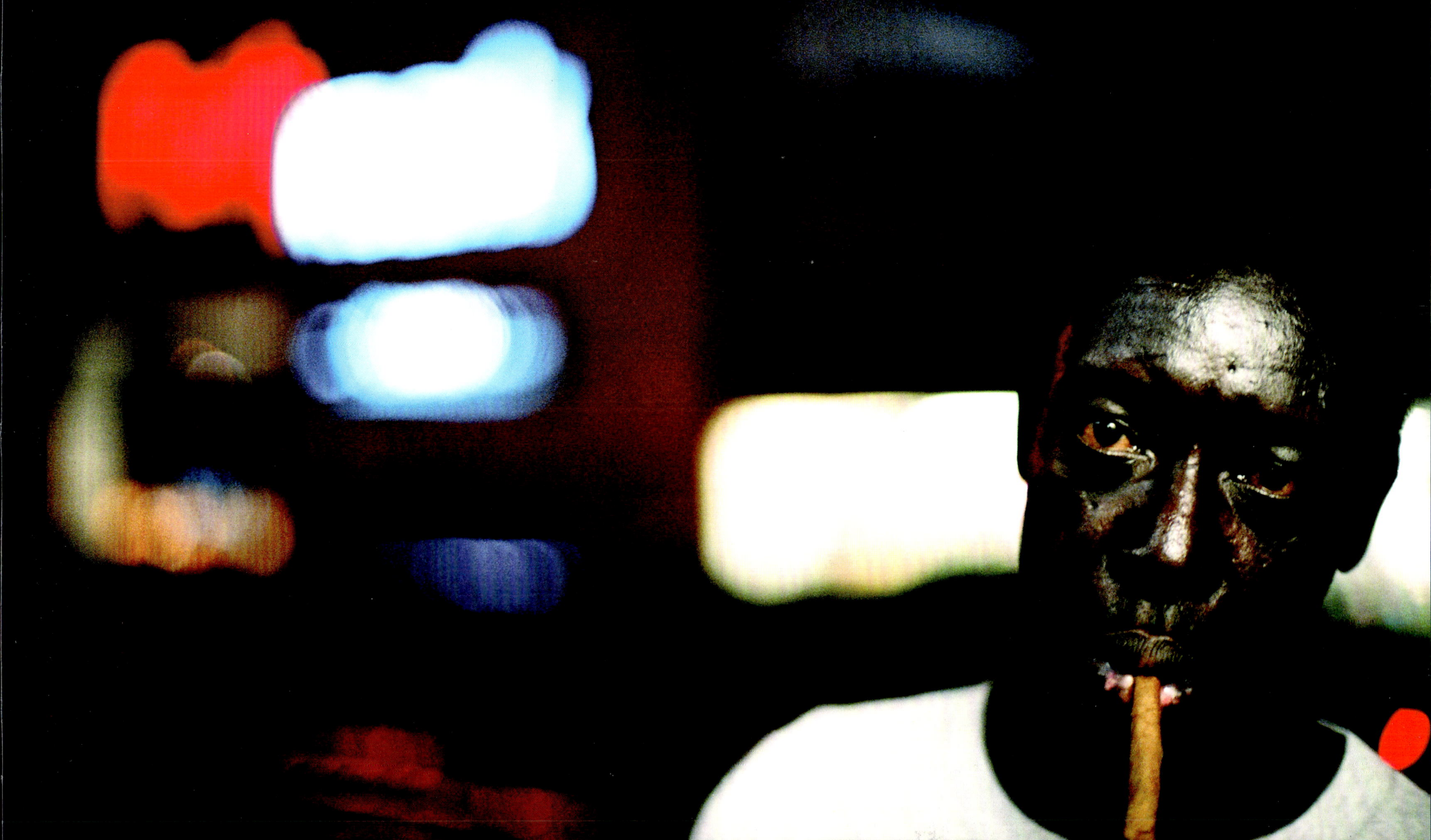

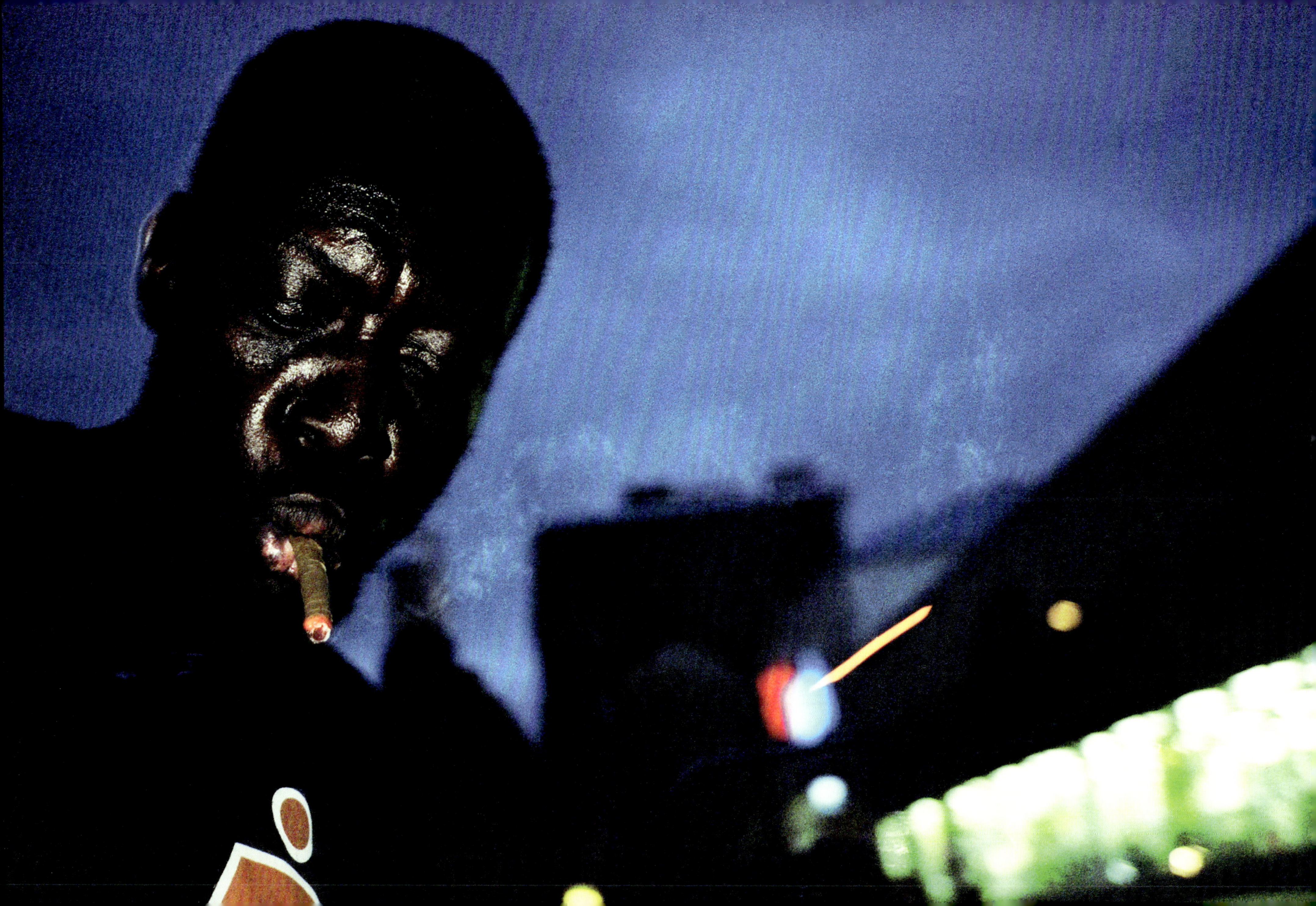

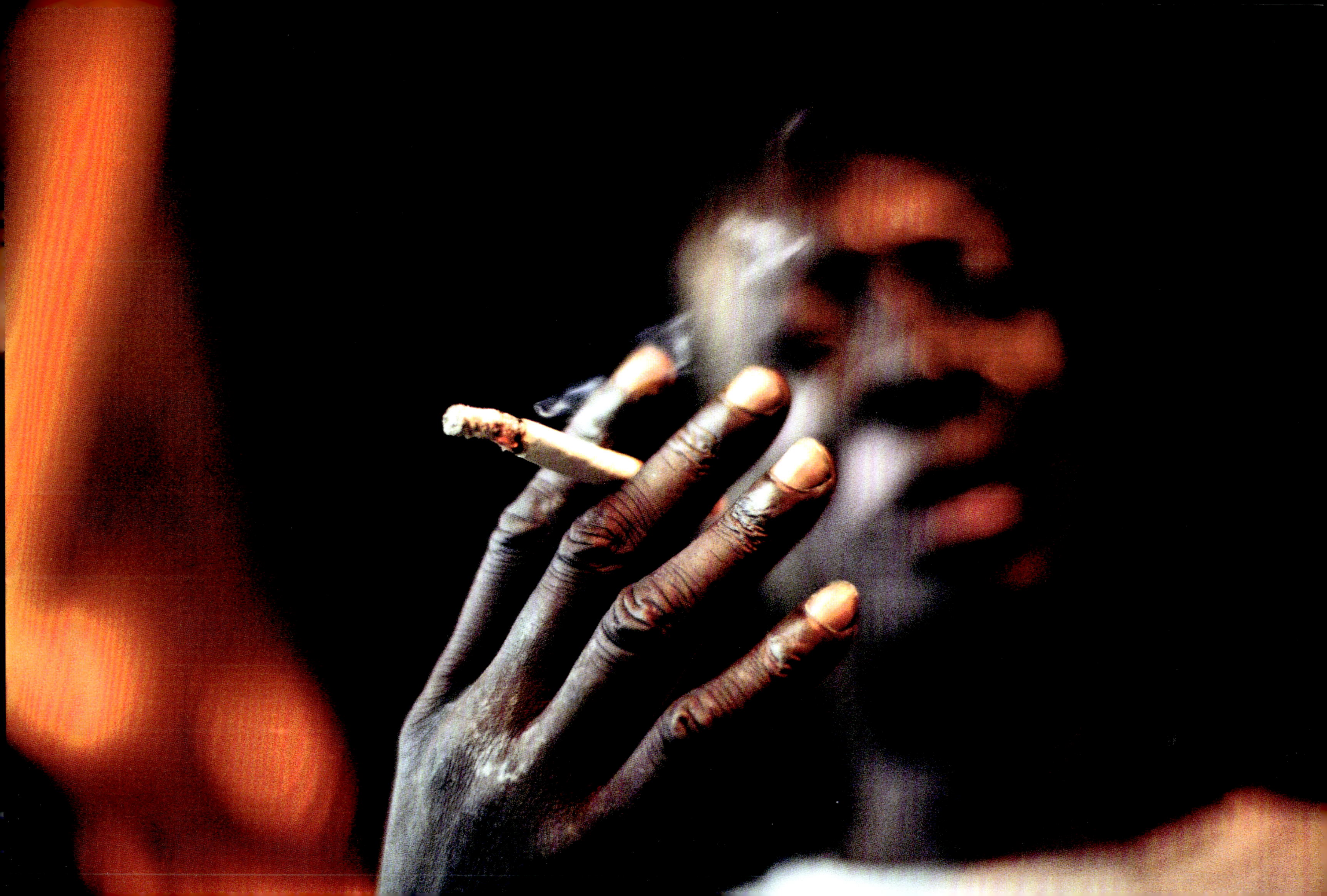

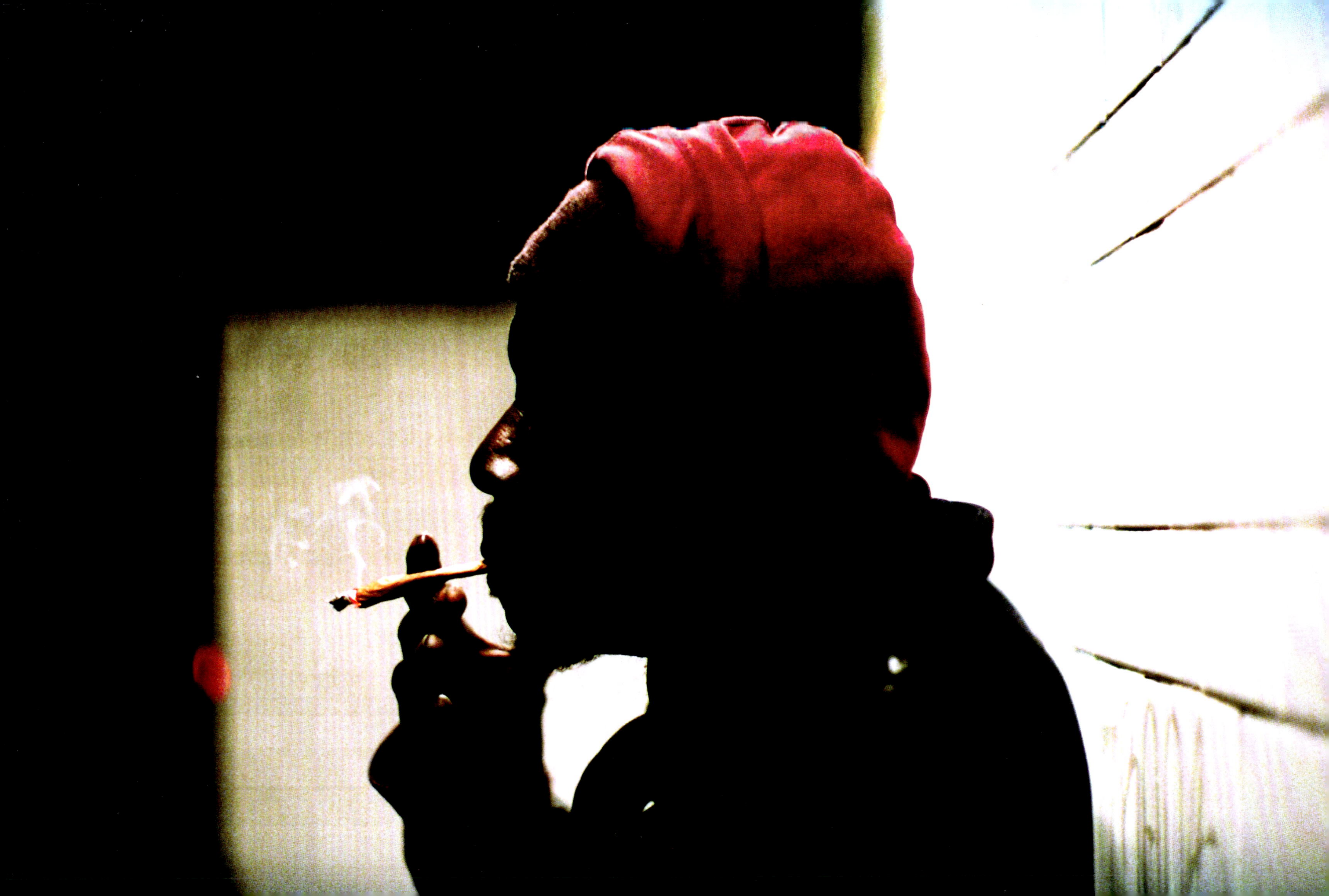

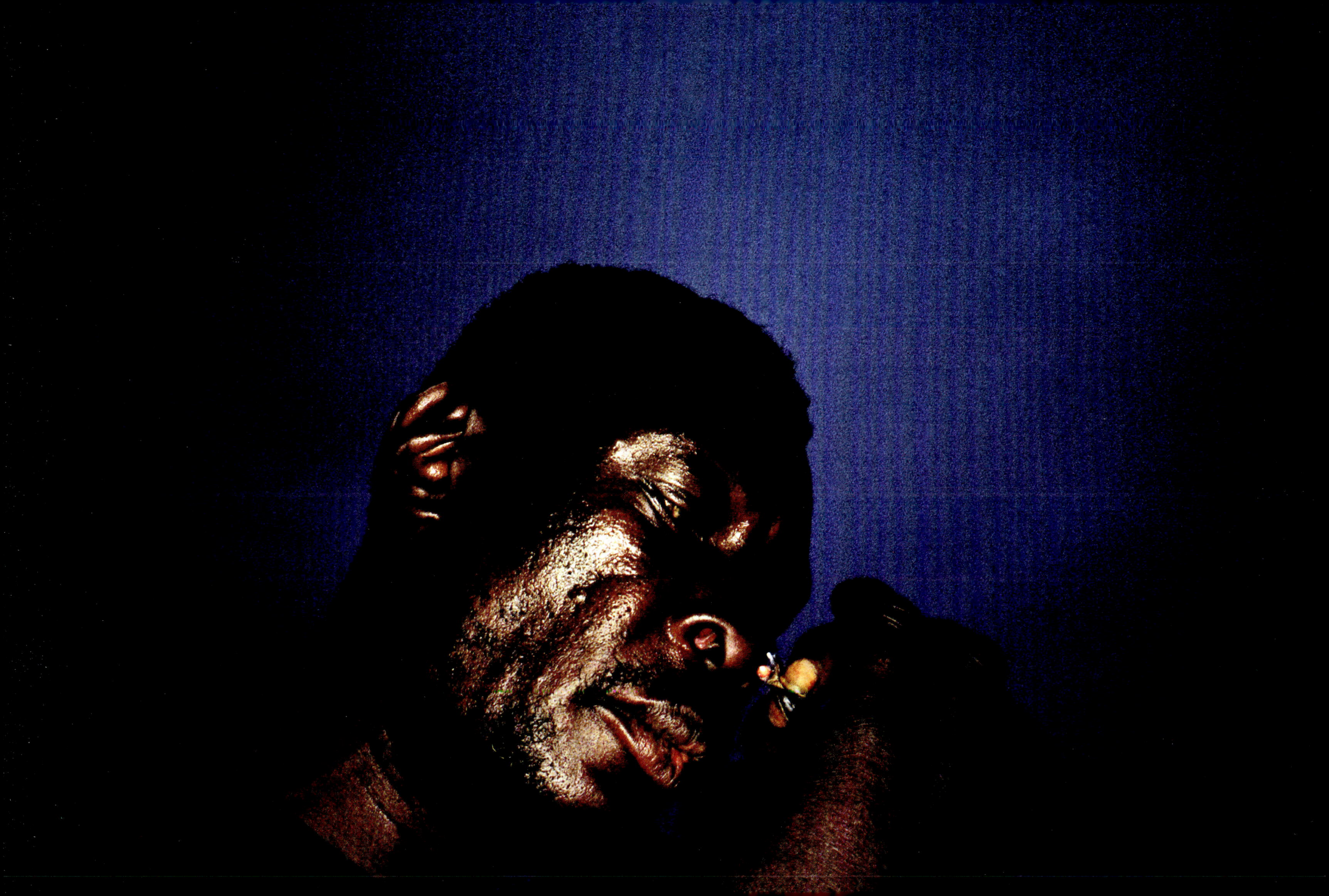

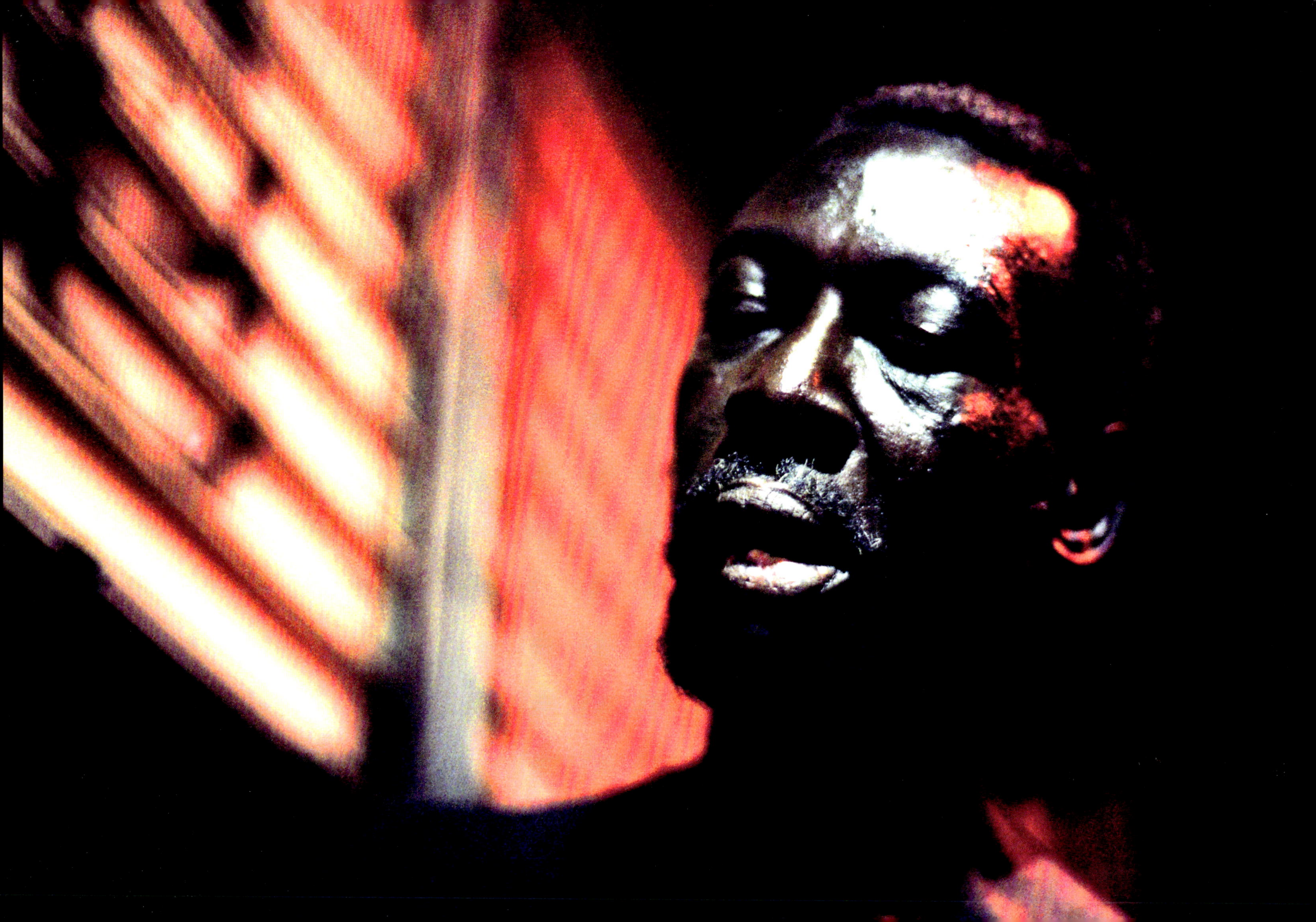

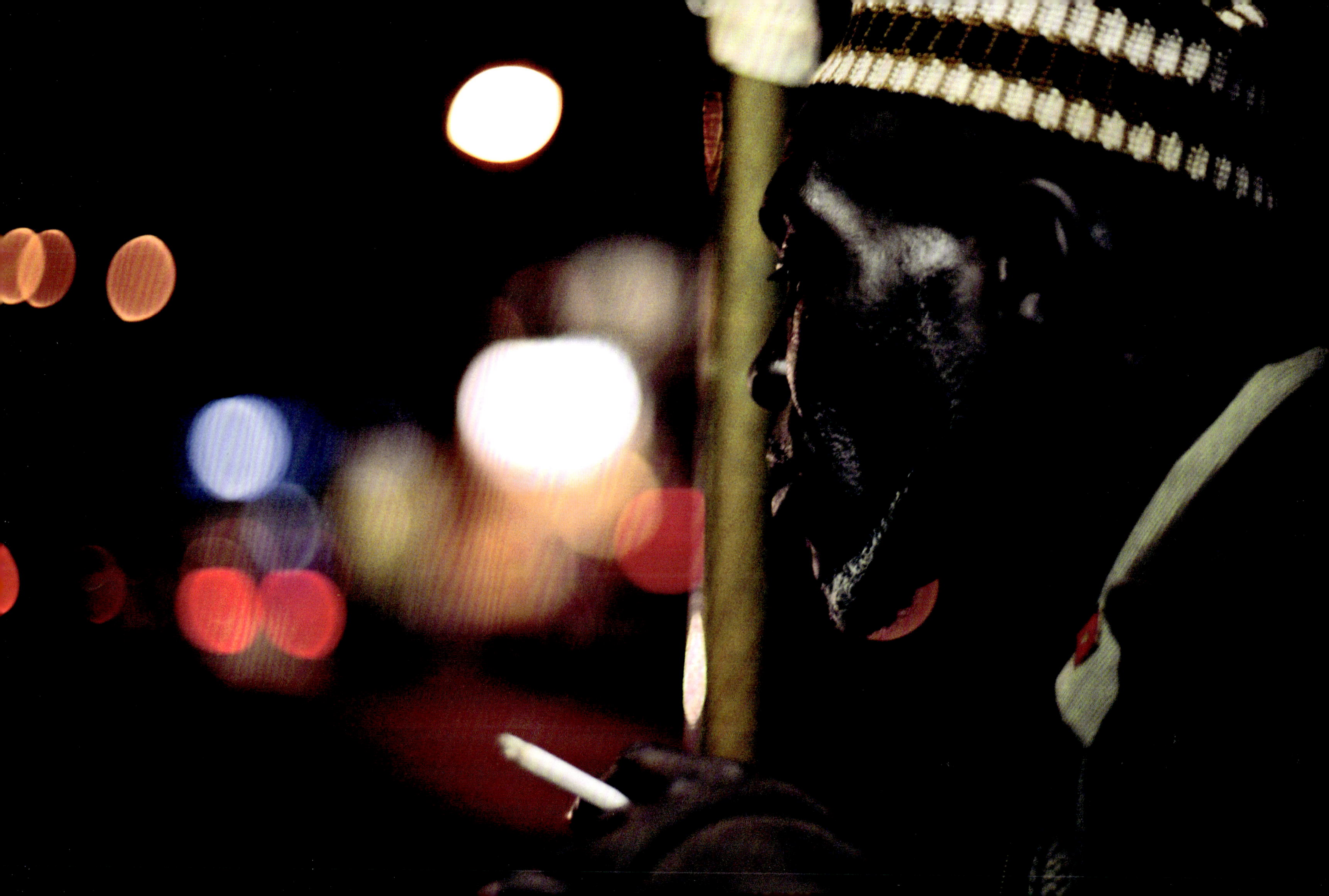

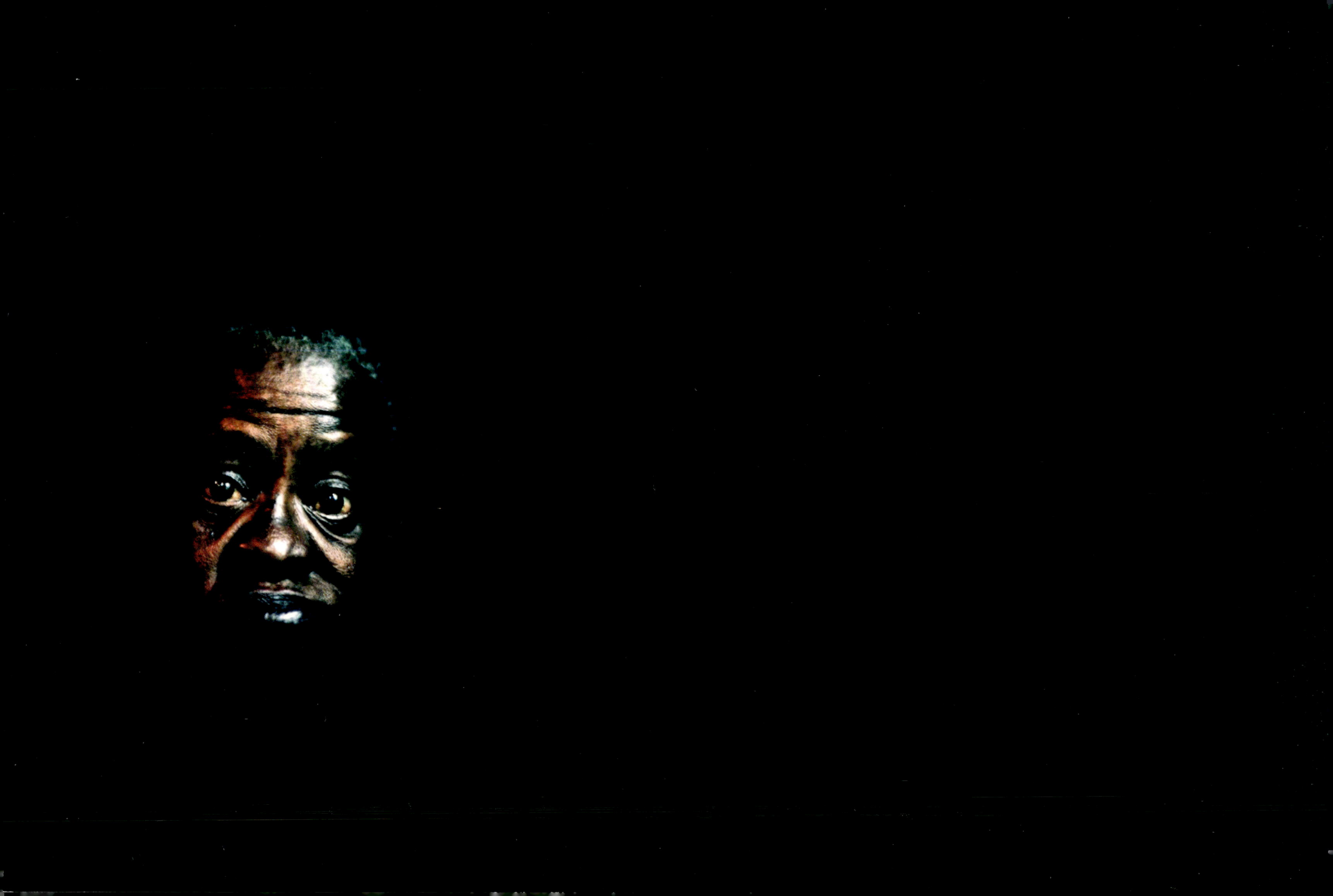

My deepest gratitude, appreciation, and respect go out to:

125th and Lexington Avenue, everyone there who co-created this work with me, the corner store, Harlem, Allah the Father, Justice, CeeAaquil Allah, Black Sun, Father Bushawn, all the Gods and Earths, Allah School, Allah Justice, DJ Allah Mathematics, Jamel Irief, Jamaica, Jamaica Queens, East New York, Vikki Tobak, Heaven Razah, Bro. El-Divine Bey a.k.a. 4th Disciple, Tragedy Khadafi, Noble Drew Ali, Mecca, Rondoo, Manuce Dulcio a.k.a. Frenchie, Sapphire, Angie, K2, Nas, NoLedge, Original Author, Eduardo Donoso, Chris Gurinsky, Gino Donatelli, Denair Carrol, Mario, Florence Ngala, Lovely Parker, Christopher Allen, Gow Mosby Junior, Ace Swipe, NYC Subway, Long Range, PheOnix RuachShaddai, Marcus Garvey, John Michael Kinberger, Michael S. Pollack, Fab 5 Freddy, Nobuyoshi Araki, Malcolm X, Tabitha Jackson, Jamel Shabazz, Rachel Chanoff, Deana Lawson, Akintola Hanif, Kitty Green, Saul Williams, Heron Arts, Tova Lobatz, Mark Slee, Randall Scott, Jed Dietz, Spike Lee, Charlie Rose, Daid Moriyama, Baltimore, Montreal, Roger Spence, John Gossage, Rachel Bosch, Jon Courtney, Nat May, Peter Williams, Lauren Jaben, Agave Print, Charlotte Selb, RIDM, UnionDocs, True/False Film Festival, Chris Boeckmann, Cynthia J. Fuchs, Ann Hornaday, Wayne White, Rodney O'Neil, Leah Giblin, Eldridge Cleaver, every professor who had me speak to their classes, all the students, everybody waiting for my next works, RaMell Ross, Chico Colvard, Sundance, Cinereach, Gil Scott Heron, Gordon Parks, IFP, Michelle Satter, Karuna Sagara, South Country Library, John Cardellino, North Bellport, Freedom Allah a.k.a. Popa Wu, Medina, Brookhaven, Jace Graf, Amherst Cinema, Dave Hamrick, Kahlil Joseph, West Coast, Shabazz Palaces, Vancouver, Seattle, Marfa, Art of Nonfiction, Brett Story, Jacob Burns Film Center, The Desert, Reel Works, Pelan, Angel Evans, AMC Networks, Mitch Margolin, Adam Davi, Mike Zmuda, the old crew, David Donovan, Rob Leonard, Sanjit Tibrewala, David Celestin, Haiti, LOUD, Mathew Molinaro, T. J. Weber, Joey Grasso, Elena Iaconis, Japan, Calgary, Josh Furey, British Columbia and Alberta, Yerba Buena Center for the Arts, Strictly Roots, the place where I spent the days of my youth – the court, Victoria Circle, my mother and father (Sonia and Aziz Askaripour), my physical brothers/teachers (Darius, Dave Mate, Mateo Fifth God), my grandmother (Mrs. Clarine Emily Case) and grandfather (Mr. William Case), my guides.